Psychopathology of the Psychoses

THOMAS FREEMAN, M.D.
Holywell Hospital, Antrim, Northern Ireland

TAVISTOCK PUBLICATIONS

First published in 1969
by Tavistock Publications Limited
11 New Fetter Lane, London E.C.4
Set in 11 on 12 pt Bembo
Printed in Great Britain by
The Camelot Press Ltd., London and Southampton

SBN 422 73060 2

Psychopathology of the Psychoses

By the same author, with John L. Cameron and Andrew McGhie

CHRONIC SCHIZOPHRENIA

STUDIES ON PSYCHOSIS

Contents

Acknowledgements

The clinical material described in this book was obtained while the author held the posts of Consultant Psychiatrist at Glasgow Royal Mental Hospital, Glasgow, Scotland, and at The Royal Dundee Liff Hospital, Dundee, Scotland. He would like to thank Dr Angus MacNiven, Professor I. R. C. Batchelor, and Dr P. G. Aungle for providing the facilities which made this work possible. Finally he must thank Mrs Joan Cormack, Miss Valerie Kelly, and Miss B. Steele for typing the manuscript.

EDITORIAL NOTE

All quotations from Freud's writings in the present work are taken from the Standard Edition (*S.E.* in the list of references), published in 24 volumes by the Hogarth Press Ltd, London, to whom acknowledgement is made.

CHAPTER 1

Introduction

The study of psychopathology as a means of deepening and widening knowledge of psychotic illness has been overshadowed by a concentration of interest on physiological research, epidemiological investigations, and family studies, as in the case of schizophrenia. The fact that the results obtained from physiological and epidemiological research are dependent on clinical concepts is conveniently glossed over. Physiological studies are undertaken in the belief that the patient population under investigation is a representative sample of a disease entity – schizophrenia or manic-depressive psychosis. It is inferred that the patients form a homogeneous group with a nearly identical symptomatology. In the case of epidemiological investigations the tacit assumption is made that there is a general agreement about the identification of specific nosological entities.

The situation is somewhat different in the case of family studies. The nature of these investigations results in detailed accounts of individual cases, which help to emphasize the great differences in symptomatology that exist between patients apparently suffering from the same illness (Wynne and Singer, 1963 a, b; Lidz, 1967). These studies highlight the environmental conditions which have led to the onset of the illness and which can be traced back into the patient's childhood and even into the life-history of the parents and grandparents (Scott and Ashworth, 1965, 1967). The repeated demonstration that new and old symptoms are brought to life by disturbances in the patient's relationship with his family has inevitably led to the patient's becoming obscured as a person suffering from an illness. He becomes submerged within the family and it is the family that is designated as sick and requiring treatment. The concept of a disease leading to the psychotic phenomena is rejected by the family study workers as vigorously as it is advocated by those who pursue physiological and epidemiological investigations.

Psychopathology has a wider subject-matter than the study of 'conscious psychic events' (Jaspers, 1963). To be comprehensive it must take account of psychoanalysis – the study of the way in which unconscious mental activities influence conscious experience and behaviour. It must also be based on certain aspects of neurology and internal medicine because mental functions and bodily processes arise from common roots (Schilder, 1950). This does not mean, as Jaspers (1963) has so clearly stated, that psychopathology should attempt to imitate the models that the study of physical disease has provided. The affirmation of the somatic basis of mental life in no way contradicts the need for a purely psychological approach to the patient, utilizing concepts and a means of investigation that are unique to psychopathology.

The controversy that has raged over whether or not psychotic illnesses are diseases (Roth, 1963) has been provoked and aggravated by the narrow conception of disease entities which psychiatry has borrowed from internal medicine. This demands that clinical states can be categorized as belonging to a disease entity only when certain criteria are fulfilled, namely, a common aetiology and pathogenesis, identical symptoms and physical signs, a similar course and response to treatment. All attempts to fit psychotic illnesses into the pattern provided by the disease concept of internal medicine have failed. One consequence has been the rejection of the disease concept by many psychiatrists. Its advocacy by others has been more an act of faith than a judgement based on knowledge. Certainly, psychotic illnesses are not diseases in the strictly physical sense. It seems necessary to suggest that mental diseases exist but that their very nature makes them refractory to the simple classifications appropriate for physical illnesses.

Patients who suffer from psychotic illnesses may indeed be suffering from diseases. The disease concept must be a wide one. It is not limited to conditions that are brought about by infections or caused by abnormal bodily processes. It also embraces conditions in which the symptoms are the outcome of an interplay between external and internal factors. Psychotic illness must fall into this category. These states are not caused by environmental events alone, although it is as a result of these circumstances that the symptoms find expression. Similarly, the clinical phenomena are not the direct outcome of abnormal brain functioning.

Bleuler (1963) has shown, on the basis of an unequalled clinical experience, that knowledge about the causes of schizophrenia is limited to two facts – heredity and psychogenesis. Hereditary factors result in an individual whose capacities to reconcile inner needs with the restraint required for socialization are limited. His responses, from infancy onwards, evoke noxious reactions from his environment. A continuous process of interpenetration of stimulus and response takes place over years, leading eventually to the illness. In this formulation, room is left for the concept of a disease process operative in the patient, one that is moulded not only by past and present experience but also by innate drive attitudes and fantasies. Yet this conception of the cause of psychotic states does not overplay the role of psychogenic factors.

Although the original psychoanalytical contribution to an understanding of the aetiology of, and of symptom formation in, the psychoses was considerable, it was never envisaged as providing the final solution to the problem of causation. Nevertheless, psychoanalysts have continued to interpret the clinical phenomena in terms of the model originally constructed for the neuroses. Thus all recent psychoanalytical theories on psychosis (Rosenfeld, 1952; Bion, 1957, 1958, 1959) are based upon the concepts of conflict, anxiety, and regression to fixation points. The model is a structural one, in which endopsychic objects struggle with one another. Inherent in this approach is the idea that symptoms are the expression of a defence against anxiety and/or guilt. It proposes that the patient's withdrawal, his cognitive defects, and his delusional reality constitute a means of avoiding even greater dangers which exist outside himself. It is assumed that what remains healthy in the patient (a true self) is hidden behind the façade of the psychotic symptomatology. No one can dispute the presence of a healthy element in the psychotic patient but no one knows its relationship to the illness itself.

This psychoanalytical theory, based on the writings of Klein, Fairbairn, and Winnicott, has found its most extreme expression in the writings of some existential psychiatrists (Laing, 1960, 1967; Cooper, 1967) who assert that there is a lack of basic unity in the patient who suffers from a psychosis and especially from schizophrenia. According to this theory, the predisposition to the illness is brought about by subtle pathogenic influences exerted on the patient. These noxious influences emanate from parents who are identified with their own seriously disturbed, yet not necessarily psychotic, parents and grandparents. These identifications arise from a series of introjections and projections. The patient is thus subject to the whole weight of pathological identifications, the result of generations of twisted relationships. These identifications make up the patient-to-be's horrifying and grotesque internal world. This internal world is repudiated by the patient although it makes its influence felt on his relations with others in the pre-psychotic period. A false self has been created through which he adapts to his environment. The true self is terrified of both the internal world and the world of reality. It is the irruption of the internal world into awareness that constitutes the psychosis.

The existential approach to the psychoses has the virtue of emphasizing all aspects of the patient's experience. It underlines the importance of his inner world, which is so vastly different from that of the healthy person. While the existential view acts as a corrective to the mechanistic interpretation of mental illness, its concentration on the individual patient and his mode of existence leads to the elaboration of theories of the type described. In common with those proposed by the students of Jung and Klein, they take the path of 'the slide into endlessness', to use the phrase coined by Jaspers (1963). Concepts and theories proliferate on the basis of limited observational data. The gap between hypotheses and phenomena is filled in and cemented by supplementary explanatory theories. The result is a comprehensive system which is internally consistent and able to withstand the demands made upon it for the explanation of any and every clinical manifestation. While it can explain everything it is incapable of offering new points of departure for a fundamental understanding of psychosis or its treatment. Impervious to the facts of experience, these theories are self-perpetuating and incapable of contradiction.

Psychogenic theories of psychosis promote the view that psychological factors are paramount in the causation and perpetuation of these illnesses. They encourage the idea that a psychological treatment will, if pursued persistently and conscientiously, eventually lead to the patient's recovery. The only proviso made is that the therapist employs a specific technique correctly and that he is not blinded by countertransferences. The facts of experience have revealed that this therapeutic optimism is not wholly justified, particularly in the case of the schizophrenias. While life experiences and inner reactions to them help to establish the predisposition and immediate stimulus for the illness they cannot account for the form that the clinical manifestations assume. This can only be attributed to some alteration in the underlying physiological functions, which subserve mental processes. This, it can be thought, results from some special characteristics of the genetic (hereditary) material brought to expression through environmental experiences of the type already described.

The psychoanalytic and existential study of patients with psychosis has revealed the sick individual behind the symptoms. These approaches expose the mental conflicts which possess the patient, and the psychoanalytic method in particular helps to trace out their history from childhood onwards. All this is necessary and essential. Any investigation or treatment method which neglects or ignores these individual problems cannot be regarded as providing a comprehensive view of the illness upon which therapeutic measures and prognosis can be based. However, the detailed knowledge of individual patients does not provide the data from which general laws regarding the development of psychotic symptoms may be formulated. Knowledge of a patient's adolescent fantasies, for example, and of their later expression in delusions, does not give any insight into the mechanism of delusion formation in psychosis or why in these states patients abandon their relationship to the world of objects.

At the present time there is little prospect of the elaboration of general principles which will be applicable to groups of patients, thus providing understanding of symptom formation and offering specific guidance for treatment. The history of modern psychiatry shows that a beginning can be made towards the discovery of these principles by studying the phenomena presented by a series of patients and by devoting attention to the phenomenological similarities and differences that exist between them. This necessary progress will never be achieved by concentration on the symptoms, problems, and conflicts of the individual case.

One aim of this book is to review the various phenomena that occur in psychoses and to present a means of ordering these manifestations. These data are readily available and it is easy for anyone to confirm their presence in comparable cases. This reliability does not characterize other aspects of patients' mental content. Thus little attention is given in this book to material other than that directly observed by the author or his co-workers. No records are given of early life experiences, fantasy life, or even the patient's account of his recent past beyond what is necessary for a comprehensive description of the case. Although this material is of the greatest significance in the context of therapy, it must be excluded here.

Chapter 2 describes the concepts necessary for the construction of a scheme that will accommodate all facets of a disordered patient's mental functioning. Chapter 3 presents the relevant details and considers the methodological problems which the employment of such a scheme entails.

Psychotic states are not homogeneous entities, and the designation of a disease or syndrome does not vitiate the fact that the patients allocated to it may not necessarily present identical phenomena. Catatonic states are taken as illustrative, and in Chapters 5 and 6 a detailed account is given of how these patients vary in the way they relate to others, in their cognition, in their motility, and in their psychotic reality.

Those who have had experience with both patients suffering from chronic schizophrenia and patients who have sustained cerebral damage due to vascular accidents, trauma, and degeneration, from whatever cause, have been impressed by the similarities which may exist between some of the clinical phenomena. It is likely that these similarities may be due to a derangement of similar mental functions even although the underlying pathology may be different. In Chapter 7 a description is given of certain varieties of organic mental state and in Chapter 8 a comparison is made between these conditions and chronic schizophrenia.

Chapter 9 examines the problem of the relationship between depressive states and psychosis. Can straightforward depressive illnesses be regarded as psychotic? How are atypical depressions with delusions and hallucinations to be classified? Chapter 9 provides an introduction to Chapter 10, which scrutinizes the concept of schizophrenia and the problem of diagnosis. Finally, Chapter 11 shows how knowledge of the psychopathology of the individual case can provide a framework for treatment.

Only the study of psychopathology, with its emphasis on the way in which patients experience their thoughts, feelings, bodily sensations, and the world around them, can provide the material that will give a reliable foundation for clinical, physiological, and biochemical investigations. The major contribution to this psychopathology comes from psychoanalysis. Psychoanalysis directs attention to the unconscious forces which participate in the production of the symptoms. Concentration on the unconscious elements in behaviour and symptoms, particularly when they consist of the expression of real or fantasied childhood transferences, prevents the physiological psychiatrist from overlooking a variable which can radically influence the results of his study.

Psychoanalysis provides an understanding of the illness and offers a guide for management and treatment. The phenomena that appear in functional and organic psychoses demonstrate the nature of the 'unconscious'. Not only do they reveal its content but they show something of the form and characteristics of the mental processes which operate in this 'region' of the mind.

The views expressed in this book are drawn from the writings of Hughlings Jackson and Freud. Their theories and concepts give due recognition to the place of endogenous factors and environmental events in leading to what must be regarded as diseases and as modes of maladaptive behaviour.

CHAPTER 2

Hughlings Jackson's 'Factors of Insanities and Freud's Theory of Psychosis

The purpose of this chapter is to present an account of the psychopathology of the psychoses in both its descriptive and its theoretical aspects. This requires a statement of the phenomena to be encountered in psychosis and of the concepts which have been created to account for them. The concepts, descriptive and explanatory, which compose these formulations are derived from descriptive psychiatry (phenomenology), psychoanalysis, neurology, and developmental psychology. Psychopathological conceptions are qualitative in nature and inevitably inexact when contrasted with the precise quantitative measurements which may be obtained in the different forms of physical disease. However, recognition of this in no way belittles their value as a means of providing an understanding upon which the management and treatment of a patient may be based.

This chapter consists of an account of the psychopathological knowledge upon which classifications of clinical phenomena and evaluations may be made. The psychopathological evaluation must be founded on a comprehensive account of the state of all the patient's mental functions. At the outset, however, a distinction must be made between descriptions of psychopathological phenomena and the formulations which offer explanations of these manifestations. The employment of clinical, descriptive concepts provides a means of detailing the phenomena which can be observed in the consulting-room and in the hospital ward. Distractability, resistance, and assimilation are illustrative of descriptive concepts taken from clinical psychiatry, psychoanalysis, and developmental psychology respectively. These descriptive concepts must be supplemented by explanatory concepts if a meaningful psychopathological assessment is to be achieved, upon which recommendations can be made. Recourse to psychopathological considerations should not be interpreted as a negative reaction to empiricism but rather as a means of refining this inherently clinical approach.

The keystone of contemporary psychopathological theory is that manifestations of mental illness result, first, from a disorganization of healthy, adult mental processes, and, second, from the intrusion of modes of mental activity appropriate to early phases of psychological development. The origins of this theory can be traced to Hughlings Jackson, who regarded healthy mental and nervous functioning in the adult as the end-product of an evolutionary process. This evolution transformed processes of a simple, organized, and automatic nature into those which are complex, little organized, and of a voluntary character. According to Jackson (1894), there is a dissolution of the highest cerebral centres in mental illness. Complex functions under voluntary control are lost. As a result, healthy nervous arrangements left intact by the disease make their appearance. These provide the striking manifestations of the illness.

Although Jackson derived his theory from the study of neurological disease he also applied it to mental illness. In his paper, 'The Factors of Insanities' (1894), he says,

> 'We must not speak crudely of disease causing the symptoms of insanity. Popularly the expression may pass, but properly speaking disease of the highest centres no more causes positive mental states, however abnormal they may seem, than opening flood gates causes water to flow or cutting the vagi causes the heart to beat more frequently. Disease only causes the negative element of the mental condition: the positive mental element, say a delusion, obviously an elaborate delusion however absurd it may be signifies activities of healthy nervous arrangements, signifies evolution going on in what remains of the highest cerebral centres.'

In Jackson's formulation the clinical phenomena encountered in psychotic states can be classified according to whether they are the result of dissolution (the negative symptoms) or the outcome of activity in the remaining healthy 'nervous arrangements' (the positive symptoms). First, therefore, are the negative symptoms, and then there are the positive symptoms attributable to the emergence of less differentiated, less complex, and more automatic (involuntary) forms of mental process. In the case of the schizophrenic psychoses, clinical data can be categorized as follows: (i) negative symptoms: withdrawal, loss of interest, psychomotor blocking, disturbances of identity, hypertonia, loss of reflexes, and loss of sensation; (ii) positive symptoms: misidentifications, delusions, hallucinations, distractability, catalepsy, and perseverative signs. The nature of the mental symptoms, both positive and negative, will, in Jackson's view (1894), depend upon four factors: the depth of the dissolution; the speed at which dissolution takes place; the type of individual in which dissolution occurs; and the influence of local bodily states.

The importance of Jackson's dissolution-evolution theory for clinical psychiatry has been largely overlooked, probably as the result of the advent of psychoanalysis and the pragmatic value of Kraepelin's classificatory scheme. Only a few psychiatrists (Delay, 1957; Ey, 1959; Levin, 1960; Angel, 1961; Power, 1965) have attempted to revive interest in Jackson's views and demonstrate their applications to clinical states. Nevertheless, Jackson's influence was not to be denied, and it is found most clearly in Freud's theory of psychosis (1911). His general outline closely follows the principles of dissolution-evolution enunciated by Jackson. The major difference is that Freud's model is a psychological construct having no connection with neural functioning.

A fundamental feature of Freud's theory of psychosis is the concept of regression. Regression is an intrinsic aspect of the entire psychoanalytic theory of mental functioning, particularly in the spheres of the development of the instinctual life and of those functions which are brought together under the concept of the ego (Freud, 1923). Regression describes a backward trend in the developmental series, and refers to a situation in which there is a revival of an earlier phase of the instincts or the ego. Freud (1916) described two forms of libidinal regression and, as will appear later in this discussion, this differentiation is of value in making a clear distinction between the different kinds of phenomena which arise in psychosis. The first kind of libidinal regression is concerned with the relationship with objects, the second with the sexual organization: '. . . there are regressions of two sorts: a return to the objects first cathected by the libido which, as we know, are of an incestuous nature, and a return of the sexual organization as a whole to earlier stages' (Freud, 1916–17, p. 341). Regression of drives or ego will take place more easily if in the course of mental development a difficulty arose which disrupted the smooth evolution of the specific function. Freud designated such disruptions and their effects fixations.

Initially Freud was principally concerned with such interferences in the development of the instinctual drives, and the concepts of regression and fixation were therefore created to describe the vicissitudes of the libidinal tendencies. On the basis of his clinical experience Freud stated that regression of the libido may take place when the instinctual drive, in '. . . the exercise of its function – that is, the attainment of its aim of satisfaction – is met, in its later or more highly developed form, by powerful external obstacles' (Freud, 1916–17, pp. 340–1). Freud continues, 'The stronger the fixations on its path of development, the more readily will the function evade external difficulties by regressing to the fixations – the more incapable, therefore, does the developed function turn out to be of resisting external obstacles in its course' (Freud, 1916–17, p. 341).

Although regression and fixation are concepts which at first sight are absent in Jackson's dissolution-evolution hypothesis, their presence is soon discerned. Regression, whether affecting the instinctual drives or the ego functions, is an aspect of the effect of dissolution. Fixations which can only with difficulty be disentangled from the products of regression can be regarded as 'evolution going on in what remains intact of the mutilated higher centres' (Jackson, 1894). Dissolution is a wider concept than regression in that it encompasses those manifestations, both positive and negative, which arise from the disorganization of adult mental processes.

Freud went to some lengths to clarify his usage of the term regression and this elucidation is of value in categorizing phenomena which can be designated products of regression. According to Freud a distinction must be made between instinctual or libidinal regression and ego or psychological regression. Freud named three varieties of psychological regression: First topographical regression, a process whereby verbal ideas are replaced by visual images, as in the dream or in hypnagogic hallucinations. Second, temporal regression, where early patterns of drive activity, cognition, and affect reappear in adult life. The transference neurosis which occurs in psychoanalytical treatment is an instance of temporal regression. Finally, there is formal regression. This describes the process whereby adult, differentiated mental processes are replaced by primitive means of representation. Concrete thinking and synaesthesias are examples of this category of psychological regression. In fact, all these forms of regression are an expression of the same basic process. Freud (1900, p. 548) adds, 'All these three kinds of regression are, however, one at bottom and occur together as a rule; for what is older in time is more primitive in form . . .'

In his first formulations dealing with psychotic states, Freud (1911) regarded many of the clinical manifestations as the direct result of libidinal regression. The libidinal investment of real objects and their mental representations was withdrawn and returned to fixation points at the narcissistic or autoerotic levels. The return of these libidinal cathexes to the self led to a pathological exaggeration of narcissism. The self was enhanced at the expense of objects. Freud's designation of the functional psychoses as narcissistic neuroses reveals his conviction that these conditions were characterized by a regression of the libido '. . . not merely to narcissism (manifesting itself in the shape of megalomania) but to a complete abandonment of object-love and a return to infantile auto-erotism' (Freud, 1911, p. 77).

The theory of narcissistic regression has proved of value in enabling the clinician to relate a number of clinical phenomena which occur in almost every psychotic illness. The concept has had a unifying and integrating influence. Delusions of grandeur, magic thinking (omnipotence of thought), certain forms of auditory and visual hallucination, alterations in bodily awareness, withdrawal of interest in the world, and complete self-preoccupation can all be understood as the result of regression to a narcissistic form of mental organization.

Freud (1911) based his theory of psychosis on the model he had elaborated for the neuroses. In neurosis, the return of repressed libidinal tendencies in the form of symptoms followed repression of these trends with their regression to fixation points. The psychosis model had the same two-phase development. A description has already been given of the first stage, where withdrawal of libido from objects and their corresponding fantasies (the equivalent of repression) is followed by regression to narcissism or autoerotism. A difference was envisaged between neurosis and psychosis, in that in neurosis the withdrawal of cathexis affects only real objects, and does not affect their mental representations, as in psychosis. Again, the fixation points differ. In the neuroses, the fixation points lie at the phallic or anal levels of the sexual organization, leaving the area of self-object relations intact. In the psychoses, fixation points have been set up just at those sites where the organization of the self and object is still rudimentary.

The second phase of the model, equivalent to the return of the repressed in the neuroses, is the phase of restitution. In this phase the libidinal trends now try to reinvest the object world. The means of carrying this out is by projection or hallucination. Delusions and hallucinations are the outcome of restitutional processes. Through projection and denial the patient is able to ignore both the nature and the origin of his fantasies and wishes. In so far as these psychical formations are disowned, the delusions represent a kind of defence analogous to the symptoms of the psychoneuroses.

The concepts of dissolution and regression were created to describe processes which lead to changes in healthy adult nervous and mental functions. These altered functions now present as clinical manifestations. Reference has already been made to the fact that dissolution is a wider concept than regression. Regression as employed by psychoanalysts implies the revival of infantile and childhood modes of mental function, whether in the spheres of interpersonal relationships or of cognition. It is not difficult to identify many of the phenomena encountered in psychosis as having similar characteristics to the mental functions of childhood. There are, however, other manifestations which do not conform so easily to this conceptual scheme. For this reason the concept of regression is not entirely satisfactory as a complete explanation of all the clinical phenomena to be found in psychotic states. Dissolution does not have this particular handicap. While it makes allowance for the phenomena brought together under regression, it also accommodates the remaining clinical manifestations.

Taken from another standpoint, dissolution and regression can be regarded as concepts which were designed to account for the exposure of modes of mental functioning which in the adult no longer have value as means of environmental adaptation. The organization of the specific function exposed provides the positive symptoms, to utilize Jackson's terminology. The pathological narcissistic organization which is revealed in the illness provides the mode of thinking (omnipotence of thought) for the creation of delusions. While delusions can be regarded as a restitution product, it is not so easy to categorize such phenomena as alterations in the subjective awareness of the body, again presumably arising from a pathological narcissism, under the heading of regression. Dissolution is free of the restrictions implicit in the concept of regression. Here, dissolution can be invoked to account for the liberation of processes which affect the normal perception of the body.

In psychotic states it is by no means uncommon to encounter abnormalities of cognition quite apart from hallucinations, delusions, and disorders of affect. Psychoanalytical writers from Freud onwards have pointed out that whereas certain features of these disturbances can be attributed to regression – for example, magical thinking, synaesthesiae, and loss of visual-perceptual constancies – there are forms of disorganization which cannot be explained in this way (Schilder, 1926). This is true of disorders of thinking in which the use and meaning of words have become seriously disturbed, of disorders of visual perception that result in misidentifications, and of the disorganization of recent and remote memory. Freud reached an understanding of such pathological phenomena by proposing that, in psychotic states characterized by such manifestations, there appears a mode of mental functioning which normally finds expression only in dreams.

Regression affects conceptual thinking in sleep. Thoughts are converted into a preverbal, pictorial form, and find representation in the dream. In Freud's words (1916–17, p. 199),

> 'The new mode of expression . . . harks back to states of our intellectual development which have long since been superseded – to picture-language, to symbolic connections, to conditions, perhaps, which existed before our thought-language had developed. We have on that account described the mode of expression of the dream-work as *archaic* or *regressive*.'

Freud discovered through his analyses of dreams that, in sleep, specific mental processes are activated which govern the direction and fate of these archaic mental representations. He named these processes 'condensation' and 'displacement', and designated them the main agents of the dream work: the means whereby the latent dream thoughts are converted into the manifest dream content.

The impact of condensation and displacement is to accentuate the effect of the regression on the thought processes in the direction of greater distortion of the latent thoughts. Displacement eliminates connections between the sensory intensity of manifest dream images and the latent thoughts corresponding to them. Thus displacement acts in the service of the censorship, ensuring that proscribed contents do not find expression in the dream and disturb sleep. Condensation, which leads to the fusion of images on the basis of the faintest common feature, accentuates the trend towards distortion of the dream thoughts. It is of interest that Freud did not regard condensation as primarily an agent of the censorship. He said (1916–17, p. 173), 'But although condensation makes dreams obscure, it does not give one the impression of being an effect of the dream-censorship. It seems traceable rather to some mechanical or economic factor . . .' He thought of condensation, therefore, as a fundamental feature of unconscious mental activity and as describing the unifying tendency characteristic of this mode of mental functioning, quite apart from the aims of the censorship to which it might be recruited as necessary. Condensation as a form of mental process stands in contrast to the highly differentiated, discrete mental organization essential for environmental adjustment. Freud designated the former the primary process, the latter the secondary process.

The disorders of cognition to which reference has been made can be understood as due to the intrusion of the primary process. Indeed, the cognitive disorganization in the schizophrenias can be thought of as somewhat like the dream state. Identical mental processes appear to be at work, particularly condensations and displacements. The sensory intensity of ideas and images determines entry into consciousness as in the dream and not the selective attention which in normal waking life is necessary for concentration and directed thinking.

The question is whether the appearance of the effects of the primary process on adult cognition ought to be regarded as due to regression or to some other process. At the present state of knowledge, employment of the concept of dissolution helps to overcome this difficulty. Dissolution of the adult mental organization leads to the release of processes which ordinarily operate unconsciously. The impact of condensation on conceptual thinking, perception, and memory leads to the phenomena characteristic of the cognitive disorder of the schizophrenias. This formulation in no way precludes the view that there are occasions when displacement and condensation are employed in the service of defence (censorship), as in the dream. The cognitive abnormalities can be classified as positive symptoms and regarded as the consequence of 'evolution' continuing in what remains of the highest cerebral centres. Jackson's conception of evolution continuing in primitive functions exposed by disease adequately covers the idea of a continuous activity of the primary process in psychotic states. It also takes account of the fact that functions that were once complex and under voluntary control are replaced by those which are simple, repetitive, and automatic.

Freud's theory of psychosis lays major emphasis on the presence in the patient of serious mental conflict. These conflicts, as in the case of the neuroses, arise from relationships with other individuals. Wishes directed towards these objects provoke repercussions within the patient's mind and they evoke fantasies which in their turn lead to anxiety and guilt. Withdrawal of libido from these objects and the related fantasies leads in psychosis to a regression of the libido and eventually to attempts at restitution. Experience with different clinical categories shows that the withdrawal from objects need not be complete, nor need the relationship with objects in the environment be entirely dominated by the psychotic reality (the results of the restitutional tendencies). Freud (1914) suggested, therefore, that in psychotic states the clinical phenomena can be sorted out into three separate groups: first, those representing what remains of normal mental functioning; second, those representing the detachment of the libido from objects, and, third, those representing the attempt to regain the world of objects.

It has always been known that patients suffering from schizophrenic and paranoid psychoses are sensitive to their surroundings and that they react vigorously to those with whom they are in immediate contact. On the one hand, there are patients who are apparently oblivious to their environment and show no response to friendly overtures. These are the patients whose behaviour is interpreted as being due to a withdrawal of libido from real and fantasy objects. In Freud's view, such patients were incapable of establishing transferences and were therefore refractory to psychotherapeutic efforts. This judgement did not exclude the possibility that rudimentary libidinal cathexes of objects existed and that in certain circumstances reactions to environmental objects might occur. However, such reactions must inevitably be unstable and ephemeral. On the other hand, there are patients who, though dominated by delusions and hallucinations, are still capable of a sustained relationship with another person. These patients must therefore be regarded as retaining to some extent their libidinal attachment to objects. In some cases a working transference does occur which is sufficient to enable psychotherapy to be undertaken.

The advent of psychotherapeutic work with psychotic patients and their close study by nurses in the hospital ward have led to increased knowledge about those aspects of their object relationships which are not contaminated by delusions and hallucinations. All the evidence points to the presence of a drive towards objects even in the most withdrawn and detached patient. In these cases there are brief moments when the patient expresses thoughts and feelings which can only be regarded as normal. For the most part, however, the object-directed behaviour is characterized by lack of strength, and lack of tenacity and consistency. When manifest it is often only concerned with the satisfaction of an immediate need: for food or cigarettes, or a desire to return home. Lack of satisfaction may lead to an angry outburst usually accompanied by intact and comprehensible speech content or to an even deeper withdrawal. Such responses may occur when more complex wishes or affects arise involving other patients, nurses, or the psychiatrist. Different forms of non-psychotic object relationship may therefore appear in psychotic patients corresponding to various levels of affective-conative organization. They are quite distinct from the psychotic forms of object relationship which may occur simultaneously in the same patient.

The clinical evidence suggests that Freud's original classification of the phenomena encountered in psychoses is not entirely comprehensive. While making a place for the healthy remnants of the personality, it does not make explicit the fact that this 'non-psychotic layer' is not to be confined to the residual healthy adult mental life which is active in the patient. It must also include the healthy childhood mental functions which have come to the fore as the result of regression. Here again, Jackson's concept of dissolution makes room for the observable phenomena. It allows for all the kinds of object relationship which may appear in psychotic states. Relationships with the characteristics of early childhood are no less the result of dissolution than are those in which psychotic attitudes predominate, the difference being that the role of regression is far clearer in the former than in the latter. Both groups of phenomena qualify for inclusion in the category of positive symptoms.

A distinction can be made in the sphere of object relations between two groups of phenomena: those that are in a sense healthy but are inappropriate because they are a revival of childhood patterns, and those that are totally aberrant because psychotic attitudes dominate the relationship. Both patterns are in a sense pathological, but it would be more useful to designate the former as inappropriate reaction and the latter as 'pathological'. In the first case the manifestations are due to regression; in the latter to restitutional trends, to use the psychoanalytic formulation. This distinction will again be found to be relevant when consideration is given to those mental states due to organic disease of the brain.

The disturbances of voluntary movement and sensori-motor function which may occur in psychoses have not been subject to the thorough investigation which characterizes the psychoanalytic study of other aspects of these states. This omission may be attributed to the fact that psychoanalysis is almost wholly concerned with mental processes and its interest in bodily function is only awakened when somatic disorders can be regarded as secondary to a psychological upset. Psychoanalytic theorizing in this clinical area has tended to follow the approach adopted by Bleuler (1911), who regarded the disturbances of motility and posture in the schizophrenias as secondary to the primary deficit affecting thinking and affect. At first sight the contemporary absence of the more grotesque of these phenomena seems to support Bleuler's contention. However, there are some newly ill patients, and others who have never been hospitalized, who show a disorganization of voluntary movement, of posture, and of the reflex system. Phenomena frequently encountered are perseverative signs, hypertonia, echopraxia, and tonic reflex responses.

The interpretation of these manifestations has always been a source of controversy among psychiatrists. Psychoanalytical writers from Jung onwards have tended to understand them as the result of wishes and fantasies which find bodily expression. The meaning ascribed to the manifestations by the patients themselves has sometimes been taken to be their actual cause. However, the fact that a patient ascribes a certain cause to a phenomenon, as in the case of endowing a movement with magical significance, can easily be regarded as a reaction to its presence rather than as its basic determinant. Be that as it may, the clinical evidence indicates that disorders of motility are frequently found in association with special mental contents. These contents comprise conflicts regarding aggression and sexuality. As yet there has been no satisfactory answer to the question of why the response to these conflicts should appear in the sphere of motility, that is, assuming the psychological component of the illness is paramount. Once again, the concept of psychological regression has been employed to explain that in these cases there is a revival of an early infantile phase, characterized by omnipotence of thought, in which bodily movements have a magical signficance. This magic of movement is the mode of object relationship appropriate to this phase of childhood.

Psychological regression, appearing under the term primitivization, has been used by genetic psychologists to provide explanations not only of cognitive disorders in psychotic states but also of disturbances of motility. According to this approach, the psychological defect allows the emergence of a mode of interaction between cognition and motility, never present in the healthy adult, but signs of which can be seen in the infant and child. Just as the child responds to perceptual stimulation with bodily responses, so do many schizophrenic patients react to verbal stimuli with bodily movements. Echopraxia belongs, in this view, to this category of phenomena. No limitation is imposed upon the response to the visual percept of the other person's movement. This is an automatic process occurring outside conscious awareness.

Regression is a descriptive concept. As it affects the libido, regression is not, in Freud's words, 'a purely psychical process and we cannot tell where we should localize it in the mental apparatus. And though it is true that it exercises the most powerful influence on mental life, yet the most prominent factor in it is the organic one' (1916–17, pp. 342–3). Regression is, however, most commonly employed in its psychological sense, and the different forms which Freud discerned have already been described. Difficulties arise when attempts are made to employ psychological regression as a means of explaining the disorders of motility referred to above. It is applicable only in those instances where the clinical manifestations appear to result from a disorganization of psychological processes themselves without any contribution from somatic sources. Such a differentiation is not easy to make, and for this reason regression never seems to be a very suitable concept to employ in this sphere of symptomatology.

It is when disorders of voluntary movement exist alongside disturbances of mental function that a disorganization simultaneously affecting both psychological and somatic processes is indicated. In these cases the close relationship between speech and voluntary movement is lost or disordered. Thus the patient responds only with echo reactions or echolalia; or he responds to the instruction after a latent period of varying length. In some cases the response takes the form of a repetitive, perseverative act. The ability to initiate, sustain, and complete a voluntary act is suspended and instead movements occur which seem to be dissociated from volition. Postural mechanisms are disorganized and they appear to be related to tonus changes in the limb musculature. These manifestations are usually accompanied by inattention, withdrawal, and loss of the capacity to attend selectively. Speech obstruction (blocking) is common. The interesting fact is that in certain conditions these pathological phenomena may temporarily disappear and be replaced by apparently normal or bodily activity.

Dissolution is a concept which can be applied equally to bodily and to mental processes. Indeed, Jackson conceived of this theory on the basis of his work with neurologically ill patients before applying it to the phenomena of mental illness. In the present context, disorders of motility can be attributed to the results of dissolution. Normal function is replaced by an abnormal motility which has lost its connection with conscious intent and awareness of self. Many unsuccessful attempts have been made to locate within the nervous system the disorganization that leads to the observable phenomena. In the past a disturbance in the connections between the cerebral cortex and extrapyramidal system was postulated as the site of the pathological activity. Today, an abnormality of the reticular activating system is often designated as the cause of the abnormalities detected on clinical examination. Whatever the ultimate cause, these disorders of voluntary movement, hypertonia, and reflex changes comprise positive symptoms, the indirect result of dissolution.

Reference has briefly been made to the fact that patients who present with psychomotor phenomena of the type described are, at times, capable of normal speech and motility, even if only for the briefest of periods. Most often, this apparently favourable outcome occurs contemporaneously with an outburst of anger or with the expression of some wish or need. This change from disordered to ordered functioning in psychotic states has sometimes been compared with the restoration of normal motility in the post-encephalitic patient and with the reappearance of speech in the patient suffering from motor aphasia. In all these instances the restoration of normal functioning is accompanied by strong affects. The beneficial change in the psychotic patient has sometimes been attributed to the possibility that in these cases the mechanisms underlying thinking and motility are subject to a functional impairment only and that given certain conditions they may return to normal functioning. It is equally likely that, as in the case of the post-encephalitic and aphasic patient, the return to apparently normal function is the result of an automatic process apart from volition and intent. Similarly, the effects of dissolution on thinking, and self-awareness, and its links with motility in the schizophrenias, remain; but the cognitive processes which once operated at the behest of conscious intent now find an automatic expression under the influence of a powerful drive or affect. Such phenomena do not necessarily indicate the return of normalcy but are in fact positive symptoms. Similar considerations may be relevant for both delusions and hallucinations. They erupt into awareness and have a compulsive quality. They are not under the control of volition and indeed attention is attracted and imprisoned by the intensity of their presentation. One writer (Bychowski, 1943b) has reported on a patient who said, 'When I am having these foreign thoughts I am not aware of any effort as I am when my own occur.' As in the dream, attention has become passive, having lost its active quality.

Jackson's theory of evolution-dissolution when applied to psychoses offers a means of classifying the clinical phenomena. Its concepts help to avoid some of the difficulties to which employment solely of the psychoanalytic theory leads. This has been seen to be so for regression. An attempt to classify psychotic manifestations requires placing emphasis on their descriptive aspects. To some this may seem a retrogressive step in the task of obtaining a deeper and more fundamental understanding of psychosis. Such classifying may appear to detract from concentration upon the patient's inner experiences and from serious consideration of the role which unconscious conflict and fantasy play in symptom formation. There is even the suspicion that the employment of a conceptual system derived from the phenomena of neurological disease will lead to the abandonment of the psychological model of psychosis and to its replacement by neurophysiological hypotheses.

These anxieties are in no way allayed if references is made to the undoubted similarities that exist between certain cases of schizophrenia and organic brain disease. In disease of the frontal lobes, for example, the patient presents a lack of interest and drive, appears apathetic, and shows disturbances of voluntary movement (loss of connection between speech and motility, repetitive perseveration, cataleptic signs, echo phenomena, and distractability). In organic mental states an outstanding feature is a trend towards the loss of conceptual powers. There is a preoccupation in thought with immediate perceptual experience, and the patient is unable to detach himself from its impact. This loss of the abstract capacity is associated with an egocentric interpretation of events. Loss of abstraction varies from case to case and in its most extreme form is represented by a complete concrete attitude.

Dissolution in organic brain disease thus leads to negative symptoms not unlike those encountered in the schizophrenias. Loss of differentiated cognitive functions such as speech, thinking, and memory occurs freely in both groups of conditions. In organic mental states, where psychomotor deterioration is severe, a better standard of cognitive function may arise automatically on the basis of strong affects and needs, but it does not usually achieve the level found in chronic schizophrenia under the same conditions. In organic states the dissolution may be deeper and in acute cases more rapid than in the functional psychoses.

Apart from the cognitive disorganization there is, in organic mental states, a revival of modes of object-relationship and drive-activity which indicate the operation of a regressive trend. This is reflected in the content of the misinterpretations and misidentifications. The misidentifications are not due to regression but to the influence of condensation. Percepts and memory traces are merged together. The misidentifications represent the memories of real persons. The patient may believe that the psychiatrist is his brother or the nurse his mother. This content is indicative of an object-libidinal regression. The libidinal attachment to real objects has been lost (owing to dissolution) but the libidinal cathexes have reinvested the memory traces. Such phenomena (misidentifications) provide conscious and observable counterparts to the neuroses, in which the withdrawal of libido from objects and its transfer to childhood objects occurs unconsciously and can only be inferred.

Dissolution in organic mental states may therefore lead to phenomena which can be interpreted as the result of object-libidinal regression. In some instances there is a regression of the sexual organization as well as a regression in the sphere of object relations. The patient may be withdrawn, inert, and unresponsive, his instinctual life centring on the erotogenic zones in a compulsive, automatic fashion. Loss of the ego due to dissolution is accompanied by regression to a phase of auto-erotism. In other cases, the libidinal regression does not affect the sexual organization as much as it affects object relations. Here there may be a revival of early object-libidinal relations, as in the patient in whom homosexual trends make their first appearance.

The formulations outlined above dealing with the psychopathology of psychotic illness provide a means of classifying and categorizing the clinical phenomena. Data can be ordered in terms of Hughlings Jackson's categories of positive and negative symptoms and in terms of whether they are the effects of dissolution or of 'evolution continuing in what remains of the higher cerebral centres'. Simultaneously, the clinical phenomena can be examined from the standpoint of the concepts belonging to the psychoanalytic theory of psychosis. Clinical manifestations may be grouped into those which can and those which cannot be considered as resulting from libidinal or psychological regression.

The psychopathological approach to classification ensures that all the observable phenomena are given adequate attention. With the use of Jackson's conceptual scheme, the signs of neurological disorganization in psychosis will not be ignored and will be given an importance equal to that of the mental phenomena. In the sphere of object relations, adequate accommodation must be made for those manifestations that are pathological in that they are inappropriate and those that are pathological in that they are not derived from any normal developmental phase. The classification must provide room for the details of disordered cognition, motility, and affect. A place must be made for those inferential aspects of the psychopathology which are associated with object relationships, particularly for the role of the defence mechanisms and the manner in which they operate in a particular case.

CHAPTER 3

Recording Clinical Phenomena in Psychotic States

The purpose of the previous chapter was to present an account of the basic concepts, descriptive and explanatory, which constitute the essence of the psychopathology of the psychoses, both functional and organic. This task was undertaken to ensure that sufficient consideration would be given to those constructs when attention was turned to the problem of observing and recording the phenomena encountered in psychotic states. The necessity for the employment of clinical concepts is obvious enough; this is the field of descriptive psychiatry. It is not always sufficiently recognized that explanatory concepts are also necessary for the observer if he is to be alert to the possible presence of a particular manifestation. Only a psychopathology that includes such concepts will prevent the clinician from, for example, grouping all the non-psychotic manifestations which appear in a specific case into the one category as if they were a homogenous unit arising from an identical development phase.

In this chapter an account will be given of a scheme designed to present as comprehensive a statement as possible of the clinical phenomena that may be found in an individual patient suffering from a psychotic illness. The scheme, which will shortly be described, derives from two separate yet related sources. The first source is the attempt made by the present author (Freeman *et al.*, 1965) to demonstrate the manner in which psychotic symptoms may be classified independently of nosological considerations. Here psychoanalytical concepts were employed in conjunction with those from descriptive psychiatry to provide seven categories under which the clinical phenomena might be classified. They were (i) the patient's capacity for object relations, (ii) affective reactions, (iii) cognitive dysfunction, (iv) superego factor, (v) factor of defence, (vi) hallucinations, (vii) delusions. It was thought that this classification scheme, incorporating psychoanalytical concepts, would extend and deepen knowledge of the patient's symptomatology and behaviour. The inclusion of such categories as 'superego' and 'defence' ensured that adequate attention would be paid to the element of mental conflict. As a result, the phenomena arising from the dynamic factor would be regarded as no less real or significant than those clinical manifestations arising from cognitive disorganization.

The second source of the present scheme is the Adult Personality Profile for *psychoneurotic patients* developed by Anna Freud and her colleagues (A. Freud *et al.*, 1965). In contrast to the classification scheme already referred to, the Adult Personality Profile is entirely psychoanalytic in its conception. In this respect, therefore, all the clinical phenomena are ordered in terms of major psychoanalytical concepts. The observed data are organized under eight major headings, the first four of which are essentially descriptive. They are: (1) 'Reason for Referral', (2) 'Description of the Patient as directly or indirectly conveyed in the Interview', (3) 'Family Background and Personal History', (4) 'Possibly significant Environmental Circumstances'. The remaining five headings comprise the psychoanalytical categorization of the clinical phenomena: (5) 'Assessment of Drive and Ego—Superego Positions'. This category is then subdivided into (A) 'The Drives', (B) 'Ego and Superego', and (C) which is (A) + (B), i.e. 'Reaction of the Total Personality' to specific life situations, demands, opportunities, etc.

The section 'The Drives' is divided into (i) 'Libido' and (ii) 'Aggression'. Libido is in turn categorized as (*a*) 'Libidinal position' and (*b*) 'Libidinal distribution'. Libidinal distribution has two aspects (i) 'Cathexis of self' and (ii) 'Cathexis of objects' past or present. All the phenomena which are regarded as Libidinal or Aggressive in nature are recorded under these headings. Within the category (B), 'Ego and Superego', a statement is made of the ego functions of thinking, perceiving, memory, motility, etc. A note is to be made of the status of the defence organization and of the superego. Under (C), drive and ego development are brought together.

Heading (6) comprises 'Assessment of Fixation Points and Regressions'. Here an attempt is made to identify possible fixation points and regressions which may have taken place in the individual case. This assessment is based on such phenomena as the patient's mode of object relations, his fantasy life, drive activity, and characterological attitude. Heading (7) consists of the 'Examination of the Conflicts existing in the Patient'. Three different forms are specified: (a) External conflicts, (b) Internalized conflicts, and (c) Internal conflicts. Finally, heading (8) is concerned with the 'Assessment of the Need for Analytical Therapy and the Ability to Profit from it'.

The Adult Personality Profile sets out to provide a comprehensive picture of the mental processes in a case of psychoneurosis. The phenomena are therefore scrutinized from the dynamic, developmental, and structural points of view. The profile is concerned not only with the patient's behaviour but also with his inner experiences, those which are conscious and those which are unconscious. It sets out to describe his psychical reality and the anxieties to which this has given rise.

Criticism is often directed against the psychoanalytic method of investigation because it employs concepts that are essentially interpretative in type. It is true that there are no such things as cathexis, regression, or projection. They are terms which have been evolved to explain why certain phenomena make their appearance. Without them no explanation of psychic events is really possible. The psychoanalytic approach, as reflected in the Adult Personality Profile, is directed towards presenting a statement of those aspects of the patient's mental life of which he is unaware yet which play a decisive role in the production of his symptoms.

The fact that the psychoanalytical profile goes beyond the observable phenomena introduces problems which thus far have been insurmountable for the clinical psychiatrist. He is inclined to regard the explanations of phenomena as expressed through psychoanalytical concepts as arbitrary and without solid foundation. He would point out, for example, that as yet no attempt has been made to examine the extent to which two observers equally familiar with the concepts might agree on the classification of a specific phenomenon.

Thus the clinical psychiatrist is unable to go beyond what he can observe and much of the patient's mental life is left out of consideration. It could be said that it is for this reason that certain delusional experiences are regarded as true delusions (Jaspers, 1963), being without cause and not understandable in terms of the patient's experience.

The controversies that have taken place have tended to obscure the fact that psychoanalytic concepts can, at many points, help to enlarge the scope of the phenomenological study without proceeding to explanation and interpretation. This is the aim of the examination scheme to be described below. While it cannot achieve the ends which the personality profile can encompass it is a step forward in the employment of psychoanalytic concepts for the purpose of a comprehensive account of the individual case.

For practical purposes therefore it seems reasonable to discard, where possible, those headings of the profile which employ explanatory concepts and replace them by those which are predominantly descriptive-conceptual. For example, the section on libido and its appropriate subdivisions can be replaced by the general headings 'Object Relations' and 'Perception of the Self, Self-regard, and Personal Identity'. The substitution of phenomenological headings is not always possible if the principal asset of the psychoanalytic approach is to be retained, namely, the capacity to offer a means of identifying and recording mental content which does not have an immediate conscious expression.

The examination scheme which will now be described (see Appendix A) is thus based on descriptive concepts taken from clinical psychiatry and explanatory concepts derived from psychoanalysis. Clinical phenomena which arise from disturbances in object relations can be most easily categorized under the heading 'Object Relations'. The psychotic reality which characterizes serious mental illness demands that the 'object relations' category must also include the patient's relationships with delusional objects. By utilizing the heading 'Object Relations', and subdividing this into (i) 'Relationship with Real Objects' and (ii) 'Relationship with Delusional Objects', much of the difficulty encountered by using the term 'Libidinal cathexis of objects—past or present' is obviated.

1. OBJECT RELATIONS

(*i*) *Nature of the Relationship with Real Objects*

It is now appropriate to consider what phenomena are to be recorded under the heading 'Nature of the Relationship with Real Objects'. This section deals predominantly with relations with present-day objects (see Chapter 4). Data about relationships in the past should be recorded in an earlier section of the scheme. Reference was made in the introductory chapter to the fact that the psychoanalytic theory of mental functions suggests that the task of relating with others in the healthy adult is compounded of trends arising from different developmental levels. The entry of excessive childhood relating attitudes (childhood object-libidinal cathexes) into an adult relationship may lead to its disruption. In psychotic illness the nature of the patient's capacity to relate to real objects in his immediate environment will vary. At one time it may reach a healthy normal level, even if only transiently. At other times it will reach a childhood level with the associated envies, jealousies, and intensive affects. There will even be occasions when the relating has the characteristics of infancy and early childhood. The quality of the relationship with the real object may, in psychoanalytic terms, be at the need-satisfying level, at the level of object constancy, or at the Oedipal level. When at the need-satisfying level, the object is of little significance other than that of providing satisfactions. Such considerations suggest a number of questions which the observer may put on examining the patient suffering from psychosis. He will of course also note the psychotic attitudes to real objects, particularly those involving persecutory feelings and irrational over-valuation of the examiner or others.

The questions which may be asked regarding the nature of the relationship with real objects are as follows: What are the types of real object relationship that appear in the course of the illness? Is the patient interested in the object only as a source of need satisfaction? Is the object easily given up? Does the object exist in its own right apart from the patient's needs and is there concern for the object? Is there a low frustration if the need is not met? Does the relationship carry with it such features as the wish to protect the object, or jealousy or envy of the object? When interest and concern for the object arise, do they remain or are they liable to disappear? Does the object relationship remain viable following the expression of aggression arising from a disappointment with or separation from the object? A note should also be made of the kinds of object-relationship content that make themselves manifest. If the object exists in its own right, what part is played by heterosexual object-choice on the one hand and homosexual object-choice on the other hand? Is there inappropriate concern and anxiety for the object? Does the patient feel persecuted by the object? Does he irrationally over-value the object? Is the patient negativistic and unresponsive?

(*ii*) *Nature of the Relationship with Delusional Objects*

The observer who wishes to obtain a full description of a patient's relationship to his delusional or hallucinatory objects will be in the most favourable position if he recognizes that the psychotic reality is a medium for the expression of past and present interpersonal conflicts which are denied admission to consciousness. Viewed from the standpoint of psychoanalysis, therefore, the content of delusions and hallucinations can be regarded as replacing relationships which once existed with real objects. Through projection, denial, and often reversal of aim, the patient is able to ignore the nature of his drives, on the one hand, and superego reactions, on the other hand. The content of the delusions and hallucinations can generally be related to the conflicts which participated in the precipitation of the illness. In so far as the conflicts are disowned, the delusions present a form of defence analogous to the psychoneurotic symptom. It is noteworthy, however, that the delusion is not created by projection or denial.

Some of the delusional content comes from childhood and adolescent memories and fantasies, the remainder from the current life situation. The observer will quickly see that real and delusional objects can often substitute for one another. Thus it would be erroneous to overlook the connection which so often exists between the elements of the patient's psychotic reality and his experiences with doctors, nurses, and other patients. Psychoanalysis also points to the fact that the delusional or hallucinatory object represents, in an externalized fashion, the critical, and persecuting, or friendly and advising, superego.

Theoretical considerations of this kind therefore lead to the following kinds of inquiry: What is the form in which the fantasy (delusional) objects find representation? Does this occur by means of misidentification or hallucinatory experiences, through the effect on bodily and mental sensibility, or by the construction of imaginary objects? Details should be provided of the nature of the misidentifications and of the delusional objects when they are available. The modality in which the hallucinations occur and their content must also be noted. An account should be given of the patient's attitudes to the delusional objects: is he friendly to, hostile to, or dependent on these fantasy objects? Again, a description should be presented of the attitudes of the delusional objects to the patient as he sees them: are they advising, friendly, reassuring, critical, or persecutory? Are the persecutory objects related or connected to real objects that exist in the present or existed in the past? Are the delusional objects condensed with real objects in the present?

2. PERCEPTION OF THE SELF, SELF-REGARD, AND PERSONAL IDENTITY

In order to overcome difficulties in the comprehension and usage of the term 'cathexis of the self' and the associated concept of narcissism, this section of the examination scheme has been designated 'Perception of the Self, Self-regard, and Personal Identity'. It would be unfortunate if a psychoanalytical concept i.e. narcissism so valuable in description and explanation, were to be relegated to a position of secondary importance. Here again, the investigator encounters the problem of how far it is justified to separate observation and interpretation. Cut off from explanatory concepts, observational data frequently appear disconnected and meaningless. On the other hand, excessive attachment to interpretation can lead to a stereotyped explanation of clinical phenomena and to inattention to significant data.

Descriptive psychiatry has drawn attention to the various phenomena which reveal how the patient experiences the self in psychotic illness. However, the tendency here has been to categorize the various phenomena under separate headings – for example, depersonalization, transivitism, etc. – and this has led to their appearing separate from one another and without any interconnections. Psychoanalysis has corrected this static tendency by suggesting that the disorders affecting the mental and bodily self can be understood as the result of disturbance in distribution of libido between self and object. Such a state of affairs implies the presence of a state of pathological narcissism.

Many of the phenomena that appear in psychosis can be classified under the heading of narcissism because they possess so many characteristics similar to those encountered in the course of childhood development. Psychoanalytic theory proposes two narcissistic phases in childhood: First, there is the stage of primary narcissism, where bodily and mental experience are syncretic in nature. Alteration in the condition of one implies alteration in the condition of the other. As development proceeds beyond early infancy, object relations are established and this primary form of narcissism becomes progressively limited. Nevertheless in childhood it reveals its presence in a cognitive and affective egocentrism. It is this egocentrism that is universally encountered in psychotic states—sometimes obviously libidinized, sometimes not. The advent in childhood of an awareness of personal and sexual identity, with an implication of stable identifications, constitutes the stage of secondary narcissism. In contrast to the primary phase, objects exist in their own right although they can still be the recipients of narcissistic cathexes.

According to the theory outlined in the previous chapter, psychosis is characterized by a dissolution of adult mental functions. This leads to the exposure of mental processes which have limited adaptive value: in this case, phenomena which reveal a disorder of perception of the self, self-regard, and personal identity. These phenomena, regarded by psychoanalysts as narcissistic, have long been the subject of discussion and controversy. What is their nature? Their resemblance to certain forms of childhood thinking and behaviour has already been referred to. Does this mean that in psychosis there is the reappearance of narcissistic phases of development – particularly of primary narcissism – due to fixations occurring at an early infantile period, or is this pathological narcissism something different only brought to light by the disease process? The latter was the view taken by Schilder (1926). Such a view dispenses with the need for regression and fixation. While this problem is not particularly relevant in the present context, it stresses the importance of taking into account the known facts of development when approaching the symptomatology of the psychoses for the purposes of classification.

With such considerations in mind, the following questions may be asked: is there an adequate investment of the boundaries of the self and the self-representations? If so, is this constant or is it subject to derangements during the course of the illness? Is there evidence of a loss of stability of the self as reflected in disturbances of self-object discrimination, resulting in a projection (externalization) of self-representations and/or a merging with the object leading to transient identification? Are there specific changes in the physical characteristics of the body as experienced subjectively, and loss of autonomy of the self as indicated by such phenomena as flexibilitias cerea and automatic obedience? Is there a disturbance of personal and sexual identity? Are there indications of a disorder of the self as evidenced in increase in intensity of bodily sensations, perceptions, thought, and affect, in hypochondriacal preoccupations, in changes in the body-image, in an over-valuation of the self, and in an exaggerated belief in the effect of thought and action? Is there an awareness of disintegration of the self, a weakness or loss of bodily or mental functions?

3. STATUS OF THE COGNITIVE FUNCTIONS

In the Adult Personality Profile cognitive functions are described under the ego. This is consistent with the psychoanalytic theory of the ego, which regards it as a '. . . coherent organization of mental processes' (Freud, 1923, p. 17) much of which is unconscious in both the descriptive and the dynamic sense. The organized and differentiated ego-functions are contrasted with the unorganized, undifferentiated processes of the id. Attention, concentration, speech, thinking, perception, judgement, memory, motility, and defence are designated ego-functions. Here attention is directed only to those phenomena which indicate a disturbance of cognition. Motility and defence are described in later sections of this examination scheme. The title of this section has been altered from the earlier one of 'Cognitive Dysfunction' (Freeman *et al.*, 1965) to 'Status of the Cognitive Functions'. The reasons for this alteration are that there is no definite knowledge of the nature of the disturbance and that the changes are rarely consistent or uniform.

In psychotic states, with the exception of manic-depression, there is loss of high-level discrimination in the use of words, in thinking and perceiving, and in memory. Words may be altered in their form quite apart from changes in their meaning. Neologisms and paraphasias are not uncommon. Concepts are altered so that they are no long autonomous and independent of wishes and affects. Similar considerations apply to percepts. In Chapter 2 this trend was explained as resulting from the intrusion of a primitive mode of mental function – the primary process.

In this approach interpretation is subordinated to accounts of abnormal cognitive function as encountered in psychosis. The following inquiries must be made.

(*a*) Is there a disorder of verbalization as expressed through speech? Is grammatical construction adequate? Is there obstruction or 'derailment' or omission in the flow of associations? Are words changed in form? Is there a naming difficulty? Do paraphasic phenomena occur? Is there evidence of perseveration of speech content? Does echolalia occur? Are there indications of a fluctuation between normal and abnormal speech? Does obstruction of speech ever give way to fluent verbalization? What is the content of speech when this occurs? What are the conditions under which blocking becomes manifest? Is there any indication that the patient fails to comprehend the speech of others?

(*b*) Information should be sought about those instances where thinking has assumed a magical, omnipotent quality. Examples should be provided of cases where concepts have lost their independence and gained new meanings as a result of condensation. Note should be made of instances of concrete thinking.

(*c*) Is the patient able to sustain attention for purposes of ordered thinking and for appropriate reactions to environmental stimuli? Are there signs of distractability? Does this distractability emanate from the patient's attempt to understand his experiences or is the external stimulus registered passively outside consciousness, only secondarily making its appearance in speech? Is there a fluctuation between states of inattention and purposive directed thinking? Is the change to normal attention related to the anticipation of the satisfaction of a need or to delusional or hallucinatory experiences?

(*d*) What is the state of the perceptual functions? Are the modalities adequately differentiated? Is there evidence of synaesthesiae? In the sphere of visual perception, is there any disturbance of size, shape, or distance constancies? Is the stability of visual perception influenced by bodily movement? Are percepts experienced more intensely than normal – for example, noise or colour? Are percepts experienced concretely? Does the eye or ear have a symbolic significance for the patient? Does the patient perceive a physical change in his body? Can he discriminate one individual from another? Are there condensations of visual percepts and memory traces leading to misidentifications? Is there evidence of hallucinations in one or more of the sensory modalities?

(*e*) Is there any obvious defect of short-term or remote memory? Are memories deranged with respect to their temporal sequence? Is there a repression of significant life experiences prior to the onset of the illness? Do memories make their appearance in the hallucinations or delusions?

(*f*) Is there faulty judgement arising from anxiety or guilt – leading to various forms of misinterpretation of environmental events?

4. MOTILITY

Disorders of motility occur commonly in psychotic states. They may appear in voluntary movement or in posture. They may find expression in a generalized overactivity or in stereotyped repetitive movements of head or limbs. These disturbances can be seen in the consulting-room or in the hospital ward. Interruption of voluntary movement, after its initiation, is the counterpart to the obstruction of speech usually described as blocking of thought. In this motor blocking, patients become fixed at some stage of a voluntary movement, and it is not brought to completion. Sometimes it is easy to see that this interruption of movement is an expression of motor ambivalence (ambitendency).

The posture of some patients is awkward and unusual. Head, neck, and arms may be held rigidly in uncomfortable positions and repetitive movements of the limbs are often to be seen. Postural persistence is thus a common feature. Many of the automatic movements and stereotypies which occur in the schizophrenias can be regarded as due to motor perseveration. This form of perseveration consists of a compulsive repetition of a motor act. It may arise spontaneously or as a response to an instruction. It can be elicited by asking the patient to perform a simple act. The patient will continue with the movement indefinitely. A second form of motor perseveration can also be found in schizophrenic states. Here a response evoked under a first stimulus continues when a second stimulus is offered. This form of perseveration is not as common in the schizophrenias as it is in organic mental states.

Clinical observation alone can lead to the recording of all the disorders of motility. However, this may be possible only over an extended period of time and with the cooperation of nursing staff. What phenomena are to be looked for? Briefly, are there disturbances of voluntary movement? Is the patient able to act on and complete an intention or command? Does motor-blocking occur during the course of a voluntary act? Is there evidence of ambitendency? Note the presence of motor perseveration, repetitive movements, and echopraxia. Describe any disorders of posture. Note whether there is flexibilitas cerea or postural persistence. Are there periods when voluntary movement occurs normally? What kind of verbal content and affect are associated with the transition from abnormal to normal motility and vice versa? Note the fantasies associated with the disorders of motility if they can be elicited. Is voluntary movement disturbed by auditory or visual percepts?

In those circumstances where it is impossible to observe the patient over a long period of time, an assessment of the extent to which motility is disordered can be obtained by the administration of a series of simple tests. These tests (see Appendix B) are similar to those administered to patients suspected of suffering from organic brain disease (Luria, 1966). Their function is to elicit delay in response, postural persistence, perseveration, and disorganization of voluntary movement.

5. SENSORI-MOTOR ORGANIZATION

It is sometimes forgotten that the schizophrenic patient exhibits disturbances of bodily function which are reflected in physical signs. Several years ago, Shattock (1950) and Hoskins (1946) described changes which appear in the different bodily systems in the schizophrenias. More recently, interest has been revived in the neurological abnormalities which can be detected in some schizophrenic patients. There is some evidence in favour of the view that both positive and negative neurological signs are encountered significantly more often in schizophrenic patients than in healthy controls (Lemke, 1955).

Patients who demonstrate psychomotor phenomena almost always present disturbances at the sensori-motor level also. Although these phenomena are transient in nature and variable in expression, particularly in the recent case, it is essential to record their presence. On the motor side, hypotonia, hypertonia of the limb musculature, diminution or absence, accentuation, and asymmetrical reactions of the tendon reflexes have been recorded. The hyper-reflexia is sometimes associated with a tonic reflex response which can be most easily elicited during the examination of the biceps tendon reflexes. The biceps muscle progressively shortens with successive blows of the tendon hammer until the forearm is quite unsupported, making an angle of various degrees with the upper arm. Here there is a persistence of posture akin to the cataleptic phenomenon. It can, like the latter, be regarded as due to tonic or static perseveration. This can be contrasted with the other form of perseveration already described in the section on motility (clonic or kinetic perseveration), which occurs in the course of voluntary movement.

On the sensory side, inattention to tactile stimuli is a common finding in some cases of schizophrenia, and generalized analgesia may be encountered. The localization of tactile stimuli is often disturbed, displacement occurring from one body-part to another. This takes place at random, the stimulus not being transposed to the symmetrically opposite part of the body. With regard to sensory organization, schizophrenic patients have been found to show a face dominance when examined by means of double simultaneous stimulation. Sensory signs, like the motor phenomena, show a striking variability of response – a positive sign being obtained, disappearing, and then re-emerging at a later time.

In the course of a neurological examination special attention should be paid to the presence of tonus changes in the limb muscles – asymmetrical states should be noted. Similarly, a record should be made of hyper-reflexia and asymmetrical reactions of the tendon reflexes. Attention should be paid to the possible presence of tonic reflex responses, particularly in those cases presenting with hypertonia of the upper limb musculature.

Similarly, investigation must be made of inattention to tactile and painful stimuli. Are there indications of displacement (disturbed localization) of sensation from one body-part to another? Is there face dominance?

During the course of a routine neurological examination perseverative signs frequently make their appearance, particularly when the patient is asked to carry out simple instructions. Such signs should be recorded.

6. MANIFESTATIONS OF 'INSTINCTUAL DRIVE' ACTIVITY

In both organic and functional psychoses, autoerotic and object-directed sexual behaviour make themselves manifest. The autoerotic phenomena may be oral, anal, or phallic in nature. The object-directed behaviour may be homosexual or heterosexual in aim. Similarly, aggressive drives, which in the healthy state are under control, often find expression in action.

These phenomena, which can be classified under the headings 'Libidinal' and 'Aggressive', should be examined for as follows:

(*a*) *Libidinal:* Indications of autoerotic behaviour should be described. Is there evidence of heterosexual or homosexual behaviour? Does the patient manifest exhibitionistic or scoptophilic tendencies?

(*b*) *Aggressive:* Manifestations of overt outwardly directed aggression should be detailed. Note possible stimuli for the evocation of aggressive outbursts. Is there an association between the expression of aggression and changes in such signs of disturbed motility as catalepsy, motor blocking, stereotyped movements, and ambitendency? Are aggressive outbursts followed by these disorders of motility? Is aggression directed to the body or to the mental self in the form of self-reproaches?

7. AFFECTIVITY

Elation, depression of mood, anxiety, and dread are common manifestations at the outset of a schizophrenic illness. Self-criticism may appear and depression of mood may persist for some time before delusions and hallucinations make their appearance. In the established case, depression of mood and a sense of hopelessness are sometimes reported when delusional experiences of a wish-fulfilling type are threated by real circumstances. A depression of mood can occasionally be seen arising from the non-psychotically involved part of the patient's mind and this can be regarded as an appropriate reaction to his plight.

It is absence of affectivity or inappropriate affective responses which is regarded as characteristic of schizophrenic psychosis. A result of the psychotherapeutic work conducted over the past twenty-five years has been to show that there is no impairment or weakening of affect in the schizophrenias. Instead, it is the manner of expression that is disturbed. It is of some interest that anger is the most commonly observed affect, particularly in patients who are for the most part withdrawn and inaccessible. As in the case of thinking, perceiving, and voluntary movement, a latent period is interposed between the stimulus and the overt reaction.

It is necessary to describe all expressions of affect. Are these manifestations appropriate or inappropriate? Detail the accompanying ideational content. If there is an absence of affect, note the form of object relations and motility disorder, if present.

8. DEFENCE ORGANIZATION

The concept of defence is unique to psychoanalytic psychology. It is the corner-stone of its theory of neurosis. Its use immediately introduces a complication of which earlier sections of this examination have been relatively free, namely, the vexatious problem of interpretation of clinical phenomena. Employment of the defence concept implies a commitment to a theory of mental function. It requires the use of a series of concepts elaborated to describe mental processes whose aim was envisaged as that of alleviating anxiety provoked by internal dangers. These concepts – identification, repression, displacement, reversal, turning on the self, introjection, and regression – delineate processes which cannot be observed; their activity can only be inferred from the appearance of certain phenomena. It is true that acceptance of the theory of defence is a precondition for the recognition of the activity of these defensive processes. However, this acceptance need not be regarded as leading to a state antagonistic to a realistic account of the patient's clinical status because by its use certain clinical phenomena achieve recognition and a prominence which they might otherwise have forgone. This is true of the mental conflicts which exist in every patient and which are so easily ignored. Conflict and defence are interrelated and one cannot be considered without the other. In the present context of description of phenomena, use of the defence concept is permissible as long as a sharp distinction is made between phenomena on the one hand and concepts on the other.

According to psychoanalytic theory, defence is a function which arises from the ego. Defences, according to Hoffer (1954) are '. . . patterns of a prescribed automatic and compulsive nature, comparable to the well organized nervous reflexes; hence the name defence mechanisms. They have a definite direction, towards the interior, and a circumscribed aim, the prevention of mental pain'. This concept of an automatic defence against the instincts in mental illness is consistent with Jackson's theory of dissolution. The psychoanalytic theory of psychosis proposes that in these states the disorganization which affects the ego leads to the disruption of the most stable and permanent defences, namely, repression and (secondary) identification. This theory is firmly based on a series of clinical observations. It is well known that in many psychotic states patients consciously experience fantasies which remain unconscious in the mentally healthy. The content of these fantasies may consist of data belonging to the Oedipus complex or to other developmental phases of object relationships (see Chapters 10 and 11). These fantasies are often accompanied by appropriate libidinal tendencies. Sometimes these fantasies are expressed in the delusions. Again, there are patients who present evidences of a return of interest to earlier stages of sexual development. Overt homosexual drives appear in some cases, varieties of autoerotic activity in others. Finally, the appearance of delusional objects and hallucinatory voices is taken as evidence of a dissolution of the identification mechanisms within the ego which ordinarily provide so much of its stability.

Psychoanalysts do not believe that the disorganization of repression and identification is synonymous with the loss of all defensive function in psychosis. Indeed, clinical observation shows that even the most deteriorated patient, whose object ties are virtually nonexistent, cannot fully gratify all his instinctual needs. According to psychoanalytic theory, the functions ordinarily undertaken by repression are replaced in psychosis by other defences which usually play only a secondary role. The less stable defensive processes find expression in phenomena which can be regarded as positive symptoms. Psychoanalysis suggest that these defences belong to what have been described, in normal development, as 'pre-stages of defence'. They occur in infancy and before the ego reaches its full development. At this time there is activity of such mechanisms as reversal, displacement, regression, projection, introjection, and turning in on the self. All these are closely linked with the primary process. In cases of schizophrenic psychosis the effect of these mechanisms can be discerned. As a result of the employment of these concepts, certain aspects of the patient's behaviour, speech, and thinking, achieve the status of significant phenomena.

It is incumbent on the observer to examine, with the aid of such clinical phenomena as are available, the status of the patient's defence organization. As this organization is always disrupted to some extent in psychosis, details must be provided of those phenomena which indicate a far-reaching disturbance of repression. A record should be made, first, of libidinal and aggressive drives which have found direct expression in action (see 'Manifestations of "Instinctual Drive" Activity', pp. 30–1 above) and, second, of fantasy springing from all levels of libidinal development. Similarly, information should be provided of adverse changes in the mechanisms of identification and reaction formation. A full account should be given of the more primitive defences which are close to the primary process and in development have their principal operation prior to the complete establishment of the ego: the activity of displacement, projection, reversal of aim, etc. should thus be detailed. Finally, attention should be drawn to those instances where control of the drives has been handed over to objects in the patient's immediate environment. It should be noted whether these are real or delusional objects or condensations of the two.

METHODOLOGY OF CLINICAL OBSERVATION

The collection of clinical observations in cases of psychosis presents many difficulties. The observing physician is rarely afforded the opportunity of witnessing the entirety of the clinical manifestations, as occurs in physical disease. In the psychoses there are few objective signs which can be recorded independently of the patient's cooperation. Most of the clinical data consist of the patient's subjective experiences, much of which he is reluctant to communicate. This reluctance is often most pronounced with the psychiatrist and therefore it is necessary to know to whom the patient is willing to unburden himself, whether a fellow-patient, a nurse, or an occupational therapist.

The fact that the phenomena are psychological in nature means that there is a variability in the clinical picture far exceeding that which appears in somatic disease. Certain symptoms and behavioural features are present one day and not the next. They are revealed to one examiner and not to another. The presence of this variability demands that the patient shall be observed over a fairly lengthy period of time if a complete account of the condition is to be obtained.

It is well known that patients suffering from psychoses frequently make their strongest attachment to members of the nursing and ancillary staffs. It is to them that they reveal their thoughts and feelings. Additionally, the nurse and occupational therapist are with the patient for long periods of the day and are therefore in a position to observe his behaviour in all its aspects. The patient's attitude to the psychiatrist is a complex one and this interferes with the patient's ability and willingness to express himself. Very often the psychiatrist becomes the recipient of fantasies which convert him into a punitive rather than a helpful figure. This may increase in intensity until he becomes part of a persecutory system. It is usually impossible to detach these fantasies by means of explanation because of the patient's lack of insight into the fact that he is ill.

The collection of clinical information about psychotic states is therefore dependent on the establishment of a team approach to the patient and his illness. In this regard, the nurses and occupational therapists have a part to play as important as that of the psychiatrist; and it is essential that they should come to appreciate the significance of the phenomena with which they are confronted (see Chapter 11). These data only become available when a constructive working relationship is achieved between psychiatrist and nursing staff. With such a background it is possible, for example, to direct their attention to the importance of recording such behavioural items as unusual posture, difficulty in the initiation and completion of voluntary movements, compulsive repetition in writing, drawing, and speech, and echo reactions. They can also observe and note the manner in which the patient reacts to their approach and continuing interest. Is the patient attentive or inattentive, responsive or unresponsive? Does he involve them in his delusional preoccupations? In order to systematize these and other observations a modified form of the examination scheme can be devised. Regular meetings can be held to discuss the scheme and foster familiarity in its use. Continuous practice with the scheme in discussions helps to provide some degree of control over the unreliability of observation that is inevitable in any descriptive technique.

The psychiatrist can gather information either by seeing the patient alone or by holding group sessions with a number of patients. Whatever method is employed, it is necessary for the observation to continue over at least a three-month period. The group situation has the advantage of providing a setting where the patient can be observed interacting with others, and there is often less restraint and more spontaneity than in the individual session. Patients suffering from psychotic illness do not spontaneously provide recollections of childhood or adolescence, as do patients with neurosis. They appear to be preoccupied with their irrational ideas and this militates against the production of information about their current life experiences. Nevertheless, the individual session gives the observer a better chance of assessing the patient's capacity to relate and the extent of the non-psychotic processes still intact. During the observation period, information obtained from all sources—psychiatrist, nurse, and occupational therapist—is pooled at weekly meetings and discussed in detail.

It is inevitable that some degree of unreliability will always be a hazard of the clinical method when it is unaccompanied by the kinds of objective measure which are commonplace in clinical medicine – the biochemical and radiological examinations. It is probably a mistake, however, to exaggerate what has come to be known as observer error in clinical examinations. This factor, observer error, will always influence the results of clinical observation, particularly in psychiatry. It can be partially controlled by the method described above where observers are adequately trained, have adequate experience, and obtain familiarity with a recording instrument—the examination scheme in this case.

Objections can be made against the technique of observation and the method of recording, and the question can then be asked: 'How far is the method reliable? Beck (1967), criticizing the author's observational approach (Freeman, 1967), wonders how, even where the observer has the necessary training to note the phenomena that are nosologically significant, the author and his colleagues go about evaluating their gathered information, and how important trends can be detected from the large file that must accumulate for each patient. Beck is critical of the author's alternative to rating scales as a method of recording and assessing clinical data: if rating scales fail to provide essential detail, then can reliance be placed on the observations made by nurses and occupational therapists?

The need for control over clinical observation, whether made by psychiatrist, nurse, or occupational therapist, is absolutely essential, as Beck (1967) advocates. However, the objective 'statistical' approach is no less vulnerable to criticism, although of a different kind. It has difficulty in producing significant information about the patient beyond identifying the presence of certain signs and symptoms. It is uncertain what the method is extracting from the clinical milieu – a criticism that can to some extent be made also of the clinical approach, although here a degree of control is exercised over the attitudes of the observer. Again, the objective method is quite incapable of throwing light on those subjective experiences which may be associated with the data recorded on rating scales. Finally, this method takes no account of influences operating on patient and observer at the time of sampling.

The examination scheme described in this chapter is an attempt to begin a process of building a reliable and comprehensive method of recording and evaluating the manifestations of psychotic illness. The points that Beck (1967) has raised must be taken into account. It would, however, seem logical to begin with an account in qualitative terms of a scheme which has been built on the foundations of clinical experience with psychotic patients. The research for the future would then consist of developing this scheme so that it would eventually achieve sufficient reliability to be employed to assess mental status before and during research procedures, or to estimate changes in symptomatology before and after therapy.

CHAPTER 4

An Illustrative Case of Functional Psychosis

The material for this illustrative case is based on data obtained from three sources and gathered over a twelve-week period. The first source was daily interviews with the patient, which continued over the twelve-week period; the second was daily reports compiled by nursing staff; and the third was reports made by an occupational therapist.

CAUSES OF REFERRAL

The patient was first seen by a psychiatrist in the medical ward of a general hospital. According to the mother of this patient, he had been perfectly well until four days earlier. At the beginning of this period he had complained of feeling tired and unwell. The general practitioner was called and he suggested that the patient stay off work for a few days. The mother noticed that he was weeping from time to time but did not give any reason for this. He could not sleep at night and would wander about the house. During the day he refused to go out. He gave the impression of being mixed up and puzzled. His speech was indistinct and slurred, and he seemed to tire easily. He said that he could not concentrate or think clearly – 'something is blocking my mind.' The sleeplessness continued and was accompanied by unusual behaviour. Ordinarily he never discussed sexual matters; now he said, 'I can't understand women – what's all this about sex?' He said the men at work were getting him down: '. . . the men at work are giving me wrong ideas about women, we are not animals.' He began to express irrational ideas. He told his mother that strange and unusual things were happening, in which he was involved. He was worried that he might have implicated his family and that some harm might befall them. His mother became alarmed and asked the general practitioner to call again. He arranged the admission to hospital.

When seen in the general hospital, the patient was quite cooperative, talked freely, and did not give the impression of complete self-preoccupation. He reported that his thoughts were being constantly influenced by the thoughts of those around him. He was convinced that all environmental events had a significance. He misinterpreted what he saw and heard in the ward. He was self-reproachful, believing that he was responsible for what was going on. He said that he would be better dead. He was without insight into these ideas at the time of the interview. As the symptoms had appeared so suddenly, the possibility of a toxic or drug cause of the illness was suspected. However, no such cause was found. At times he was not sure if he was really in a hospital or if the doctors and nurses were really doctors and nurses. There was no indication of memory defect. After twenty-four hours he was transferred to the mental hospital for investigation and treatment.

DESCRIPTION OF THE PATIENT

At the time of admission to the mental hospital the patient presented as a slimly built young man looking if anything younger than his 19 years. He was restless and agitated. The slightest sound caught his attention. He found it difficult to remain seated, and wandered about the room. He seemed on the point of bursting into tears, but would suddenly smile instead. He would cover his face with his hands. His movements were quite normal and he did not maintain postures or assume uncomfortable positions. His manner was friendly, but his anxiety and apprenhension could not be restrained. His speech was slow and there were often pauses. It was frequently disjointed, which made it difficult to follow.

The following excerpt is illustrative of his speech content at the time of admission to hospital:

> 'I have been reading stuff and it is different . . . think someone is annoying me . . . hear banging noises when waking up . . . it's not really a banging noise, I feel a pressure in my head. I've been feeling confused ever since the summer holidays. I think I've been poisoned because of the way my stomach reacts . . . it gives me a pain . . . I asked my mother and she said "I'll give you

pills." I've got the pills and I didn't feel very well... the pressure in my head, that's what bothers me . . . it affects my vision, it's not too sharp, if I sleep I'll be better. I've not been sleeping well at all . . . 1966 . . . I've got the impression there will be an explosion . . . if I don't go back to 1947 this place will be shut. Loud-speakers singing carols the whole time . . . if I listen I can hear them . . . the voices say I've died already . . . that's if I don't read the Bible . . . the Bible seems against me, no it isn't, it depends which I read. I've been thinking about life, I can never understand it, I can't make it . . . left me for a week . . . then wouldn't speak to me much for a week . . . I went to work on Monday and they started making a fool of me . . .' Later, he said: 'I feel I'm being got at by the Russians, I've been injected with syphilis . . . my teeth are suddenly going to fall out because they will be kicked in by the nurses. All the people in the ward are priests . . . there is a purge against religion, isn't there?'

FAMILY AND PERSONAL HISTORY

The patient's father is aged 50. He is an engineer and in good health. He is an illegitimate child. He is regarded as a very quiet, retiring type of man. The mother is 56, also in good health. She is very religious and belongs to a mission-hall church which imposes many restrictions on its members. The husband does not share his wife's religious interests and this has been a cause of friction between them. Religion is talked about a great deal by the mother. She told an interviewing psychiatrist that she did not really love her husband, marrying him merely to get away from home. The mother had a brother who was a patient in a mental hospital in 1947. He was discharged after about a year. In 1963, he committed suicide. The mother was pregnant with the patient at the time of the brother's hospitalization. She visited him frequently and kept a diary of what he said. She stated that the patient didn't know about his uncle's illness and suicide. (In fact this was not so.) She was concerned lest her son should turn out like her brother. The family are in comfortable financial circumstances.

The patient has a sister of 24. She is single. About eighteen months earlier, she obtained an honours degree at the University of Edinburgh. She was teaching in London when the patient fell ill. There is another sister aged 17, still at school. Both siblings are fit and well.

As mentioned above, the mother worried about her brother throughout the pregnancy. She suffered from hydramnios and possibly a mild pre-eclamptic toxaemia. The labour was long and difficult, but the patient was born normally and weighed $9\frac{1}{2}$ lb. No unusual events occurred in the first year. The mother was well physically but there seems little doubt that she was in an anxious, somewhat depressed state because of her brother's illness. When the patient was a year old he contracted whooping cough. At eighteen months he was ill with measles. This led to a middle-ear infection which left him slightly deaf in one ear. This deafness was not discovered till he started school. He was not hospitalized with these childhood illnesses. He was not dry at night till he was 4 years old. He was a quiet, unaggressive child. This lack of aggressiveness has characterized his personality up to the present time. He is known as gentle in manner and considerate to others. He had friends at school, played football, and joined in the ordinary activities. He was in no way different from the others. It should be noted that he began to speak rather late, but that once he had started no abnormalities appeared. He was found to be left-handed.

As far as can be ascertained, the home was reasonably stable in his childhood, apart from the mother's nervousness and the occasional arguments about religion. He did well at school and obtained four 'O' Levels. He began an apprenticeship as an engineer when he left school. He has done well at this, being considered the best apprentice in his factory. He has passed several examinations. He is a conscientious person, with interests outside his work and family. He is very enthusiastic about outdoor pursuits and is a member of a yachting club. He has a number of male friends but has never had a girl-friend. He is described as outgoing, energetic, and cheerful – a good organizer. Unfortunately it was impossible to obtain any further material about the patient's childhood. In the interviews which the author had with the mother she spent most of the time talking about her brother's illness, its effect on her, and her present nervousness, which she said was heightened by her son's illness.

SIGNIFICANT CURRENT EVENTS

A few days before the illness began, the patient was transferred to another department of the factory. The day prior to his complaining of feeling unwell, the men at work organized a kind of initiation ceremony for the patient. This took the form of a mock trial, the patient having the role of prisoner. This upset him quite a lot. He thought the men considered him unmanly. He felt he ought to have challenged another apprentice to a fight. This mock trial was only the culmination of a series of stresses which had existed since the summer holidays of

1966. For some weeks he had been worried by the talk of sex that is so common in factories. Reference has already been made to his complaints on this score. It also appears that he had been caught up in a conflict about masturbation. After the summer he had decided to abandon the habit but had not been completely successful. He was guilty about this and reactions to masturbation occurred during the illness. Concurrently he became interested in a girl, a friend of his sister. Unfortunately the girl went about with a friend of his. He did not want to try to 'cut in' in case he upset his friend. A further possible source of stress was a suspicion that the patient had discovered his mother's diary of her brother's illness sometime in the late autumn.

With respect to historical material which may be relevant in this section, it is worth recalling the mother's concern with her brother during the patient's infancy. She was preoccupied with religion throughout his boyhood and adolescence. She condemned sexuality and all evidences of aggression. She regarded the expression of these drives as wicked and sinful. Her attitude in this respect left their mark on the patient, and he in turn found it difficult to tolerate the demands of his sexual and aggressive drives.

I. OBJECT RELATIONS

(*i*) *Nature of the Relationship with Real Objects*

Some of the phenomena now to be reported could equally well have been allocated to the section dealing with perception of self, etc. The following material is illustrative: 'I don't seem to have a personality of my own. I'm just a conglomoration of all the men in the ward. If one of them is angry, I'm angry too; if someone is happy, I am happy too. Do you know, there are ten men who have passed through my hands. I've seen lots of men come into the ward and more go out cured. It is not right . . .' At a later point he said: 'It's like talking to yourself, you become me.' A further illustration of the same phenomenon was as follows: 'Your eyes keep roving about.' Asked whose, he replied, 'Mine', or again, 'It was the last person that touched me . . . I'd taken on his character . . . it's like talking to myself, I've become you.'

He wanted to know, 'Are you a man or a woman or both? . . . suppose I'd better go . . . you're a fake as well . . . you're turning . . .'

Some days later, he announced that he was half-man and half-woman, not quite human. Delusional objects – to be described later – were similarly hermaphroditic. Changes in appearance of patients, nurses, and the observer were also based on the state of his perception of the self. The observer was also changed by him: 'You have taken on my character.' As was to be expected, the patient completely identified, although transiently, with other patients, behaving as they did and claiming their names as his.

Alongside these forms of object relations, the patient showed less disorganized patterns of relating to others. Again this was not limited to any one individual but occurred in relation to patients, nurses, other patients, occupational therapists, and the author. The content of his thought often had a depressive colouring. Directly or indirectly he expressed the fear of damaging the author either physically or mentally through contact with him: 'I'm beginning to rip you up . . . I'm betraying you.' He explained his inability to describe his experiences as follows: 'I can't tell you, you would be . . . I can't tell you; if you understood you'd become like me. When I swallow or breathe men are absorbed into me, they become me . . . If I look in your eyes you will be broken-hearted, like the men in the ward . . . I mustn't trouble you, I'll break your spirit.'

He feared he had harmed his parents. He had aimed too high, he had spread rumours. At one time he believed his parents had been murdered because of him. He said, 'I'm damaging people, I'm damaging the world.' He had to disappear; otherwise his sister and his family would be wiped out. He was distressed by the fact that he had caused disasters he had heard about on the wireless or television. He was very worried about the other patients. He warned a nurse, 'Don't touch me, you'll get a shock.' He would not let nurses or patients come too near. He refused to see his sisters: '. . . it's too dangerous for them.' He was afraid of harming the occupational therapist also: 'Don't come near me, don't come near me . . . I don't want you to look into my eyes as you might crack and I don't want you to crack.'

When his sister arrived from London about six weeks after his admission to hospital it became apparent that he had a very positive attachment to her. He was friendly and talkative in her presence, and the detachment, hesitancy, and negativism which characterized his attitude at that time towards the author and nursing staff were strikingly absent. He was, however, responsive in those circumstances where the object appealed for his help or cooperation, particularly if it was a female. One morning he refused breakfast and insisted on staying in bed. The ward maid reminded him that he had promised her to help to polish the floor. He promptly got up, got dressed, and polished much of the ward floor. The occupational therapist was able to get the patient to return to the ward when she explained that she was responsible for him and that she would be blamed if he ran off. This responsiveness was limited to the occupational therapist, the ward maid, and his sister.

No apparent difference existed between his concern for the safety of men or women. He expressed great anxiety about contact with men. He believed that he was being forced to come close to men all the time. He wanted to be alone because he influenced them adversely. Reference will be made in a later section to his concern about bisexuality and to his fear of homosexuality. Reference has already been made to the fact that before his illness he was interested in a girl but did not press his advances because he did not want to upset a male friend who was also interested in her.

Object relationships, whatever their organizational level, were unstable. This was shown in his constant anxiety about the fate of the world and about individuals. With regard to the former he said, 'I hear the world blowing up . . . I've got to go; the world is being over-run . . . I think there's a nuclear explosion.' One evening, while having a bath, he commented on the weight-loss of a patient who had recently been discharged. In the patient's mind he was dead and this would be his fate too. All the patients who left the ward were dead. He wanted to know why all his friends had disappeared.

(*ii*) *Nature of the Relationship with Delusional Objects*

Delusional object relationships did not appear until about ten days after the patient's admission to hospital. The first sign was an unwillingness to speak to the author: 'I've said too much, I'm a marked man.' He was reluctant to enter the consulting-room or sit down. He would stare at the wall and put his hands to his ears as if to indicate that both he and the author would be overheard. As he did not speak he was given a piece of paper and a pencil. He wrote, 'They are listening.' Then he said, 'I am quite well; they're a great lot in the ward.' He showed a great interest in the author's watch. Only later was it understood that watches had a special significance. He told the nurses that he heard voices from watches. One evening he tried to take his watch to pieces to find the source of the voice. He believed watches were harmful to him. He threw his away and was very suspicious of the watches belonging to nurses and other patients.

Delusional qualities were attributed to the author and other doctors.

He had asked the author if he was a man or a woman. Later he told a nurse that he was surrounded by 'paranoidals' who were half man and half woman and who preyed on humans. He believed a woman doctor was a vampire. This idea was stimulated when he saw her take a blood-sample from a patient. During the remainder of his stay in hospital the author remained as a delusional object, at least during the course of the interviews. Although it was known from occasional remarks and from nursing reports that he believed he or some other influence had harmed or changed the author, there was little sign of interest and contact to indicate the presence of an affective, real relationship.

The following excerpt from an interview illustrates his attitude to the author and to the meetings. He spoke in a very low and distinct voice with many pauses. 'Am I sitting here again . . . I think I had better go away . . . I had better not . . . I think I'd better . . . I'll just go away outside and walk . . . I seem to be . . . I'm annoying people . . . I'm very ashamed. . . . Can I go away outside . . . hear the watch . . . let me away . . . now quick . . . I'm not kidding you [he stood up and repeated this] . . . before it's too late . . . I haven't got my watch wound up . . . this is . . . come on [he looked at the author's watch] . . . can I go out . . . the sun seems to be shining an awful lot . . . shining too much . . .' His next phrase could not be heard. He said, 'Can you not hear me?' 'What are you saying?' At this time a tendency to repeat questions or statements made to him was very common. This echolalia also occurred with the occupational therapist and nurses.

The circumstances of the author being in charge of his case, the patient's knowledge of this, and his having to remain in the hospital, undoubtedly provided an extra stimulus for his withdrawal after the first week or two in the hospital and for the heightening of the delusional ideas. It seemed as if all the circumstances encountered in the hospital were employed as material to elaborate his delusional reality.

2. PERCEPTION OF THE SELF, SELF-REGARD, AND PERSONAL IDENTITY

In this case there was abundant evidence of serious disorders in the patient's awareness and evaluation of his bodily and mental self. The phenomena to be reported below can be grouped into five categories. First are the changes which the patient experienced in the physical characteristics of his body; second are the changes in bodily sensation; third are disturbances of personal and sexual identity; fourth, hypochondriacal anxieties; and, fifth, the over-valuation of the effects of thought and action. Reference has already been made in the section on 'object relations' to phenomena which suggested a difficulty in self-object discrimination.

According to the patient, changes had taken place in his bodily structure. He believed that his bones had altered in their consistency and that he had shrunk in size. He expressed the idea that he was no longer completely masculine but instead half man, half woman. This belief has been referred to above (p. 47). He insisted that he had some foreign substance inside his body that must be cut out. He thought it must be a hyena because he laughed too much. He was convinced that he had a hole in his stomach caused by electricity being passed through his body.

Changes in bodily sensation were suggested by his complaint that his body was charged with electricity. On this account no one must touch him for fear of electrocution. He had a transmitter located in his head between the right and the left sides of the brain. 'There's too much electricity in my body, that's why I sit on my bed. It has rubber wheels and does not conduct electricity.' At another time he complained that his body was effected by gamma rays. They had some connection with worms and grubs which were consuming his body. At other times he showed no anxiety about the effects of rays or electricity, saying, 'The gamma rays can't harm me; I'm well earthed.' He experienced his body temperature as elevated: 'My body is running far too high a temperature . . .' When asked how he knew this, he replied, 'The windows in the ward are covered with steam . . . I'm too hot . . . I must get cool.'

He had doubts about his sexual identity. He was confused; was he a man or a woman? For a while he had thought he was turning into a woman: 'Can they change from one to the other?' He thought a patient called him a 'poof' – was he homosexual? His own personality had gone: 'I reflect people's attitudes; they correspond too much to me . . . I take on other people's personalities.' He never lost his sense of identity, although there were fleeting moments when he behaved in exactly the same manner as another patient, calling himself by the name of the patient in question. All these experiences were closely connected with other patients, nurses, and the author.

He overvalued the effects of his thoughts and actions on others and on the world in general. At the second interview he spoke as follows: 'I'm able to do more than I should be . . . I'm able to influence people . . . I'm not touching you.' When asked what would happen if he did, he replied, 'I tend to shatter you a bit . . . unless you are a priest or a monk

. . . I'll have to go and be a monk. I've been influencing television and radio, transmitting signals at a high rate, that's what's exhausting me. . . . The television show is specially prepared for me. . . . Everything I see or touch seems to be affected.' Later he said, 'When I look at men they are shattered.' On this account he refused to look at the author. He asked the occupational therapist not to let him look at a bus which was passing by: 'Don't let me look at the bus or I'll be switched on.'

He believed that the wind had begun to howl while he was at the lavatory defecating. Attention has already been directed to his belief that breathing and swallowing had the most far-reaching effect on those around him. He also thought that on the day of his admission to hospital he had saved the world of mortals from rockets. There was no one like him, no one could beat him. If he was kept in the ward he would kill someone and then everyone would kill. He had seen Christ. He would say no more about it because: 'You will pick on him like the others.'

Only on the one occasion mentioned above did this patient ascribe a beneficent influence to himself. His megalomania consisted almost exclusively of destructive effects he was having on people. Thus he was preoccupied with self-reproaches. He felt himself to be a menace. He wanted to be put into solitary confinement or left at the North Pole. He became increasingly agitated when he was not allowed to be alone or to get out of the hospital away from others. He was without a sense of well-being and his self-esteem was low.

3. STATUS OF THE COGNITIVE FUNCTIONS

During the first week in hospital the patient's speech was normal in quantity and in grammatical construction. As the delusional reality came into the foreground a radical change took place. It was often difficult to hear what he said, because he spoke indistinctly or in a whisper. Sentences were started but not completed. The following is illustrative: 'Don't listen to them . . . I've tried to help you . . . don't . . . this country's getting wrecked . . . the Russians have won . . .' He was asked what was wrong. He echoed 'What's wrong?' and looked at the ceiling with a fixed stare. After a pause he continued, '. . . Turning into a race of giants . . .' He was asked, 'Who has?' He replied, 'Who has? . . . You're as bad . . .' He looked at the author's watch, as he often did. He muttered something. The author said that he could not hear him. He replied, 'I can't . . .', again beginning to echo the author's statement. There was a pause, followed by 'Are you . . . are you a man or a woman or both?' 'I suppose I'd better go, you're a fake as well . . . You're turning . . . You'd better keep . . . Why did you open the windows? . . .' His lips moved but no sound emerged. Later he said, 'I've been brain-washed . . . You're changed . . . Your hands have changed . . .'

Obstruction of speech occurred in two circumstances. In the first, the obstruction appeared to be due to an actual difficulty in thinking and words. He said, 'I can't think . . . someone is trying to . . . putting a tremendous pressure on my brain and not letting me think.' Some weeks later he said, 'Somebody blocks my mind.' He told a nurse that he found it difficult to speak. In contrast to this awareness of a difficulty in thinking, interruption of speech and a reluctance to talk must be considered the result of the predominant psychic reality. He must not speak to the author, for example, because the latter would become like him. He said to the occupational therapist, 'I don't know why I can't speak . . . I get sort of blocked . . . maybe I was switched off . . .' Thinking was omnipotent, and many illustrations of this have already been presented.

The patient was unable to sustain attention for speech or for simple tasks. He was easily distracted by sounds or movements. It was a distractability which led to the interruption of speech or of any activity in which the patient was engaged. He appeared to interpret these extraneous stimuli in terms of his delusional reality. He would speak as follows: 'I made a fool of myself in front of my parents asking them about sex.' Just then, air in the hot-water pipes made a gurgling sound: 'Is that gas?' he asked anxiously. Another time a window creaked and he said, 'You'd better watch yourself.' This form of distractability must be distinguished from a second type which also occurred in this patient. Here the patient did not seem to be conscious of the fact that he had registered a visual or auditory impression, which then determined the content of his speech. The author happened inadvertently to crack his knuckles while the patient was saying that he thought the egg he was given at breakfast looked poisonous. He continued '. . . there's something lacking in my diet'. He was asked what. He replied, 'Calcium – I think my bones are too thin.' A second instance has already been quoted. The wind whistled outside the consulting-room. This led him to leave the topic on which he was engaged to relate the fact that he believed he had caused the storm the day before when he was defecating.

In the sphere of perception, both visual and auditory sensations were intensified. The sun, the sky, and colours all seemed brighter than usual. Sounds were louder and difficult to tolerate. All this was attributed to the Russians, atomic influences, and so on. He found the talk of the other patients deafening. He seemed to suffer considerably from any kind of loud noise or shouting. His perception of words and his comprehension of them were frequently faulty. He could not always understand what was said to him – it seemed incoherent. He did not necessarily recognize his own speech: 'My lips utter words which I don't understand.' For a long period he continually responded to questions or statements made to him with an echo reaction (echolalia). For example, the occupational therapist recorded the following instances: 'Were you out for a walk today?' The patient replied, 'Was I out for a walk today?' Then again, 'What's wrong with your arm?' Did you enjoy your game of badminton?' 'Did you enjoy your game of badminton?' was the reply. When a nurse asked him why he did this he replied, 'The words just bounce back. I can't keep them in . . .' Echolalia occurred with the author as well as with the nurses and occupational therapist.

There was no evidence of visual misidentifications. On several occasions, however, visual and auditory perceptions were misinterpreted. He thought he saw his mother being dragged into the hospital. For a time he believed that the patients were not really patients but were men in disguise. He frequently misinterpreted overheard speech in terms of the psychotic reality. Auditory hallucinations which have already been described were reported from time to time. These voices were not necessarily persecutory but sometimes advising; for example, he was told to 'get out of the ward or be good.'

He did not show any defects of memory.

Judgement was mostly defective, as the material presented demonstrates. There were, however, a few occasions when the patient appeared to recognize that he was ill and that his thinking, feeling, and understanding of the environment were dominated by irrational ideas. This appearance of a healthy ego was also to be noted on those occasions when the patient's speech and thinking functioned within normal limits. This did not happen frequently with the author but it did occur with nurses and with the occupational therapist.

4. MOTILITY

As in the case of speech, motility was progressively disordered with the development of the illness. The patient demonstrated grave defects in the initiation and completion of voluntary acts. This disorder was reported by nurses long before it became apparent in the consulting-room. As in the case of speech, movements were started but stopped before completion. When eating, he would bring food to his mouth and then take it away. He would do this several times and then suddenly get the food into his mouth with a hurried movement. He took a sparking-plug out of his pocket, went to put it on the table, but only got part of the way, took it back, started again, and the process was repeated several times. He half laughed and cried as he did this. This ambitendency was also noted in his inability to stand up or sit down. He ended up neither standing nor sitting, with hips and knees flexed. He took a mouthful of water, retaining it in his mouth for a long time, neither swallowing it nor spitting it out.

He would remain stuck in the middle of a voluntary act. This was particularly so in dressing, and he was always having to have help. He began to wash his hair, put shampoo on it, but proceeded no further, standing immobile in front of the wash-basin. This behaviour also occurred in the occupational therapy department. It took him a long time to stick a few tiles on a box. He sat with a tile in one hand and the box in the other, and when asked to carry out an action he sometimes responded with an echo-reaction: 'Please get on with your work': 'Please get on with your work.'

Associated with this inability to begin an act was the fear of injuring people. This suggested that on some occasions the inability to act had a defensive aim, activity being replaced by passivity. The nurses reported that he stood motionless for periods of up to half an hour. It was also observed that he had difficulty in responding to a second simple instruction after responding correctly to an initial request. This perseverative behaviour was noted only during a period of about a week when the patient was extremely withdrawn and almost impossible to contact. Finally, reference must be made to the fact that the patient was incontinent of urine on two occasions. There was also a phase of overactivity when he identified with restless patients. He jumped about, falling on the floor, and rushed up and down the ward. Unfortunately there was no opportunity of finding the kinds of circumstances or mental content which appeared contemporaneously with the onset of the motility disorders.

5. SENSORI-MOTOR ORGANIZATION

Routine physical examination at the time of the patient's admission to hospital revealed no physical abnormalities. A week later he was submitted to a neurological examination and this also proved negative. At this time he was cooperative and the disturbances which were to affect speech, movement, and posture had not yet occurred.

A further examination was carried out three weeks later, when a series of abnormal phenomena were observed. The patient was slow in responding to simple instructions and he showed evidences of repetitive perseveration, that is, he appeared to have difficulty in terminating an action once initiated. There was a definite increase in tone of the upper and lower limb musculature. He showed echolalic responses when spoken to. These phenomena occurred contemporaneously with the delusions of persecution already described.

A third neurological examination was conducted two weeks later. In addition to the phenomena just described, he showed signs of persistence of posture, and the repetitive perseveration was even more pronounced. For example, when asked to shut his eyes he did so; asked to open them and put out his tongue, he responded by protruding his tongue and shutting his eyes. After resuming the normal position of eyelids and tongue he closed and opened his eyes several times. Again, when his upper limbs were passively flexed and extended he continued this movement himself. Shortly after the eye-tongue test he was asked to carry out another simple instruction but responded by shutting his eyes, thus demonstrating the presence of the 'switching' variety of perseveration. He had at this time great difficulty in carrying out the tests described in Appendix B, showing difficulty in the smooth execution of voluntary movement.

At the time of discharge, when the psychotic manifestations had receded into the background, there was no evidence of the above phenomena.

6. MANIFESTATIONS OF INSTINCTUAL DRIVE ACTIVITY

(*a*) *Libidinal*

In psychoanalytical terms, this patient had reached the phallic stage of libidinal development. This is borne out by a statement that he had a conscious conflict over masturbation. He said that he had stopped masturbating about three months before his illness began. He had been interested in girls but had no physical contact with them. Shortly after admission to the hospital he showed how much masturbation disturbed him: '. . . If I touch things they go wrong. I touched myself (he pointed to his penis) . . . If I lose my self-respect I'm done for.' He was afraid he was a homosexual. He maintained on several occasions that his persecutors were bringing him into contact with men all the time. Although he emphasized the destructive aspects of such contacts with men, the libidinal element was to be noted in the incorporative aims and subsequent identifications that he made with them. His fear of homosexuality could be traced partly to his belief that he was changing from a man into a woman.

Reference must be made to the frequency with which scoptophilic manifestations were encountered. Looking assumed great importance but it had a destructive connotation. Thus he must not look. Curiosity and a fear of the curiosity of others were also pronounced. Details of the way in which the aggressive drives found expression through this scoptophilia will be described in the next section. At no time did he show any overt homosexual interests.

(*b*) *Aggressive*

The material already described shows that the patient felt that his aggression was out of control: 'I drive people to crime by breaking their hearts.' However, he had not abandoned the struggle to regain control, as is reflected in the following statements: 'I must control myself. I've got to get away from here and leave this earth in peace.' One day, at the occupational centre, he said to the therapist, 'I want to go for a walk among the trees. You'd better not come with me. I'm going to get lost.' When the therapist persuaded him not to go, he replied, 'I'd better not touch you . . . you're a nice girl.' Later, he added, 'I've disillusioned you . . . I'm bad really . . . I might wreck the place. I must go for a walk.' At this he ran out of the door. He never became violent and only on a few occasions did he show any anger (which lasted seconds and passed away).

Reference has already been made to the fact that overt aggression never appeared during the period of hospitalization, and anger rarely; but destructive fantasies comprised much of the content of the delusions. He was afraid that he had been poisoned; the food was drugged; the seagulls who ate scraps looked ill. The delusional objects, the 'paranoidals', preyed on humans. He swallowed the spirits of men and changed them for the worse. Reference has already been made to his belief that when he defecated he had caused a storm. Finally, a number of illustrations had already been given of his belief that when he looked at anyone or anything he or it was damaged or destroyed.

Aggression seemed to be aimed directly at the body or through a heightening of conscience (superego). With respect to the former he reported that voices told him to open his stomach with scissors. The occupational therapist found him trying to push an awl into his abdomen. It had penetrated into his jumper and shirt when she stopped him. As for the latter, his constant self-reproaches revealed an overactive conscience.

7. AFFECTIVITY

As the illness developed there was a general loss of affect, apart from the expression of anxiety, which reached considerable intensity. There was no indication of inappropriate affective expression. As recovery took place he became somewhat overactive and elated. This elation was particularly noticeable in his relations with his sister but was not seen with the author or with other members of the male staff.

8. DEFENCE ORGANIZATION

The predominance of psychic (delusional) reality showed that repression was seriously disorganized. It would appear that the principal defence was initiated by an anxiety that he was out of control. This was indicated in the fear that arose prior to the onset of the symptoms that his car was getting out of control while he was driving: 'When I was driving my car I felt it was against me . . . getting out of control . . .' He feared that he could not control his urine or resolve his conflict over masturbation. He dreaded the effects of his aggression.

The clinical phenomena suggest that in the absence of effective repression the two major defences employed were reversal of aim and projection. Supplementary defences were turning in on the self and introjection, particularly with respect to the aggressive drives.

Reversal of aim – the replacement of active by passive aims – was seen most strikingly in the motility disorders presented by the patient. The interruption of voluntary movement, the maintenance of postures, and the ambitendency all reveal a state where active aims are initiated through the voluntary musculature and then abandoned, being replaced by passivity. The motor acts were not necessarily endowed with magical (narcissistic) significance, although this was so in the case of breathing and swallowing. The motor paralysis seemed to have the purpose of protecting objects from the impact of the drives. By abandoning active aggressive aims, he became passive and inactive. Before he fell ill he was known for his energetic behaviour and was described as 'always on the move'. The change was reflected in his motility. Turning on the self was noted in his wish and attempt to injure himself.

Projection appeared in different forms. First, there was the straightforward projection of aggression, no different from that encountered with healthy or psychoneurotic individuals; he said, 'People hate me.' Second, aggressive drives and scoptophilic trends were discounted through projection on to delusional objects who were persecutors. This defence was not very effective since it did not relieve him of guilt or of the dread that he had damaged his family and those about him. Reference has already been made to the way in which the patient externalized positive and negative aspects of his physical and mental self on to the author, the nurses, and other patients. It is difficult to regard this form of projection as defensive in aim since it did not alter the patient's intrapsychic situation. There was no easing of his anxiety or guilt. Similar considerations can be applied to the introjective tendencies which also occurred. However, introjection of aggression as defence took place, leading to increased self-reproach.

The defence was effective in so far as objects were preserved from the effects of the patient's drives, particularly aggression; the motor paralysis ensured this. It was ineffective in that it did not preserve the patient from constant awareness of the psychical reality with its anxieties and guilt. The reversal of aim, acting through the voluntary musculature, leads to disruption of environmental adaptation.

Throughout the period of observation, the patient revealed through self-reproaches that the superego remained operative as a psychic structure. The material described in earlier sections indicates that it retained only a critical function. Some small degree of externalization and loss of differentation was suggested by his feeling of being watched and by some of the characteristics of the persecutors. The intensity of the self-reproach matched the intensity of the anxieties regarding his aggressive drives. Condemnation of libidinal drives occurred, as has been described.

CHAPTER 5

The Heterogeneous Nature of the Catatonias

I. Object Relations

In this and the following chapter, a detailed account will be given of the variety of clinical phenomena that appear in patients categorized as catatonic. The purpose of these descriptions is to demonstrate that the base for such a categorization is very narrow, consisting of no more than the fact that these patients present a somewhat similar disorder of voluntary movement and posture, and varying degrees of negativism. When the object relations, perception of the self, cognitive status, affectivity, and psychomotor functions are scrutinized, great differences are found to exist between individual patients. This suggests, as Kleist (1960) and Leonhard (1965) proposed, that the catatonias are by no means a homogeneous group but are rather a collection of syndromes, having in common a motility disorder which varies in its mode of expression and intensity.

The clinical phenomena to be described in these chapters are drawn from four patients who were studied for periods ranging from three months to over a year. Their medication consisted of a small dose of phenothiazine drugs and the amount was held constant. At first sight all four patients appeared similar. When observed in the consulting-room or in the ward they were inattentive and unresponsive, showing signs of active or passive negativism, and disorders of movement and posture. They had all been ill for several years. Two had had remissions early on, but had relapsed. Their ages ranged from 22 to 30. No account will be given here of the history of the illnesses.

OBJECT RELATIONS IN THE CATATONIAS

The first case will be presented in greater detail than the remaining three, to demonstrate the kind of interaction that characterized all the patient-observer contacts at some point during the study period.

CASE I

Miss A was a young woman of middle height with a pale complexion and sullen appearance. She frequently screwed up her eyes and in so doing her face assumed a threatening expression. She sat hunched up in a chair, her limbs held in a rather fixed, rigid position. She did not speak or make any spontaneous movement. She was quite neatly dressed but her hair was not properly combed and had an unkempt appearance.

(*i*) *Nature of the Relationship with Real Objects*

The following material consists of an account of the manner in which the patient related to the author and others as real objects over a ten-month period. The patient refused to sit alone with the author in an interview room. In the early days she often refused to have a meeting at all. When she did she was inattentive, uninterested, and completely turned in on herself. When she agreed to an interview she did not allow the meeting to last very long. Although she would frequently say, 'I've got to go now', she generally made no move and would not leave for another five or ten minutes. She made few spontaneous utterances but occasionally might say, 'It's nice of you to come', or, 'You can come again.' Occasionally she asked for a cigarette. Only later did the author learn from the nursing staff that she had a voracious appetite for cigarettes. Refusal usually led to an angry outburst. This reaction, however, did not occur when he had to tell her that he did not have any cigarettes.

From time to time she seemed a little more pleasant and some warmth appeared in her attitude. On one occasion she offered the author a sweet. This friendliness was usually transient and was easily replaced by anger and a subsequent withdrawal. While the patient was asking if she could go out with her sister who was coming to visit, the ward sister entered the room. Miss A stopped speaking and said, 'You can go now.' When asked why, her response was one of anger. She repeated, 'You can go now . . . I prefer my own doctor.' Only later did it become clear that her 'own doctor' referred to a delusional object and not to the doctor who had previously undertaken her care.

The anger which she had shown towards the author was quite absent when he next saw her. This interview took place in the afternoon instead of the morning, which was the usual time. As soon as she saw him she said, 'I missed you not looking in this morning.' This interest in the author's visits became a constant theme throughout the following months, namely, an anxiety as to whether or not he would come and see her the next day. At the same time this concern was connected with a need to tell him that it was time to go; for example: 'It will soon be time for going away.' When she was asked if she meant herself or the author she answered, 'I won't be going from here . . .' Following a pause, she said, 'Perhaps you will come another day.' This positive feeling was reflected in his again being offered a sweet and her speaking a little more openly. She said, 'It's terrible to be locked up, but I'm not now . . . I've forgotten all about it. . .' Towards the end of this particular interview she added, 'You will not be coming back . . .' She had no idea why she should have thought this.

The first lengthy break in the interviews occurred at New Year 1966. She had no apparent reaction when told about the impending break and her behaviour both with the author and with others remained as before. When seen after the holiday she was quite friendly. She made no comments on the break but when he happened to mention it she said she had missed his visits. Her behaviour in the next two weeks remained much as before, combining a lack of interest with concern that he should come to see her. Unfortunately he suffered from an attack of influenza and did not see her for about two weeks. When she was encountered accidentally in the corridor on the author's first day back he found her shouting, 'I don't like you! Don't follow me! I like my own doctor!' When seen later that afternoon she was silent but not hostile. The next day she sat flicking through a magazine throughout the interview, quite ignoring the author. Before she left she said, 'Come again tomorrow if it suits you.'

The call for morning or afternoon tea and the possibility of getting a cigarette from the ward sister always had a priority over the meetings. For example, when found standing outside the sister's office she said to the author, 'I've nothing to say to you . . . I'm waiting for a cigarette.' In view of her pleasure in smoking he decided to offer her a cigarette daily. During the first meeting in which she was given a cigarette she was friendly and apparently concerned lest he did not come back the next day. She spoke as follows: 'You'll be going for good, away on holiday.' (The author had been out of town for a day three days earlier.) When asked why she thought this she replied, 'I don't think you like me . . . I'm fed up . . . The drawing (at occupational therapy) will cheer me up . . . You'll be going now.'

The next meeting (a Monday) found her more cheerful and alert. Often enough she sat slumped in a chair with eyes half-closed, paying little attention to her surroundings. She said that she was feeling much better. People thought her mad but she was really quite all right. She would just have to be understanding. For the first time, she asked several questions: 'Is that a new watch you've got? . . . you told me you'd several watches (this was incorrect) . . . do you live in Dundee?... do you live alone? . . . are you keeping well . . .?' This was her first reference to the fact that the author had been ill with influenza several weeks earlier. It was impossible to avoid thinking that the cigarettes had perhaps made her more communicative and interested in the meetings.

The next day, although mostly silent, as was her habit, she wanted to know if he was going out of town again. She continued, 'You'll not be coming back . . .' When asked why, she replied, 'You'll be going on holiday . . . you're good to me . . . you help me.' After this expression of gratitude, she asked for another cigarette. This amiability continued throughout the following meeting. She offered him a sweet, saying, 'My doctor is very good to me. . .' Here it was difficult to know to what doctor she was referring, although it obviously had reference to the author. She continued with the preoccupation about his leaving: 'Are you going away on your holidays? . . . I thought you said you were going away for a few days.' She was obviously still under the influence of the author's visit to London, which had occurred about two weeks earlier.

At this time the patient's Saturday visits home had to be cancelled because she had repeatedly attacked her elder sister. This was about four and a half months after the meetings had started. Not long before this incident she had said that she was a nuisance to everyone. It was noticeable that whenever she was friendly and interested the volume of her speech increased and what she had to say was much more clear and coherent. Following the attack on her sister, she said that she would not be going home the next Saturday: 'I don't mind.' After saying this she lost all interest in the meeting and began flicking through a magazine. She continued to do this until the author took out a diary to make an entry. Then she said, 'You've got your notebook out . . .'

Once again she withdrew into her paper. Just before she left she repeated, 'You'll not be coming back . . .' When asked why, she said, 'You'll be busy . . . I'm glad you're coming back . . . if I get on with this (pointing to her magazine) I'll get better. . . .' She continued, 'You've very intelligent . . . I must find a picture before you go . . .' She eventually turned up an advertisement illustrating a little girl in a dressing-gown helping her mother to wash the dishes.

The change in her attitude to the author had no doubt some relationship to her being given cigaretes. She was even willing to come along for an interview when found waiting outside the ward sister's office for a cigarette. Once again she said that she would not be going away for the weekend. She continued, 'You'll be having the weekend off . . . you'll be away . . . will you be in Dundee? I was thinking you must be a traveller when I saw your briefcase . . . travellers used to come into the shop (where she worked) . . . they used to come to my uncle's shop . . .' It should be noted that this was the first time that the author had brought his briefcase into the interviewing-room when seeing her. After a silence, she said, 'I don't care if I don't get home at the weekend . . . I'll go next week.' This meeting not only revealed her concern about getting home for the weekends but also showed that she was not always clear in her mind about the author's identity.

About five months after the meetings commenced, the author decided to ask the patient to continue them in an interview room instead of in the ward where they had taken place up until that time. To his surprise she agreed quite readily. In the following weeks she continued to express concern for him and anxiety lest he fail to return to see her. Typical of her comments were: 'You're very kind to me. Be careful on the roads . . . will you come back to see me? . . . will you want to be going now?' At the same time she revealed once again that her recognition of him was particularly unstable. She said, 'You'll be going to your work . . . in the town . . . are you in business? . . . have you a job in the town? . . . do you work in a shop?'

A fortnight before the Easter holidays, she was told that the author would be away for about two weeks. A few days before the break was to take place she was reminded about it. She had obviously quite forgotten. The next day, she spontaneously said, 'You'll be going off on your holiday . . . You said you were going to America . . . Scottish . . . Scottish-American place . . .' (She had actually been told that he was going to America when she had inquired where he was off to.) She continued, after a pause: 'Will I get home this weekend . . .?

I must get home for good . . .' When he did not respond positively to her statement, saying that it would be better to see how things were at home first (at this time the patient was still not allowed home at the weekends), her mood changed. She became angry and shouted, 'Everything's all right at home. You could let me go home . . . it's nice to get away from the hospital.' She was now unhappy and almost in tears, and continued, 'You miss your home . . . it's nonsense to keep me here . . . I should be at home.' When she left, she called the author by the name of her delusional object (Dr H).

In these days, the content of her thought was as before: 'You'll be wanting to go away . . . it's up to yourself . . . will you come to see me . . . I'll have to go now and finish my dishcloth . . .' She still had doubts about the author's identity: 'I'll see you tomorrow . . . will it be the same man? . . . I thought maybe there were two of you . . .' Although rather apathetic and withdrawn, she continued to speak as she had been doing for the past six weeks, although the volume remained small: 'You'll be going on holiday . . . have you a shop? . . . I thought you had a shop as well as going on holiday . . .' She asked questions: 'What school did you go to? . . . have you been to the pictures? . . . are you keeping well? . . . you're having a good rest sitting there . . .' She was pleasant, appreciative, and yet curious: 'Thanks for the nice time . . . I mean, coming to talk to me . . . it helps me . . . you'll get a cup of tea brought in here . . . are you keeping well? . . . do you eat well? . . . what do you drink? . . . can you be bothered with me today?' She went on: 'When are you going on your holidays? . . . I'll be back at work . . . you'll be working on your holidays . . . I'll probably not be here when you get back.'

When she was seen after the fourteen-day break, no appreciable reaction could be discerned. Her behaviour as recorded by the nurses during the two weeks had remained as before. She welcomed the author, asking if he had had a good holiday: 'Were you in America – British America or something?' She wanted to know if today was a public holiday. Her attitude towards him over the next weeks continued to vary between lack of interest and a concern about whether he was going to visit her: 'I was wondering if you would come to see me today after I said cheerio . . . I thought you may not come back.' It seems fairly reasonable to assume that her fear that the author would not return to see her arose in part from her concern that her indifference and irritability would lead to the end of the meetings.

The data now to be reported are drawn from three successive meetings. She had been told that the author might not manage to see her the next day. As it turned out, he was able to get along after all. She said, 'I wasn't expecting you today . . . I just thought Dr F would come today . . . my mother's coming today . . .' She was silent, and then said, 'Do you get fed up? . . . I thought you may get fed up . . .' When asked why she thought this she said, 'If you're ill . . . I'm not fed up . . . will you come tomorrow? . . . See you're careful on the roads . . . mind the traffic.' At the next meeting she looked aggressive. She refused to come from outside the sister's office where she was waiting for a cigarette. She shouted, 'Go away! . . . I don't want to speak to you! . . .' The next day (the third meeting), she came to the room but was unfriendly. The author said, 'It's a nice day.' She responded, 'It's a nice day . . . don't say that to me . . .' Then her manner changed. She became amiable and interested: 'Are you keeping all right?' When asked what was wrong yesterday, she replied 'I was upset . . . I am sorry for being angry . . . people get angry sometimes . . . I wanted to do the jig-saw puzzle my sister gave me . . I don't know why I was angry.' She smiled (quite an unusual occurrence) and asked, 'Are you going on your holidays? will you come again tomorrow?'

Interspersed with the apathy, indifference, anger, and concern about the author were brief phases when she showed some slight animation which led to her asking questions about him or telling him something about her life before the illness. Then she would speak more than usual. More often than not the content of her speech was not well organized, for example: 'I often get the blame . . . of course everyone knows it's not my fault . . . they get angry with filth.' She paused, and then said, 'My friend and I used to go dancing . . . we used to exchange clothes . . . she is married now and hasn't been to see me for years. I used to go to church with my uncle . . . I painted the windows when the minister was giving the sermon . . . I didn't die.'

As was so often the case, this friendliness gave way to anger and withdrawal. The circumstances occurring at the time often suggested a possible explanation of the change in attitude, as in the following instance. An arrangement had been made for the author to see her mother and as a result the patient was not seen till the late afternoon. At the outset the patient was extremely pleasant. She asked about the weekend: could she go home? Arrangements had been made with her mother for the patient to resume her home visits at the weekend. The patient said, 'Maybe I'll be home for the holidays.' The author said that she could look forward to getting home when she was better. She replied 'I've been ill . . . I've forgotten all about it.' Her appearance had changed dramatically. She looked angry and said, 'You don't need to come unless you want to . . . to tell you the truth, it'd be better if you didn't come . . .' She was silent, and then complained of a headache: 'I prefer my own doctor . . . I don't like men doctors.' When asked why she would feel better if he didn't come, she said, 'I thought you didn't like me. I thought you couldn't be bothered with me . . . can I go now? . . . I'm not ill . . . you're upsetting me . . . there's nothing wrong with me . . .'

From time to time she would say that her mother or sister was due to visit (they came at least twice or three times a week) but only on one occasion did she make any comment about them. She was saying that her sister was coming to visit her: 'My sister's coming to see me tomorrow – my stand-offish sister . . .' After a pause: 'She is a very good sister.' She had become more talkative and it seemed possible that this was related to the fact that she had resumed her home visits. She said, 'I'm very quiet, like you . . . I was very worried maybe you wouldn't come . . . don't you like to see me? . . . do you like to see me? . . . would you like this more comfortable chair? . . . are you keeping well? . . .' After a pause, she continued, 'There are fine glasses you've got . . . have you had them for a long time? . . . I like your tie . . .'

After another silence she went on, 'Thank you for your company . . . I get frightened here.' When she was asked to talk about this she replied, 'Do you get frightened too?' This was followed by 'My uncle George has a lovely car. He came up last week . . . have you a mother? . . . is she alive? . . . uncle George's mother is alive . . . have you a family? . . . you must look after them.'

This positive attitude did not last long. She reverted to her inattentive and withdrawn self and spoke little. She remained affable, nevertheless, but even this vanished, leaving her irritable and aggressive. One day, when offered a cigarette, she shouted, 'Cigarettes are not everything!' When asked what was wrong her anger increased and she shouted, 'Two students told me to forget my illness. It's a sin my being in hospital. I should be at home at work . . . I'm not bothering with that bugger again . . . you know all about it . . . I am going away now.' At this point she stamped out of the room.

This sullen unpleasant manner gave way to a more friendly state in a matter of a few days. This fluctuation of feeling was characteristic, as the material already described illustrates. She said, 'My mother is a good sort . . . so are you . . . I was just asking, would Dr F be coming along this morning . . .' She expressed regret that she didn't have a sweet to give him: 'I said to myself, you'll come to see me . . . will you come tomorrow? . . . you'll be tired; it's a long walk . . . you don't need to come; it's up to yourself.' A bell rang for tea but she did not use this as an excuse to run away, although she said, 'I'll have to go for my tea.' She sat for a further ten minutes in silence, then left. This concern for the author continued in succeeding sessions: 'You must look after yourself . . . if you are not well go to the doctor . . . who is your doctor? . . . do you ever go to Dr H? Do you want to go now?' Her friendly attitude was reflected in her telling him about the times when she and her friends went out together. At the same time, she did not forget to add that her friend had now forgotten all about her. In spite of what appeared to be an interest, concern, and involvement in the meeting, she quickly turned away in annoyance if, for example, she was asked a question, saying: 'I am past that stage . . . I am quite well . . . I need to go home . . . I'm finished with being asked questions . . . they used to ask questions . . . I don't care . . . I'm quite well now . . . I don't need to be asked questions . . .' After saying this she would become silent and then leave the room.

Her vulnerability, expressed so often in the fear that the author would not come or would want to end the meetings, was unexpectedly revealed when for a change he had to say that he must end the session early. After the meeting had proceeded for about twenty minutes he said, 'I'm sorry I must go away now.' The patient burst into tears, saying, 'I'm not feeling well.' She agreed that she thought he had meant that he was going to go away for good. She asked 'Will you wait until I finish this cigarette?' This direct expression of attachment soon vanished from sight and was not seen again before the end of the period described here. Within a day or so she was saying once again, 'I've nothing to say to you today . . . you can go away now.'

However good the relationship was with the author or any other individual in her environment, it was easily destroyed by disappointment. She was liable to fly into a rage if, for example, she was refused cigarettes. The ward sister reported that she had to serve the patient her meals first because if she was kept waiting too long a furious outburst often resulted. On one occasion the patient shouted at her sister while they were waiting for tea in the hospital canteen. It appeared that the patient could not tolerate delay in satisfaction, particularly if some other stress was superadded. This view received support from the fact that she did not always fly into a rage when at the canteen or when the author did not comply with her request for a cigarette. It is of interest that aggressiveness might break out against the object once the need was met, for example, the patient pleaded with the ward sister for a cigarette: 'You're a lovely woman . . . I like you.' Once she had the cigarette she shouted at her, 'You've a face like a hen . . .'

Reference has already been made to the numerous occasions when she became angry with the author. The immediate stimuli were being asked questions, expecting her to stay when she decided to terminate the interviews, his missing meetings, and his arriving when she was hoping for a cigarette from the ward sister (interfering with her needs). Her anger was not generally sustained. Sometimes it passed in a matter of minutes – for example, when she was seen in the ward at one time she said angrily, 'What do you want? . . . I don't like you . . .' Nevertheless, she came to the room and, once sat down, said, 'I do like you . . . will you come tomorrow?'

(*ii*) *Nature of the Relationship with Delusional Objects*

It was difficult to obtain extensive details of this patient's delusional objects because of her reluctance to speak about her subjective experiences. Reference has already been made in the previous section to her hostile reaction when her attention was drawn to these matters. There fortunately were a number of occasions on which she expressed herself sufficiently well to give some information about her delusional ideas. The first indication of a psychotic relationship was given when she misidentified a patient as her elder sister. She frequently attacked this patient. During one meeting this patient passed through the sitting-room where the patient was being seen. The patient said, 'That's my sister Jean . . . my sister's at home . . . I have two sisters . . . I have two uncles . . .' This condensation of sister and fellow-patient was noted from time to time throughout the period of the meetings.

The misidentification of fellow-patient and sister declared itself through the patient's behaviour and was therefore fairly obvious. Less apparent was a more important psychotic relationship which the patient conducted with her general practitioner (Dr H). At first the author was confused by her referenced to 'my doctor'. He thought she was referring to the doctor who had looked after her prior to his involvement in the case. Only later did he come to realize that 'my doctor' was her former general practitioner, a woman doctor whom she had not seen since the first weeks of her admission to hospital. Only with this knowledge in mind did he understand that when, in a positive state with him, she said, 'My doctor's good to me' she was condensing Dr H and himself. This condensation was confirmed when, as was mentioned earlier, she ended a meeting saying 'Goodbye, Dr H'.

The author had been told by the nursing staff that the patient was occasionally to be found shouting at the wireless and television or turning them off. On one such occasion she shouted out, 'I'll use my own sense, Dr H.' It was only later that she revealed that she was in daily communication with Dr H by means of the wireless and television. Dr H apparently told her how to conduct herself, when to go out, when to wash and keep clean. It would appear that Dr H had a kind of supervisory and governing role for the patient, for example: 'I'm not a worrier . . . my doctor doesn't let me worry.' There were occasions when the patient objected to conforming to Dr H's requests, as for instance washing her hair or disposing of menstrual tampons. By chance, the author, on one occasion, discovered the stimulus for a preoccupation with Dr H. The evening before, the elder sister, Jean, had said to a nurse, in front of the patient, that she (the patient) should have her hair washed. This evoked an aggressive response in the patient. The elder sister took a great interest in the patient, bringing her clothes and encouraging her to keep neat and tidy and take an interest in everything that went on in the hospital. The ward sister had the task of keeping the patient attentive to her toilet and generally getting her moving about. Both sisters were fused in the patient's mind – 'I have two sisters (true) . . . Sister F (the ward sister) arranges . . . I should speak to my doctor . . . Dr H will arrange my weekend at home.' It seems a reasonable interpretation that the patient transferred the demand that she should wash her hair from the sister to Dr H and the subsequent rage reaction also. Dr H, the elder sister, and the ward sister were condensed, and the assaults on the elder sister were the physical equivalent of the verbal attacks against the delusional object, Dr H. It is likely that her periodic anger against the author was sometimes motivated by a condensation of Dr H, the sister, the ward sister, and the author. Anger with them led to anger with him. The condensation of Dr H with the ward sister and nurses was confirmed by the nursing staff.

CASE II

Mr B was a single man who had been ill for about eight years, only one remission occurring a year after the onset of the illness. He was about average height and slimly built. His movements were stiff and lacked spontaneity. He might begin a movement and then cease half-way through. His clothes were untidy and stained. He was seen daily for over a year.

(*i*) *Nature of the Relationship with Real Objects*

When the observation period began, Mr B was inattentive and unresponsive. His reaction to a question was often to turn his face away or close his eyes. On the rare occasion when he spoke he would break off in the middle of a phrase or sentence. Sometimes he muttered noiselessly, his lips articulating words which were inaudible. From time to time he would ignore the author's presence and examine his own face in a mirror hanging on the wall of the interviewing-room. It was reported by nurses that he was in the habit of standing in one position for quite long periods. The negativism that found expression in his refusing to comply with simple requests was also to be seen in occasional utterances he made in response to the author. For example, when asked why he did not want to speak, he replied, 'It's not why.'

As the weeks went by, the lack of interest in the author's attendance for interviews lessened. At first there was only an increase in his telling him not to use certain words: '. . . It's not (etc.).' Then he began to speak about his delusional preoccupations, a few of which had a persecutory content. He was inclined to over-value his abilities and he regarded himself as an exalted and influential person. Much of what he said was difficult to follow, partly because of blocking of associations and omission of connecting links between phrases, and partly because of his speech disturbance arising from the disorder of thinking. Details of his cognitive functions will be described in Chapter 6.

His relationships with real objects were of two different kinds. The first reflected an aspect of his inner world. He was for ever assimilating (introjecting) those around him: fellow-patients, visitors, nurses, doctors, even television personalities, into his own self-image. This category of phenomenon has been described as a form of primary identification. He would say: 'Billy Jones (a fellow-patient) is part of my leg and an opera singer, his left leg is part of mine, and a girl also. The rest is Billy Jones, not so much Billy Jones. It's much more complicated than that. I have another complaint . . . my arm was stripped bare in the swimming pool . . . I was feeling terrible . . . my face is looking terrible . . . I am the first serious patient to have this composition . . . I am made up . . . the first patient to have a complex tissue . . . I am composed of different people . . . I am a critical patient . . . I am so ill . . . there is no doctor who understands it yet . . . I am cold . . . I am not strong enough without my jacket . . . my feet are complex too . . . I have the same mouth as a black nurse and another black woman . . . not a nurse.'

He did not confine his assimilatory trend to parts of objects. He also made transient identifications with entire persons, thus becoming that individual: 'Did I tell you how I became Dr F . . . just as I was the man who bolted I was you.' On another occasion, he said, 'I was a Mr P (a male nurse) the week you were away . . .' These transient identifications represented a primitive form of relating with objects, for they were usually with individuals of significance to the patient in one sense or another.

Apart from this form of object relationship, he behaved to the author and nurses in a realistic manner, acknowledging them as distinct from himself. He treated the author as a confidant. He told him about the problems and difficulties which arose from his delusional ideas. As time went by it became apparent that the patient had little concern for him as a person in his own right. He had no interest in him other than as someone to whom he could talk and someone who would help him to fulfil his irrational ambitions. When this was seen as impossible the patient's attitude changed entirely, as will become apparent later. Although he was mostly friendly in manner and communicative, there were frequent occasions when he withdrew into an unresponsive, inattentive state. Occasionally he flew into a rage if he felt he was being contradicted or misunderstood. These bouts of rage, during which his speech was quite normal, were followed by withdrawal and the appearance of cataleptic manifestations.

A drastic deterioration in the relationship with the author occurred when the inevitable disappointment with him took place: for his failure to procure the pension which the patient believed he was entitled to for saving the hospital from destruction. According to the patient, the hospital was disintegrating when he arrived and he, alone, had undertaken its restoration. 'It was,' he said, 'Mr X's opinion that it demanded wages for life. He is the only one with me all along.' Only with the granting of a pension could he leave the hospital and be in a position to marry the girl he had loved from afar prior to the illness.

There was, at first, no outward sign of discontent with the author for his failure to arrange the pension. However, he was noticeably quieter. He repeatedly complained of assaults on his face by the television and by other patients. A depressive affect began to appear in association with these fears. He complained of the cold; it was penetrating the skin of his face. He said he was tired; his sister was clever but he had exhausted his intelligence in 'perfecting' art and love.

The depression declared itself more forcibly when he said, 'I am a very miserable and unhappy person.' As the days passed his utterances became more fragmented and difficult to follow. There were, however, exceptions; one morning he said, 'I am a most unfortunate person, I've always been unfortunate. I lost a ring, I haven't been given the pension and I've been martyred three times. . . . All my work is taken for granted.'

At this time he returned to banning words and expressing doubts as to whether he should continue the meetings. He was constantly preoccupied with his face, touching it and looking at it in the mirror. He said that seeing other patients unclothed at bathtimes was altering the shape of his face. The hospital was no place for Eva (the girl he had loved prior to his illness). This remark showed that he regarded Eva and himself as a unity. His attitude became increasingly threatening and domineering, particularly if any of his prohibitions and instructions were ignored. When a meeting had to be cancelled he accused the author of disturbing him through the television. Some days later his mother reported that on the day of the cancelled interview he had criticized her violently as they walked round the hospital grounds. He cursed her and shouted that she did not care about him; that she did not come to see him. Nor did it matter that he had been shut away for six years. The mother said he had never spoken to her like that before.

This phase reached its climax with an outburst against the author. This resulted from an unwitting failure on the latter's part to conform to some of the patient's instructions. He accused the author, who was buying cigarettes at the canteen in the patient's company, of interfering with his speech. He insisted that the transaction be repeated so that everything could be made all right again. Unfortunately the canteen had closed for lunch a moment or two after they had left and so the patient's request could not be carried out. This led to outbursts of fury. The author was coarse and crude. He must obey and open the canteen immediately. Eventually Mr B quietened down but became quite inaccessible.

(ii) Nature of the Relationship with Delusional Objects

This patient's delusional reality consisted primarily of wishful fantasies. He performed great deeds, was handsome, and in all ways perfect. As will be noted in Chapter 6, he experienced his body as changed and distorted. While he was hopeful and contented with his grandiose ideas he did not feel persecuted. Only when he was depressed did he attribute his altered bodily perceptions and sensations to persecutors. As was noted above, the author was included among these enemies. At such a time, patients and nurses whom he often criticized became condensed with the delusional persecutory objects.

CASE III

Mr C was a single man of 23 who had been unwell for a period of four years. His face was expressionless. He was untidily dressed, and his clothes were rather shabby and neglected. He made no response and it was only with much encouragement that he was prevailed upon to speak. When this occurred he could not sustain his utterance for more than a short period. Sometimes he would answer a question and then break off in the middle of a sentence. He sat rigidly and uncomfortably. He continually examined his right forearm. Such voluntary acts as he initiated were generally broken off prior to completion, the limbs remaining in a fixed position. These postures were held for varying lengths of time. His behaviour was further characterized by inattention. Unresponsiveness, inattention, and catalepsy typified the manner in which he presented himself.

(i) Nature of the Relationship with Real Objects

During the illness, he was mostly withdrawn and only rarely did he show interest in persons or activities. He was extremely sensitive to his contact with the author. He had a dread of the relationship developing a sexual character. He said, 'I am a homosexual, I'm frightened of real sex . . . I am afraid of grabbing men.' This fear arose most vividly in relation to the author when the latter had occasion to undertake a neurological examination. He said that he was frightened he might pervert him if he touched him by accident.

He also regarded the author's presence as an intrusion. This is well illustrated by the following instance. At a particular interview he did not speak for some time. Eventually he commented on the new canteen which was being built on to the hospital. He asked when it would be finished. The author said he did not know. A few minutes later the patient smiled. As there was no apparent reason for this he was asked why he was smiling. He reacted to this question by turning his head away. He looked angry. It was suggested to him that this question had made him angry but he was frightened to admit this. Once again he ignored the statement, sitting for some minutes with his head bent in his chest. Eventually he said '. . . it lowers a man to speak all his thoughts . . . I like to keep my thought to myself . . .' When asked why he should feel this way he replied, 'I get upset if I speak about my thoughts . . . doctors ask too many personal questions . . . it makes me worse . . .'. He agreed that he was angry and added that thinking made his hands stiff. While he had been quite relaxed at the beginning of the session, by the time it was over his whole posture was characterized by rigidity and lack of movement. The nursing staff reported that for the remainder of that day the patient did not use his right arm, which he held in a state of rigid extension. His state was described as 'catatonic, tense, and resistive', quite different from the condition prior to the interview.

As the weeks passed, a very weak attachment developed. This was evidenced in his asking the nurse when the author was coming to visit the ward. There were also times when he would remember to return to the ward in time for his interview. This interest in the interviews and in the author never developed any strength or intensity.

He over-valued himself and attributed a similar over-valuation to the author. During a session when he referred to himself as a genius he told him that he must be a genius also because one of his eyes was bigger than the other. In his opinion geniuses were not necessarily famous and well known – 'Just one of the crowd like you and me . . .' He continued, '. . . the way you sit shows that you have special powers . . .' Indeed he was the one who was specially concerned with posture and bodily position.

He was aware of the limited control he had over his aggression and this was a source of anxiety to him. At one meeting he asked if there was an operating theatre in the hospital. When asked why he wanted to know, he replied, 'I'm frightened I may punch someone . . . no, I wouldn't punch anyone.' This fear of attacking people and of breaking windows led to his asking to go to bed – he made the cause of this request quite explicit, again demonstrating how little confidence he had in the control of his aggression.

(*ii*) *Nature of the Relationship with Delusional Objects*

This patient was subject to auditory hallucinations and there were times when he was prepared to describe them. He attributed his outbursts of violence to God's commands; for example, he said, 'God told me I'd be all right if I broke the cups.' He also heard his parents' voices telling him that he must do as the doctors instructed. He believed that his thoughts and his movements were controlled by some unknown agency. After a time the author became involved in his delusional ideas. He revealed that he was afraid that the author would control him by means of hypnotism. This was the cause of his fear of shiny objects. He had said at a previous time that the ashtray and the lights in the consulting-room had made him frightened. Only several weeks later did these fears become understandable when in response to the author telling him that he was afraid of him the patient said '. . . I'm frightened of your hard eyes . . . you can be hypnotized by hard shiny objects (ashtray, light switch) . . . I can hypnotize myself . . . it can happen by accident . . . hypnotism is dangerous . . . you might hit your head against the door . . . fall on the floor or throw yourself out of the window . . .'

CASE IV

Mr D was a young man aged 20 who had been ill for a period of two years. When seen for the first time it was noted that he demonstrated unusual mannerisms and would adopt unusual postures. He would remain silent for long periods. He was frightened and apparently without insight. He only made one or two spontaneous utterances. He complained of giddy spells, that his mind was 'playing hell', and that noises upset him. He added, 'They're always after me.' He was inattentive and would not reply to questions, typically fixing his attention on something other than the author. He maintained postures for a considerable length of time, and repetitive movements of the hands were frequently observed. There was little affect apart from the initial anxiety which passed away after a short while.

(*i*) *Nature of the Relationship with Real Objects*

This patient avoided contact with other patients. He sat or lay on his bed. He did not want to eat in the ward dining-room and would sometimes bring his food to the bedside. He was compliant but quite inaccessible. His only expressed wish was to leave the hospital and return home. He said to the author at one of the first interviews, 'You can't touch me with talk,' or, 'I shouldn't be here, I've always been like this.' He would not speak and after a few minutes got up and walked to the door.

The only trace of real interest in another person occurred when an occupational therapist came to see him and to suggest that they might work together. The few remarks he made to her indicated that he was for ever misidentifying those around him. He confused his mother, the occupational therapist, nurses, and the author with fantasy (delusional) objects. It was of interest that for a short period he would emerge from his delusional experience and recognize the real person to whom he was talking. This occurred with the occupational therapist, on one occasion with the author, and from time to time with nurses.

He was negativistic and ambivalent. The following represents a statement which he made to the occupational therapist: he said, 'They decided yes. I don't know why but they decided yes. . . . What if I say yes? Will I get away with it? . . . I can't help saying yes to them.' The occupational therapist asked him why he was afraid to say no. He replied, 'I'd have had it then wouldn't I?' A few days afterwards he said, 'I'll still be standing here in six years' time and saying yes, I do, and something inside of my head will be saying no. I'm not going to stand here and be questioned. It's made my mind wrong and I just say yes. Look at that! He just stood there and told me he wouldn't spare me.' After a pause he continued, 'I can't tell them yes like a man, can I? No, of course I can't.' One day he pinned a piece of paper to his bed with a large NO written on it. When he was asked by the nurse what it meant he said angrily it was his own business and then shouted, 'No, No, No, No . . .' After this he ran across the ward, shouting over his shoulder, 'Bugger off, bugger off.'

The attachment which had been formed with the occupational therapist increased in intensity if not stability with the passage of time. He looked forward to her visits, asking when she would be coming again. He also went across by himself to the occupational therapy centre. One day he said to her, 'You belong to me now – what are you going to do about it?' During these meetings with the occupational therapist the patient frequently had delusional perceptual experiences. The therapist was sometimes able to help him to recognize the unreal nature of these experiences and he obtained comfort from this. One day he looked behind a radiator and screamed with fright. He responded to the occupational therapist's reassurance by saying, 'You're right, there's nothing there but dust.' On another occasion he shouted out, 'Look at these shining things – they are watching me.' Again he calmed down after the therapist had talked to him.

The fact that the patient could be influenced in the direction of insight suggested that there was some significant object relationship at that moment. These instances which have been quoted, and others, are reminiscent of a mother calming her frightened child. Mr D had made a relationship with the occupational therapist although, as time was to show, this attachment was extremely vulnerable and easily lost. He was concerned for the therapist's safety and welfare, as was illustrated in the following instance. He entered the occupational therapy room, walked straight over to the therapist, put his hands on her shoulders, and addressing the ceiling, announced, 'You mustn't interfere with this one.'

Although he developed this tenuous relationship with the occupational therapist, it was easily submerged within his delusional reality. One day, when walking with her he suddenly began to shout and curse her. A few minutes later, he said, 'I'm sorry, I thought I was talking to someone else, I didn't know it was you.' As far as could be ascertained, the occupational therapist had not provided the patient with any cause for such a reaction. His attitude to her was at times also one of distrust; and this appeared clearly in his remark, 'I wonder what goes on behind those pretty faces.'

His behaviour with the author changed very little throughout the clinical contact. The only thing he had to say was, 'I want to go home.' He rarely spoke and there was only one occasion when he expressed himself freely; and that was when there was a joint meeting with his mother. This meeting took place so that arrangements could be made for the patient to have weekends at home. A month or so later he reacted sharply to a weekend being cancelled. He withdrew to his bed and refused to get up except when the occupational therapist came to see him. Most of what he said to her concerned his wish to get home. These requests were accompanied by a depressive affect and threats of suicide. He asked her, 'Am I going home on Saturday? I'll threaten to kill myself if they don't let me home. That will make them let me go.' The therapist asked him how that would help. He replied, 'I'll go myself then; I could, you know.' Shortly after this, a pronounced change took place in his attitude to the occupational therapist and he refused to see her. When she came to the ward to see him, he said, 'I'm not coming over [to the occupational therapy department] . . . I don't feel like it.' A day or so later she managed to persuade him to come to the centre but he left in a short while after having a row with her. Unfortunately the centre had run out of the very materials he needed. This was enough for him to retreat in anger to the ward. From this time on he was quite inaccessible to her. He stayed in the ward, remaining huddled up in bed and refusing to speak to anyone.

(*ii*) *Nature of the Relationship with Delusional Objects*

Reference has already been made to the fact that this patient constantly misidentified those around him. He was therefore constantly mistaking members of the hospital staff for his delusional objects and vice versa. The persecutors comprised a condensation of fantasy objects and the hospital staff. Limitation of his freedom, the general restraints, and the treatment probably provided a reinforcement from the environment for his psychotic reality. Over and above this he felt himself persecuted by unknown forces. He frequently showed signs of great fear, and examples of this have already been described.

It was not easy to get a clear picture of the delusional or hallucinatory content, since the speech was often disorganized and without logical form. The following statement which appeared in the joint interview with his mother and the author is illustrative; 'I'd rather be dead than where I'm going . . . it takes four hundred years to come off the stocks . . . they threw one on the fire . . . an archangel . . . they got them specially made and threw one on the bloody fire . . . they threw one on the bloody fire . . . that's why I'm going on the fire . . . it's true . . . you have to sit in a chair and it goes along a rail . . . I'll live till 45, he says . . . that puts it down to nothing . . . I ask him . . . he went mad because of me . . . the Pope has these things . . . an element between the soul and meat . . . he did it to their minds . . . they're all running around . . . this bloke who did it to my mind is up there with the birds . . . he lives in another world and has a flat face . . . he nearly went mad and put the blame on me . . . there you are [turning towards his mother], one just came and warned her: go your way, you'll be safe.'

At times he became frightened and this was so when he expressed some persecutory idea, for example, 'They are going to plaster me against the wall' or 'They're after me.' On several occasions he would run to his bed and hide under the blankets.

OBSERVATIONS ON THE CLINICAL DATA

The data presented in this chapter demonstrate that patients who manifest disorders of motility and negativism and who are categorized as catatonic vary in the manner in which they relate to real objects and fantasy (delusional) objects. Patients like Miss A and Mr B came to develop an interest and attachment to those who took time to get to know them. For the most part, this object relationship bore the characteristics of the 'need-satisfying' type of relationship which is appropriate to infancy and early childhood. It was weak and tenuous. As long as the patient felt the object was satisfying a need, whether physical or emotional, the relationship continued. A disappointment or frustration led to its disappearance permanently or for a short time. For brief periods the relationship seemed to strengthen and reach a level where the object existed in its own right, with the patient beginning to show some concern and regard. This occurred with Miss A, but again it was only transient.

There are patients who at first sight do not seem to relate at all, even at the 'need-satisfying' level. They are withdrawn and apparently inaccessible. This was the case with Mr D, until he was introduced to the occupational therapist. From this time a relationship did develop but it was not sustained. It is quite possible that in some cases a relationship is only possible with a member of the opposite sex. In the case of Mr C, homosexual fears precluded any kind of relationship with a male figure. His case, and others which have been observed and documented in the literature, show that homosexual tendencies may make a striking appearance in catatonic states. These patients are aware of their homosexual urges and they dread them. This leads to a withdrawal and to aggressive outbursts against men, to be followed by catatonic signs. In these cases, the level of object relationship is much more advanced than that described as 'need-satisfying'. The object exists as an entity representing a constant threat and not as a source of satisfaction which is no longer of interest once the need is alleviated. Apart from this difference, patients who relate on the 'need-satisfying' level, may like Mr B demonstrate an 'assimilatory' form of relating with others (primary identification).

The differences which appear with real objects also occur in the sphere of delusional object relations. In some patients the appearance of delusional objects varies, depending on the patient's mental state. In Mr B's case delusional objects only made their appearance during the period when he felt hopeless and depressed. Then he attributed his bodily discomforts and dissatisfactions about his appearance to his persecutors. When optimistic about his delusional prospects, he was free of such persecution and any delusional object was helpful or advising. A similar kind of association existed in Miss A's case. She was more inclined to be conscious of delusional objects when she was disappointed and angry. Misidentifications and hallucinatory experiences of all kinds may occur and there does not seem to be any consistent pattern. It is important to note in the cases of Miss A, Mr B, and Mr D that delusional objects were easily condensed with real objects (author, nursing staff) and thus a displacement occurred from one to the other. This condensation was not found in Mr C, nor is it a uniform occurrence in cases of catatonia. When present it has important implications for the day-to-day management of the patient.

It would appear that catatonic manifestations may make their appearance in patients whose object-relations capacity operates in quite different ways. In all, there is the ability to relate at the 'need-satisfying' level. This may or may not be accompanied by ephemeral 'primary identifications' which have no relation to the interaction necessary for adjustments with real people. Then there are those patients whose relations with real objects are more complex. The patient may show concern for the object, he may become jealous or envious, and he may develop homosexual or heterosexual urges towards the object. All kinds of object-relating may appear in the one case. In conclusion, it is worth recalling that catatonic manifestations – perseverations, catalepsy, negativism, etc. – may arise in patients with organic cerebral disease and who do not show any disturbance in their object relations (see Chapters 7 and 8). This in itself suggests that catatonic manifestations are phenomena which may appear in different forms of cerebral disturbance – whether functional or organic – and by themselves cannot be considered to constitute a homogeneous group of conditions. Catatonic signs may be regarded as a symptom complex (Jaspers, 1963). A symptom complex, however, is not a disease entity but only a step in the path towards the delineation of such entities. It merely draws together heterogeneous manifestations under the wing of phenomena common to all the above-mentioned states.

CHAPTER 6

The Heterogeneous Nature of the Catatonias

II. Cognitive Status and Perception of the Self

As in the case of object relationships, patients categorized as catatonic show a wide variety of cognitive abnormalities and defects in the perception of the self and in the sense of identity. The material described below is drawn from the same patients as in the preceding chapter.

CASE I

(*i*) *Cognitive Status*

Miss A presented a pronounced disorder of thinking, as expressed through speech. Grammatical construction was often incorrect and there was no logical connection between phrases and sentences. When told in reply to a question that the author was going to the United States for a few weeks she said, 'Will you walk there or will you go in the car . . . it's very far, America is in Scotland . . .' She repeated this and continued, 'There are a lot of Scottish people in America. Why do you not take your holidays in Balgay Park, it's nearer.' She laughed at her joke. The next day she continued in the same vein: 'You'll be getting off on your holiday . . . you said you were going to America . . . Scottish . . . Scottish-American place. . . .' She failed to go on (blocking) but eventually said, 'I must get home for good.' More often than not the disconnected nature of her speech made it impossible to remember for purposes of recording. There was frequent evidence of blocking, as in the instance quoted above. It was the rule when she spoke rather than the exception. Deflexion of verbal themes was often to be observed and they sometimes appeared to serve a defensive function in so far as they seemed to have the aim of avoiding a particular topic.

From time to time there was a clear indication of perseveration of speech content. Phrases would be repeated automatically when they were no longer appropriate. This perseverative trend was sometimes employed in those instances of deflexion of speech when a defensive aim could be inferred, as in the following example. In the course of an interview, a vacuum cleaner started up outside the consulting-room. This caused the patient to say, 'They never stop.' When asked if she helped with the housework she replied, 'I used to do housework at home.' There was a pause, and she continued, 'You're a very quiet person . . . so am I . . . people are different.' When it was suggested to her that she disliked confiding in others she replied, 'We helped one another . . .' There was a block in her associations. When asked, 'With what?' she answered, 'With the housework . . . cleaning and dusting . . .' She paused, and continued, 'It's better to be with your own folks . . . you wouldn't want to be ill . . .' A similar instance occurred when saying that she liked history at school: 'I had to go to hospital when I was at school,' she said. When asked what for, she replied, 'For history.' Perseveration was also to be observed in her returning to themes which were currently irrelevant. For example, she would continually ask the author about his going away several days after he had returned from a day's leave of absence which she had been told about in advance.

This patient did not devise neologisms or substitute words as Mr B did. Fluent speech was most frequently encountered under two conditions: first, when she seemed positively inclined towards the author and, second, when she was angry. A partial account has already been given of such a change from disordered speech content to rational speech under the influence of anger in the previous chapter. It is described in a little greater detail here. She had asked to go home for the weekend, but was not given a direct answer. When the author said, 'You will have to speak to your sister about it,' the patient replied, 'I have two sisters: Sister F (the ward sister) arranges it . . . I should speak to my doctor (Dr H) . . . She will arrange it . . . I'll arrange it . . . she says I need to go . . . I say so . . . Dr H says I must go.' The author suggested that they should wait and see how things were at home first, but her response was one of furious anger and from this point she spoke clearly and logically. In neither case, whether she was pleased or angry, did the coherent speech content continue for more than a minute or so.

Periodically it could be seen that concepts had lost their permanence and autonomy. The example given in the preceding chapter, in which the author was designated a traveller is illustrative. Evidence of this trend was also to be noted in her condensations of ward sister, elder sister, and the author. A further instance of condensation was her inability to distinguish the poets Shakespeare and Burns. She was looking at a book depicting Shakespeare country. When asked if she had ever been there she replied, 'I used to go to Ayr for holidays with a friend' (Ayr being Burns country). Her inability to discriminate owing to condensation was also to be noted in her joining together Scotland and America, as described above.

The patient's inability to sustain attention for the purpose of adequate verbal communication is a feature implied in the clinical illustrations already presented. Her incapacity to initiate and complete an intention has also been referred to. The inattention which characterized her behaviour was pronounced, particularly in response to comments made by the author. When he happened to remark on her slightly more cheerful manner, saying, 'You're in good form today,' she replied, 'Yes, there were fine seats at the school . . . I like the school.' Her forgetfulness of acquired information could in part be regarded as a result of an inadequate functioning of the attentive process.

She was not distractable in the active sense and she rarely sought out external stimuli. There was no direct evidence of the assimilation of environmental stimuli outside consciousness. The material described in the previous chapter illustrates the frequency with which the inattentive state was replaced by active attention, and vice versa. In nearly all cases the appearance of directed attention was associated with the presence of a particular need or with a strong affect, usually anger.

While there was no indication of fusion of perceptual modalities, there was, in the visual sphere, misidentification resulting from a condensation of visual percepts and memory traces. These have already been described. There was no evidence of a disorder of size, shape, or distance constancies affecting visual perception. Only on one occasion did Miss A give unequivocal evidence of auditory hallucinations. The response to the wireless and television might suggest that she was auditorily hallucinated. However, it seems more likely that this series of phenomena was in part misinterpretations of what was heard on the radio and television based upon her delusional ideas.

This patient showed a pronounced defect of memory with regard to acquired information and to information recently received. Long-term memory was often also deficient. A striking feature was the apparent forgetfulness of the experiences of her illness, a common occurrence in psychotic patients. She dismissed it as 'a lot of nonsense'. She was unable to give an accurate statement of how long she had been in the hospital. Nevertheless she had no difficulty in recalling the date of the month or the day of the week. References have already been made to the number of times when she 'forgot' that she had been told about a pending interruption in the meetings and forgot that the author was a doctor. The day before a ten-day break about which she had been previously warned – eight months after the commencement of the meetings – she asked, 'Are you going away today?... will you be at your work? . . . do you work in the hospital? . . .' After a pause she continued, 'I've got to go now. Will you come tomorrow?' Memories were also distorted and falsified. A few days before, she related the following experience. She had attacked her sister with some violence when at home on a Saturday. She said, in a whisper, that when she was at home she had been watching the television. There was a film about boxing. Her sister Jean was in this film: 'It was terrible; she was being knocked about.'

(*ii*) *Perception of the Self, Self-regard, and Personal Identity*

This patient paid little attention to her appearance. For the most part she had to be pressed to wash her hair and keep herself clean. Her sister brought clothes for her and thus whatever she wore was reasonably fresh. She never showed signs of obvious dilapidation. Reference has already been made to her annoyance when she was asked by the ward sister, by her own sister, or by the nurses to tidy up and in general keep herself clean. Only on one occasion did she ask, 'Is my hair all right? . . . I don't like it . . . she's ugly . . . I'm not ugly . . .'

There was no evidence of a disturbance of personal or sexual identity or any clear indication of merging phenomena with objects in the environment. The boundaries of the self appeared intact although no definite conclusions could be drawn in view of the scarcity of information. She did not over-value herself and there were no delusions with a grandiose content.

CASE II

(*i*) *Cognitive Status*

Mr B presented a serious defect of both speech and thinking. His flow of words was often obstructed, and as a result of omissions and 'derailments' it was frequently impossible to understand what he was trying to convey. For example, he said, 'I was with Waters . . . of course about that horrific thing, the way it happened was more complicated than the horrific thing itself . . . if I may talk about the penis . . . very complicated . . . not very complicated . . . made up of many creative things . . . a Goya stopper . . . Sheila Ward . . . a Sheila Ward Goya stopper . . . before the accident. After the accident it was just a Sheila Ward . . . there still seems to be some hope for me because there were so many things.'

Interspersed between such disconnected phrases, a coherent statement usually dealing with his delusional reality might appear as in the following: 'I haven't much to say doctor . . . I fell over something this morning . . . seeing paradise . . . there is just a possibility of getting your head chopped off if you see paradise . . . of course, doctor, Una is still very sincere . . . she didn't . . . remember I established someone . . . she was too beautiful to bear children . . . she could only marry the prepared person by God . . . that's me . . . isn't that so, Doctor? . . . it was a marriage made by God . . . you say to me you still nurture the hope of being a saint . . . if you marry you ruin your chances of being a saint . . .'

The disorder of thought led to an incorrect use of words, for example, 'I was rectified . . . rectified as insane'; to the creation of new words, 'quadracy' and 'sexarchy'; to paraphasias and neologisms and to the interchange of meaning of words with a similar sound, for example, 'feet' and 'feat'. There was also a deterioration in conceptual powers: 'I was no winks,' he said, in reference to the fact that he had never been flirtatious, or, 'I was a perfect art-gallery face,' to indicate that his face was like an art-gallery painting. This loss of the capacity to conceptualize at an abstract level was seen again in his description of a nurse, whose name he was either unable to use or preferred not to: 'Do you know a nurse? . . . There's a for-Christ's-sake nurse . . .' Objects, persons, and behaviour were thus represented concretely by their actions or characteristics. Occasionally he would use verbs as nouns, as in the following instance: 'It was the go-down this morning . . . They were all like devils. As I passed the last judgement and walked in the court. Rather than take any . . . meals . . . when I was . . . rather than take any meal . . . when I was in danger of the go-down, I cleared it all satisfactorily.' The 'go-down' was part of the nurse's instruction: 'You can all go down to the courtyard now.' This phenomenon, of part of a word, phrase, or sentence representing the whole, was frequently encountered and was an aspect of the defective conceptualization.

The disturbance of conceptual function also resulted in the creation of new concepts, but abnormal ones in that they possessed significances quite apart from their usually accepted meaning. The concept referred to here is the word 'masterpiece'. The patient was for ever referring to a masterpiece at the beginning of a period of observation but it was impossible to understand him on account of his inappropriate use of words and syntactical errors. In time, however, it transpired that he was alluding to a poem which he had written prior to the onset of his illness, and here he used the word correctly. Further knowledge indicated that this word had numerous other meanings which had an equivalence with one another and which were affectively significant. The masterpiece represented himself. One day he explained, 'How dare you insult the masterpiece!' when he was angry with something the author had said. It was the keystone of his delusional system. The very first time he had ever referred to the poem as a masterpiece was on giving it to the girl-friend who had ultimately rejected him, saying, 'I have written this for you, it's a masterpiece.'

His delusions centred on the idea that he had voluntarily given up the girl-friend (the reverse of what had happened) in order to undertake the restoration and salvation of the hospital. He was in the habit of separating the word 'masterpiece' into three parts, 'mas', 'ter', and 'piece'. The first component had the following significances: it stood for the mass; for master in reference to Christ with whom the patient was identified; and also represented the headmaster of his school. The patient's father was also a headmaster and their relationship was a difficult one. The second component, 'ter', was identified as the Latin word for thrice and belonged with his belief that he had been thrice martyred. In fact he had been in three separate mental hospitals. 'Piece' also meant the peace which he had brought to the hospital.

The concept 'masterpiece' not only had its correct meaning for the patient, but at other times it also had a multiplicity of connotations equally significant. In this example, thinking can be seen to have regained its magical quality.

Mr B had difficulty in sustaining attention. He was distractable and percepts were assimilated into his stream of associations outside his consciousness. The capacity to attend for the purposes of adaptation to reality was easily disturbed, particularly if it interfered with the patient's delusional reality as is illustrated in the following instance. The patient was talking about a television film he had seen the previous day. Luckily the author had seen it also. The relevant portions of the film consisted of a wedding scene during which two important incidents took place and an act of infidelity. The first was a fight between the bridegroom's friend and another character in the film. The second was later when the bridegroom, in a state of alcoholic excitement, climbed up on to the roof of the house, overbalanced, fell to the ground, and broke his leg. The patient's account of the film omitted the accident altogether. He insisted that no accident had taken place: he wanted to know how the man could fight if he had a broken leg. The patient had confused the bridegroom and his friend, thus revealing the influence of the condensation process on the perceptual function.

It was not surprising that the patient was only interested in the marriage and in the fact that the bridegroom had sufficient money to send for his fiancée and bring her to his house. This is what he would have liked to do. He said that he had taken part in the film and had helped the man to marry. In fact the marriage did not take place, the fiancée becoming pregnant by another man. Although the patient denied the accident he continually referred to the bridegroom as the 'accidental man'. This indicated that the accident had registered in the patient's mind as a memory trace but had been denied admission to consciousness. It could be compared with the day residue of a dream or with a tachistoscopic exposure.

Mr B presented a series of perceptual anomalies, particularly in the sphere of bodily awareness, which will be described later. In the visual modality he occasionally had difficulty in discriminating figure and ground. Shape and size constancy was disordered: faces changed shape and he reported that a certain woman had got smaller 'to respect her father', as he put it. This again reflected the deterioration in his capacity for abstract conceptualization. Misidentifications were common. With respect to memory, there were serious derangements, which were more inclined to appear when a memory might have led to the contradiction of a delusional idea, as in the instance of the 'accidental man' quoted above.

(ii) Perception of the Self, Self-regard, and Personal Identity

Mr B had lost the sense of unity of bodily and mental self. As in the example quoted in the previous chapter, he felt himself to be made up of other persons or parts of them. This applied equally to women and to men, indicating a disorder of sexual identity: 'It's wrong for Una (the girl-friend) to be kept in a ward with men,' he said. At another time he reported, 'I saw a man in church; it was a special Mass. When he bolted from the church I felt a part of me was made up from his semblance.' Even allowing for his individualistic mode of verbal expression, his statements suggested that he had difficulty discriminating himself from animate and inanimate objects in his immediate environment. He said, 'She (his mother) picked up a razor blade and some of it seemed to spread into me. I shouldn't have said anything. I said to her, that's a murderous thing to do. I gave her a blow. Later a cat jumped in and out of me . . . I ejected it. I don't think it contaminated me.' He did not feel the self to be autonomous: 'Do you remember that Dr F I had . . . Dr F strengthened my body . . . I was impeded in my movements by Dr F – not Dr F but Dr M . . . I am too complicated . . . I was two men who came into the ward.'

He experienced disturbing bodily sensations: his face changed in shape and increased in size; his mouth was twisted. He felt his body getting bigger and smaller. Sometimes these sensations followed a transient identification with their real or imaginary figure: 'I am the Hunchback of Notre Dame . . . I've got it . . . I saw it in my bath . . . I was looking at myself in the mirror . . . I was small . . .' He appeared to experience sensations in parts of the body not subject to stimulation; for example, he reported, 'A nurse was brushing my clothes with a big brush and made an awful mess of my face . . . clothes are really a part of you . . .'.

In spite of all his 'identifications' he never lost his identity as Mr B. He over-valued himself: he said, 'I was the most exquisite boy.' Only when he was depressed did his grandiosity disappear to be replaced by a sense of physical weakness and bodily damage. In general, he paid little attention to his appearance and was untidy and unkempt.

CASE III

(i) Cognitive Status

Mr C exhibited the blocking phenomenon in the most striking fashion. He would utter a few words and then come to a halt. Many minutes might lapse before he could begin to speak again and often he did not do so. This blocking was also to be observed in his inability to complete a voluntary act once commenced. Extending as it did to both speech and motility, the blocking indicated the degree to which the ego organization had suffered a dissolution of function.

When angry, he was able to speak normally for a short time. His thinking did not show the defects in conceptualization characteristic of Miss A and Mr B. He did, however, express ideas which indicated that his thinking had a magical quality. The delusions and hallucinations pointed to the over-valuation of thinking; and this was associated with defective judgement. He had no doubt about his own omnipotence and omniscience.

Inattention and lack of interest led to apparent memory defects with respect to short-term memory. These deficiencies vanished when he became interested in what was going on about him. He did not present any defect of visual perception, but there was evidence of auditory hallucinations and misinterpretation of overheard speech.

(*ii*) *Perception of the Self, Self-regard, and Personal Identity*

This patient's mother reported that prior to the illness he was in the habit of expressing ambitions which were quite out of keeping with his actual capacities. These fantasies of success stood in contrast to his actual behaviour. According to the mother, he was shy and self-effacing. He had a pronounced sense of inferiority and limited self-esteem. The wishful fantasies of great achievement later found an outlet in delusional preoccupations. He told the author that he must be a genius: he must be, because God spoke to him; he could swallow coins and read his mind. He said, 'You are thinking that you will not let me out of the hospital.' He added, 'Only a genius can bounce his head against the wash-hand basin.'

He showed no evidence of a defect of self-object discrimination or of the sense of identity. However, he was very concerned about his sexual identity, being quite convinced that he was in the process of developing feminine physical characteristics. Apart from this, he showed no disturbances of the body-image comparable to those observed in the case of Mr B. However, he showed great concern about his physical health, frequently complaining of stiffness in his arms and legs. He complained of rigidity of his musculature as stiffness. He was in the habit of examining his right forearm and on several occasions asked the author if he thought his hands were beautiful.

CASE IV

(i) Cognitive Status

Mr D's speech was occasionally normal in quantity and form but more often the grammatical structure was defective and it was difficult to understand, as in the instance quoted in the previous chapter. Then a perseverative trend would appear and in conversation he would show the phenomenon of echolalia. When he was in an unresponsive mood blocking of speech was extremely common.

Thinking had regained its magical omnipotent quality. He said, 'When ever I think of speed the police appear. It doesn't matter how many people are going fast I only have to sit on my bike and think of speed and hundreds of policemen appear in cars. When I sit on my green Honda and think of speed the police appear. How would you like to have a green head?' There was also evidence of faulty conceptualization, so that words had additional meanings apart from the correct ones. For example, he did not take off the reefer jacket he was wearing. When asked by a nurse why he kept wearing his jacket he replied, 'I'm just waiting to go home and let this wear off.' The word 'wear' was a condensation product, containing within it references to drug effects and delusional experiences as well as to the wearing apparel.

His speech was also disturbed by distractability. He would assimilate random auditory percepts into his communications, as in the following instance: 'Just a rubber head. Does he know that? . . . That's what did it . . . they wouldn't put them there . . . let the gun off (a car-door slammed at that point outside the room) . . . oh it's a car-door . . . he melted his car . . . that's what those guns do . . . but the car down on the ground . . . he ate it.'

For long periods of time he was inattentive and it was then that he was inclined to show evidences of blocking of speech and disturbances of voluntary movement and posture. With respect to perceptual upsets, he showed a loss of object-constancy in the visual sphere. He said, 'That table moved . . . it can't do that to me . . .' and again, 'If I stand still long enough the trees move.' He believed that the faces of those around him changed in shape and size. Misidentifications were also common, as has already been described.

(ii) Perception of the Self, Self-regard, and Personal Identity

Mr D was always self-preoccupied, even before the illness began. This self-preoccupation was heightened during the psychosis. While ill he was in the habit of examining his face and body in a mirror. He constantly examined a scar on his thigh; he called it frightening. At the outset of the observation period he appeared to have renounced the autonomy of bodily function. During physical examination he would maintain the position into which one or other of his limbs was placed. He also demonstrated a tendency towards automatic obedience. Concurrently he showed signs of faulty self-object discrimination. A coloured patient was in the bed opposite to the patient. A nurse overheard the patient say in a derisive tone as he scrutinized himself in the mirror: 'You Indian.' He was at times uncertain of his identity: he asked, 'Who am I?'; later he wondered if he was God. 'Who the hell am I? I don't know,' he repeated over and over again. His self-overestimation was revealed in his remark 'If they attacked me I'll walk around invisible', or, again when looking in the mirror, he asked a nurse if she did not think he had a wonderful appearance.

There was a constant fluctuation between pleasure and over-valuation of the mental and bodily self, on the one side, and disgust, anxiety, and criticism of the self, on the other side. He complained of a change in the shape of his body and head. He expressed ideas which suggested that changes had affected skin sensation. He said his face was covered in urine and his hands with grease. This fluctuation of attitude and feeling suggested a profound lack of stability of the sense of self.

OBSERVATIONS ON THE CLINICAL DATA

The clinical material presented shows many differences between individual patients as well as similarities. Speech may be normal in form or extensively disorganized. Perseveration may appear in some cases and not in others. Obstruction of speech occurred in every patient. A disorder of thinking also presented itself in every case but it was not always of an identical nature. This disorder had two main forms: one, a magical omnipotent type of thinking and, two, a mode of thinking characterized by a deterioration in the capacity for abstract conceptualization. The first type was present in all patients, but the second was absent in Mr C's case and present to varying degrees in the other three. It was most pronounced in Mr B, and this led to a more extensive disorganization of syntax than in the other two.

Magical thinking is an integral aspect of psychosis and its presence in a patient cannot be regarded as specific for any one psychotic state.

A disorganization of the function of abstract conceptualization, however, does not occur in all the functional psychoses and in the patients described this disorder varied in intensity. Its presence did not necessarily indicate an all-round deterioration in mental functions, so it was not associated with inattention, lack of interest, and diminished self-awareness. This 'lower' level of abstraction may be the state in which thinking proceeds in certain patients. Kraepelin's category of schizophasia might include states of this kind.

The obstruction of speech due to the blocking must be regarded as something quite different from the disorders of thinking referred to and must result from some other pathological process. It is blocking which is usually associated with inattention, sometimes of a profound degree, and diminished self-awareness; 'passive' distractability and echo phenomena are accompanying manifestations. Blocking may affect the activity of the thought processes, whether they are disordered in the sense described above or not. In catatonic states all patients present the blocking phenomenon at some stage of the illness, but not all will manifest a disorganization of abstract conceptualization. Blocking can be regarded as a negative symptom in so far as it expresses a loss of function. The loss of the capacity for abstract conceptualization is also a negative symptom. However, the appearance of concept formation at a less advanced level, as in the instances quoted, is a positive symptom, reflecting as it does the exposure of a mode of thinking not pathological in itself and showing striking similarities to the thinking of children and primitives.

All the patients were similar in that coherent, fluent, and logical speech appeared when they were angry or under the pressure of a need. This return to normal speech and thinking was never sustained for more than a few minutes. The themes were always simple and direct, and never contained complex abstractions. Most often, this 'improved' cognition appeared when the patient was in a withdrawn, unresponsive state in which blocking affected both speech and volitional movement. After the anger there was always a reversion to the earlier state. It does not seem correct to include this 'improved' cognition with the general disturbance of thinking because all that seems involved is a resolution of the blocking with a resultant ventilation of thought and affect through speech and action.

Inattention is a common finding in patients categorized as catatonic and it varies in its intensity. This phenomenon must be designated a negative symptom because it represents a loss of function. However, clinical observation has revealed that this inattention is associated with a form of distractability in which extraneous stimuli are assimilated outside awareness and obtain a mental registration. This distractability is the counter part to the inattention and it reflects the presence of a state of consciousness in which attention has different qualities and characteristics from that necessary for reflective awareness and adaptation. While inattention was present in all four patients at some stage of the observation period, distractability was not. It appeared in Mr B's case and to a lesser extent in Mr D's. Distractability is a positive symptom and should be classified as such.

Apart from the disorder of attention, the patients differed in the extent to which they experienced auditory hallucinations and misinterpreted environmental events. The same variation occurred in the way the body was perceived, and not all the patients failed to discriminate self from objects. The disorder of memory which appeared in two patients could only be discovered whenever the patient was no longer blocked and inaccessible. Under such circumstances the forgetfulness usually centred on delusional ideas (Mr B), or some topic the patient may not have wanted to discuss (Miss A). The clinical phenomena favour the view that repression is operative here. The fact that repression functions efficiently in a condition where repression is supposed to be seriously deranged raises important issues regarding the fate of repression in the psychoses.

The term 'catatonic' has become synonymous with the condition where the patient is unresponsive and inattentive, presents speech blocking, and manifests disorders of movement (motor blocking) and posture. When material of the kind described here is reviewed it is difficult to avoid the conclusion that catatonic manifestations act as a cover concealing from view a wide variety of clinical phenomena. This view is certainly supported by the effects of electroshock therapy on catatonic patients. Such a theory is in accord with Bleuler's view that catatonic signs are secondary phenomena in the schizophrenias.

When observations are made on catatonic patients over a long period by nurses as well as doctors, it is clear that catatonic signs are not fixed, immutable phenomena. They wax and wane in intensity, disappear entirely for short periods, and then return. Such changes may take place in the course of a few hours, so that a patient who is apparently catatonic at one moment is asking the nurse at another if he can undertake some task (for which he expects a reward) or may equally well be found filling in his football coupon. When patients are examined in the 'non-catatonic' state, as has occurred here, they can be seen to differ in the manner in which they relate to others and in their mode of thinking and perceiving. When catatonic they must be considered to be in an altered state of consciousness the signs and symptoms of which are reminiscent of those found in organic mental states. It would therefore be of interest to compare the cognitive, conative, and affective organizations which constitute the state of consciousness in chronic schizophrenic states with those which obtain in mental disorders due to organic brain disease (see Chapter 8).

CHAPTER 7

Organic Mental States

In the two preceding chapters the clinical material was drawn from patients suffering from catatonic schizophrenia. It was noted that there were phases of the illness when certain phenomena made their appearance that showed the greatest likeness to manifestations encountered in different types of organic brain disease. These phenomena – distractability perseverative signs, echo reactions, inattention, and transient identifications – have been observed in cerebral arteriosclerosis, senile dementia, Alzheimer's disease, Pick's disease, brain tumour, epilepsy, and mental defect. It may be of interest to record in detail the form and the manner of appearance of these phenomena and compare them with what is found in schizophrenic psychoses.

It has been the custom in the past to describe as dementia states of intellectual disorganization due to organic brain disease. The concept of dementia is a global one describing a generalized and irreversible deterioration of all aspects of personality functioning. A few exceptions are made to the rule of irreversibility but none to the idea of a widespread degeneration of cognition, conation, and affect. Today there is a greater acquaintance with patients suffering from brain disease, particularly that associated with the later years of life. This reveals that the term 'dementia' as understood above is applicable to only a section of patients with cerebral disease. Often the intellectual deterioration is entirely limited to a deficiency in short-term memory, while speech, perception, motility, and many aspects of personality remain intact. A progressive deterioration spreading to other faculties is not necessarily the rule, and there are even occasions, as later clinical illustrations will show, when the deficient function improves, even if only transiently. Again, there is no uniform disintegration of personality, and psychotic symptoms are the exception rather than the rule.

It is therefore more in keeping with current views (Zangwill, 1964; Wolff, 1963) to follow Allison (1962) and group these cases under the heading of organic mental states. This allows for the variation in the type and extent of intellectual and personality deterioration to be found in these conditions. Once again, use will be made of the examination scheme outlined in Chapter 3. Cases will not be described individually, but clinical data derived from several patients will be presented under the appropriate headings. The clinical states studied comprised senile and arteriosclerotic cerebral states, chronic alcoholism, presenile dementias, epilepsy, and brain tumour.

1. OBJECT RELATIONS

(*i*) *Nature of the Relationship with Real Objects*

A variety of forms of relating to real people appear in patients suffering from organic mental states. The presence of amnesias does not interfere with the general capacity to relate, since entirely different patterns of object relations (real and delusional) may arise in patients who have equally extensive amnesic defects. Of greater significance for the form of relating is the presence of an altered state of consciousness characterized by misidentifications and delusional ideas. The specific manner in which the patient relates to others is therefore more dependent upon the presence of positive signs than on negative manifestations, using these terms in the Jacksonian sense.

There are patients who welcome the interest of psychiatrist or nurse and they demonstrate this in their speech, even although they are handicapped by disturbances in this function. A case in point is a patient with senile cerebral degeneration who responded to an approach by the author as follows: 'My health is wonderful . . . I have worked all my life, maybe that's the reason.' When he was asked what more he could say he replied, 'You give me a hint of what to tell you . . . have you heard of Hughie Green? . . . some other grocer in Kilsyth . . . my brother Arthur is the man for pulling the boy's leg . . . you have to have patience because . . . if I knew what would interest you . . . give me a hint.' He was asked if he knew who the author was and he went on, 'I know you are clerical . . . your office here is telling me all the time . . . I know you are very well learned . . . I don't know how you got my name . . . just as we are sitting in this office conversing . . . you thought you'd like to see me in these days of wild youth . . .' When asked how old he was he replied, 'You're only a young man . . . I'm ninety and haven't got a fault in my body . . . it's thinking good thoughts . . . I've seen you twice before in your own office in the middle of the town . . . a bit off towards Glasgow . . . you're clerical and different kinds of work . . . you might be a solicitor . . . you're very exact and correct in your speech . . . in your knowledge of right . . . I'm glad you sent for me . . . you'd make a jolly good companion if I was more knowledgeable.'

When amnesic defects are extensive they exert a special influence on the way in which relating occurs and they lead to a characteristic form of object relationship. The amnesia results in a failure to relate to objects as distinct entities with their own special characteristics separate from the self and others. For example, the following conversation took place between the author and a patient suffering from diffuse cerebral degeneration: 'Do you work?' he was asked. 'No I haven't . . . we were all paid off . . . bad people used . . . we were all put away . . . they were paid, overpaid . . . sent off. Down with all wages . . .' He was asked why he was paid off and he replied, 'I didn't need to pay. I'd like to work . . . getting away from knocking about here . . .' He was asked if he knew the author and he replied as follows: 'He goes himself the boy . . .' He was asked the same question again and he said 'Does the boy know his man?' The third time the author asked the question he pointed to himself to emphasize it, asking in addition whether he had seen him before. The patient replied, 'Yes, before . . . be your heart,' clearly indicating that he perceived the author's gesture. When asked the question a fourth time the patient replied, 'Good heavens boy, I don't know his name, I don't know exactly his age.' Finally the author asked the patient, 'What's my job?' The patient responded with, 'What's my job . . . a foreman . . . good money . . . in Bilsland's Bread . . .'

In this last example the patient did not misidentify the author, but he was unable to relate to him as a specific person with his signified role distinct from any other person who would have approached him in the same way. All real objects are condensed into one without identifying characteristics. The patient responds in an identical fashion as long as the behaviour of the objects remains uniform. These patients also have difficulty in discriminating themselves from others (real objects). This was indicated in the case of the first-mentioned patient. The transient difficulty which he had in recognizing that a question was asked about him ('How old are you?' he was asked; he replied, 'You're only a young man; I'm ninety', etc. . . .), and not about the questioner, is encountered in many patients with a similar condition. This, in conjunction with other phenomena, supports the belief that self-object discrimination is no longer effective and that a process of condensation has occurred.

In contrast to the patient who welcomes personal contact there are those who are apathetic, withdrawn, and lacking in interest. This lack of interest is usually associated with inattention and an unresponsiveness. Mr X, suffering from a presenile dementia, had been most unwilling to enter conversation, gradually became increasingly self-preoccupied and refractory to efforts to interest him in discussions about himself or his family. Eventually it was impossible to reach him at all. This state appears to be quite common in patients where extensive degeneration accompanies epilepsy or occurs in the presenile dementias. It was also to be found in the case of Mr P, who suffered from a brain tumour.

In other patients, an active negativism may be encountered that expresses itself not only in the patient's reluctance to participate in conversation but in his behaviour also. This negativism, which is not accompanied by persecutory delusions, finds expression in a refusal to accede to requests, to active negativism (Bleuler, 1911), and to uncooperative attitudes, and is usually associated with defective short-term memory, perseverative signs, and a disconnection between speech and voluntary movement.

In those cases where cerebral degeneration is not so extensive, as in the instances just mentioned, patients may make a strong attachment to doctors and nurses. There would appear to be a critical point in the progress of the disease when recognition of the object to whom an attachment has been made is lost and the latter becomes merged (condensed) with all other objects. Sometimes the attachment to a special person is reflected in the patient's behaviour. Mr X, who had great difficulty in remembering the author's name but did so after several weeks of daily interviews, showed his attachment in the following manner. He was always in the habit of standing in or walking up and down a certain part of the ward. Several weeks after the interviews started he took up a new position outside the door of the interviewing-room where he was seen. He continued this behaviour for a long time after the meetings were discontinued. It only ceased when his condition deteriorated, as has been described.

The attachments patients may make have the characteristics of childhood relationships, with their strong affects and dependencies. Often enough the patient reveals in his speech that he regards himself as a child *vis-à-vis* the doctor or nurse, for example, a patient said, '. . . I'm only a boy, I've seen nothing . . . as you get older the more you can walk and find out exactly what's wrong . . . it's hard for me to say because I don't know . . . I'm a boy . . . only a boy . . . I don't know . . . I don't get out to get these things learnt . . . I can learn these things at school . . .'

(*ii*) *Nature of the Relationship with Delusional Objects*

Patients with organic mental disease may present all the phenomena encountered in psychotic states. Misidentifications, ideas of reference, and hallucinations and delusions with contents varying from wish-fulfilment to persecution may appear. Two distinct categories can be discerned. In the first, the patient's state is characterized by a denial of the reality of his environment and its replacement by a new reality. This new reality is based on misidentifications of those about the patient and by delusional beliefs regarding the real situation in life. Rationalizations and confabulations are freely used to sustain the delusional reality. Thus the patient is quite certain that he is at home going out to work at his chicken-farm every day.

In the second category, the patient primarily suffers from persecutory delusions that cause great anxiety. He may believe that his body and mind are being interfered with or his possessions stolen. Misidentifications occur, but instead of their being with relatives or friends from the past they are usually with fantasy figures who have come to punish or injure. The literature provides extensive details of these delusional beliefs as they occur in organic mental states.

Most clinical psychiatrists have had the opportunity of witnessing the development or the resolution of these delusional states in cases of organic mental disease. In one case, a patient of 70 years of age who suffered from cerebral arteriosclerosis, which expressed itself in transient but very slight memory deficits, developed a severe melancholia. At this time his intellectual functions were intact. His condition did not respond to the administration of antidepressive drugs, and as the mental state increased in severity it was decided to administer electroshock therapy. After the second treatment his intellectual functions were grossly impaired. Short-term memory was defective and he showed perseverative signs. Simultaneously he confabulated, misidentified those around him, and expressed delusional ideas. Nurses reported that the previous night he had believed he was at home (the patient was a farmer). He insisted on going out to the cow-shed and had to be restrained. Two days later the intellectual functions had returned to normal and the delusional reality had disappeared. The patient's depressive state was also much relieved.

There are, as is well known, a number of causes for the appearance of a psychotic reality in patients who already suffer from organic mental states. Apart from infections and all those factors which lead to a diminished cerebral circulation and metabolism, it is essential to recall that, whenever patients are deprived of those cues which enable them to make a veridical assessment of their environment, illusory and delusional states occur. This is most likely to occur at night. In this respect, these patients can be compared with young children whose cognitive apparatus has not developed to a state where a stable conception of the environment has been attained. Fantasy (psychic reality) can easily overwhelm their perceptions, particularly at night, thus leading to terrors and to states not unlike those encountered in certain cases of organic mental disease.

Unless the patient is dominated by persecutory delusions his misidentifications generally arise from memories of real persons. These misidentifications are a form of transference because they are indeed the revival of a lost relationship. This may be noted when the patient believes the physician to be his brother or is convinced that he is a child at school and fears he will be scolded by the teacher. One patient, after passing flatus, said, 'I hope the teacher didn't smell it.'

Above all, the patient who suffers from an organic mental state shows the capacity to relate; and the degree to which this will be deranged will depend upon the extent and intensity of delusional preoccupations when they occur. When these are minimal he will welcome the interest of the physician and rapidly relate to him, showing signs of transference that in a sense are similar to those of the psychoneurotic patient. He will differ from the latter in so far as he brings to life the memories of the past as misidentifications and misperceptions. He differs from the schizophrenic patient in so far as the distortions which the schizophrenic patient effects in the patient–physician or patient–nurse relationship are generally not achieved by the organic case unless there is a pronounced preoccupation with persecutory ideas.

2. PERCEPTION OF THE SELF, SELF-REGARD, AND PERSONAL IDENTITY

In organic mental states the patient usually retains the sense of self and personal identity. The amnesias that are such a striking feature of these conditions do not usually affect these self-conceptions. However, sometimes the patient no longer acknowledges himself to be as he is in the present but insists that he is as he once was – usually in early adult life or adolescence. This development can be regarded as a wish fulfilled and accepted by the patient as reality. In so far as it is a belief without foundation it must be considered a delusion and in essence no different from the wishful delusions of schizophrenic and manic patients. When misidentifications and confabulations are part of the clinical picture it is not uncommon for the patient to assume other identities (again, wishful thinking) as in the case of one patient who insisted that he was a doctor when he was being seen in the consulting-room.

Occasionally patients are encountered who seem to show a genuine failure in self-object discrimination not unlike that seen in schizophrenic states. The patient appears to confuse himself with the examiner. In one case the author pointed to his cheek in order to demonstrate to a patient what he wanted him to do. In this instance the patient (suffering from a senile degenerative state) appeared to have forgotten the word 'cheek'. After two or three demonstrations, the author pointed to his own cheek and said to the patient, 'You do this too.' The patient pointed to his cheek, saying simultaneously, 'That's your right cheek.' In all such instances the question of the use of language complicates the issue, and it is not always easy to be sure whether or not the patient is utilizing and allocating pronouns correctly. However, the balance of evidence favours the view that in many cases of organic cerebral disease self-object discrimination no longer operates effectively.

As a rule, the cognitive disorganization which is caused by degenerative and vascular changes in the brain does not by itself lead to complaints about abnormal bodily experiences. This only occurs when delusional complaints are present also. It is only when senile or arteriosclerotic patients are asked to identify parts of their bodies or localize stimuli that defects in bodily awareness become manifest. When such phenomena are elicited they are invariably accompanied by an amnesia for time, place, and person, defective retention and recall, defective topographic memory, and confabulation.

A variety of clinical phenomena make their appearance in cases of advanced cerebral degeneration. First, there is an inability to name body-parts, the patient having forgotten such words as hand, wrist, leg, and cheek. Second, the patient may give the wrong name to a body-part or make an echolalic response, as in the instance, 'Lift your left hand, please,' to be followed by the patient's answer, 'Lift your left hand.' Third, the perseverative tendency interferes with the patient's response, so that he continues to identify one part of the body when asked to identify another. A fourth, and last, observation can be made when certain patients are examined by means of double simultaneous stimulation.

Apart from a tendency to show varying degrees of inattention to a stimulus, some patients continue to perceive a stimulus when it has been applied to another body-part. For example, a patient will continue to localize tactile stimuli on both cheeks whenever the stimuli have been transferred to the backs of the hands. Two further phenomena are of interest here. In one case, there was evidence of a patient being aware of the hand stimuli even although he kept repeating that he felt the stimulus in the cheeks. The evidence consisted of his pushing forwards the backs of his hands as if inviting the stimulation. In another case, the tendency to give the wrong response could be interrupted and replaced by the correct one after repeating the stimulus to both hands three or four times.

This last series of observations suggest that the inattention to the second set of sensory stimuli is the outcome of perseveration. However, the explanation is not wholly to be found here because reinforcement of the second set of stimuli leads to a correct response. This indicates that a defect of the attention mechanism is also involved, in that there is a failure to inhibit the impact of the first series of stimuli. The data suggest that a close relationship may exist between perseveration and sensory inattention.

Finally, reference must be made to yet another form of inattention that is occasionally found in organic mental states, namely, the syndrome of anosognosia, the non-recognition of physical defects. Most often this is associated with the sequelae of cerebral vascular accidents affecting the non-dominant cerebral hemisphere. Anosognosia is associated with severe cognitive disorganization. On the basis of a study of twenty-two cases of cerebral disease, Weinstein and

Kahn (1950) have proposed that the non-perception was always an aspect of a generalized mental disturbance characterized by amnesias, confabulations, disorientation, paraphasias, and perseverative signs.

3. STATUS OF COGNITIVE FUNCTIONS

It is generally recognized that there is a gradual loss of vocabularies in patients suffering from degenerative cerebral states. Over and above this, however, are varying degrees of loss of the capacity for sentence-formation and grammatical construction. In more advanced cases it is often difficult to follow the patient's utterances for more than a phrase or two. An outstanding feature in speech is the perseverative trend (Freeman and Gathercole, 1966). This phenomenon will be found in nearly all the instances quoted below. Mr X, the patient suffering from presenile dementia, demonstrated this sign and a general disintegration of sentence formation. He spoke as follows: 'Janet is in the office . . . Anna, bigger than me, she is in an office too . . . the wife was telling me on Sunday . . . the office she's in, the one bigger than what I am . . . in 1950 I was taken to the infirmary in an old ambulance with double pneumonia . . . I was at my father's funeral . . . you're looked after here . . . of course I don't smoke. The ones that work get an issue of cigarettes, I don't smoke at all . . . the girls are in the office . . . the two of them . . . there's the one bigger than me . . . Janet . . . the one with the glasses also works in an office . . .' As he fell silent he was asked what he was thinking and he replied, 'I get one of the white things after breakfast and dinner . . . they are small and white. You get a small thing . . . a glass thing with cold water too . . . the mouth. It's good . . . others get the same . . . Ann and Janet both work in offices . . .' He fell silent again and then continued, 'That mark on my forehead; I fell on gravel . . . I was young at the time . . . it left a mark there . . . it left a mark there . . . are you kept busy doctor? . . . it just shows you . . . the main doctor comes round to see everyone right this morning . . . one day Tom Peters smokes a wooden pipe . . . we get out of the road of the smoke when he starts . . . it's a wooden pipe he smokes . . . he gets it in the canteen. They are building a new canteen . . . electricians working inside . . . it's a big one that's built . . . working inside, the electricians . . . they'll see it right beforehand . . . I'm doing fine doctor . . . these are my brown shoes I have . . . they live inside. My black shoes are inside . . . different leather . . . Janet wears glasses, she's in some office now . . . the other one's bigger than me . . . she works in an office now . . .'

The examination of patients suffering from organic mental states reveals the difficulty of attempting to distinguish disorders of speech from disturbances of thinking. Words may no longer be available. When the patient is aware of his amnesia for words it is possible to assume that thinking is intact. The question is, what is the nature of the thought process in cases of this type? For example, an elderly patient, suffering from a diffuse cerebral disease, could not recall the author's occupation. He had been a motor-car mechanic all his life and still thought he was working. When pressed for an answer he said, 'Aren't you for repairing machines?' Here the disease had resulted in a failure to produce the correct concept. Nevertheless, the wish to do so was present and he succeeded in elaborating thoughts in words which approximated to the concept sought after in terms of his own work experience. Concept-formation in such instances is clearly defective and thus a thinking disorder is present.

Stengel (1964) has described a type of speech defect occurring in organic mental patients who show an indifference to the nature of their verbal productions.

The following example is illustrative. In this case of senile cerebral degeneration, the patient had been told at the beginning of the interview that the author was a doctor. Twenty minutes later he was asked if he could recall the latter's vocation. He replied as follows: 'Are you not for animals? . . . they say you look after animals . . . or such . . . a vegetarian or Victorian . . . some name like that.' This patient was disorientated for time, place, and person. He denied that he was in hospital. He insisted that he was living in the country where he had spent his childhood and early adult life. He misidentified doctors and male nurses as his brothers. The word he wanted to use was veterinarian. Instead he used words with a similar sound – vegetarian, Victorian – literal paraphasias. This can be interpreted as resulting simply from an inability to recall or utilize a specific word. However, what must be taken into account is the overall thinking disorder which allowed the patient to believe that he was young and at home again. Here is magical thinking. Some might consider that asking a doctor if he was a veterinarian was a means of expressing his dissatisfaction and contempt.

Paraphasias and neologisms in organic mental states may have multiple meaning which can only be discovered through knowledge of the patient's past life, present experiences, and circumstances. The choice of substitute word may not be merely a matter of chance or of sound, as is so often assumed to be the case. In instances such as the case quoted, the disturbance of speech reflects a basic defect in the process of conceptualization and is not purely a disorder of verbalization (Bay, 1963).

In organic mental states there is a generalized deterioration in conceptual powers which arises from either the loss of or the inability to form verbal concepts. This inevitably leads to a narrowing of the range of thought, to a preoccupation with immediate experience. At times, the patient appears unable to detach himself from the impact of extraneous stimuli and this may be the cause of the distractability which is so common in organic mental states and which will be described below. This description, including the earlier references to perseveration, is reminiscent of the account given by Jaspers (1963) of the 'amentia' type of symptom complex. It is the loss of the ability to abstract the self from immediate experience which results in an egocentric interpretation of events. This egocentrism is usually associated with some degree of magical thinking. Here, thoughts are no longer regarded as a means of communicating ideas to others or as a way in which an optimal adaptation to the world of reality can be attained.

In this respect a degradation of thinking has taken place from a highly abstract to a less abstract state, as in the following example drawn from a case of senile cerebral degeneration. The patient said, 'I think I seem to be making some headway . . . I'm thinking about my work more than anything else . . .' He was asked what he was doing now and he replied, 'Nothing special, just the usual: the chickens to look after; at one o'clock with the chickens and in the afternoon clean them out; keep the place clean and tidy. If you have the afternoon you keep the place clean and tidy; by that time it's dinner time; then you have the afternoon feeding . . . you can't do much after you have the feeding done.' 'What else do you do?' he was asked. He replied, 'Of course you have the chickens: you take the chickens from the machine, from the incubator; that's about the stretch of their day's work. I don't think there's anything else after that: just the ordinary feeding . . .' In this case there was a complete denial of reality and the thought processes had an omnipotent and concrete quality.

When patients with organic mental states are asked questions or are confronted with a statement, they may fail to reply or may make an inappropriate response. Mr X, the patient suffering from presenile dementia, spoke as follows: 'I saw you round this morning, Doctor. I saw you round this morning; the other one goes to ward 8 . . . he's white-headed . . . one with glasses . . . once you're in there there's something wrong with you . . . there's a well-built chap there . . . he's paralysed on one side . . . years ago I took an epileptic fit . . . I was taken to the Infirmary in an ambulance . . . I was given something to drink . . . I had something small to take . . .' At this point the patient was asked if he did not feel disappointed that the doctors did not do more for him. He replied, 'No, the doctor is white-headed; he goes into ward 8 to see them right . . . he is white-headed, there is another doctor who goes with him.' Here the response appears to have been determined by the author's use of the word 'doctor' and by the perseverative trend.

The influence of perseveration in leading to inappropriate replies to questions can also be seen in the following instance. This illustration also shows how the perseverative trend results in a patient sticking to his theme and remaining uninfluenced by repeated questions. The patient was talking about his daughter: 'She works in an office now.' 'Does she come to see you?' the author asked. The patient replied, 'She works in an office now . . . Janet works in an office. She's bigger than me.' The author asked, 'Do you not miss your daughter?' The patient continued, 'That's the one, she's bigger than me . . . you see the amount of homework she has . . . Janet laughs at her.' The last question, 'Do you not miss your daughter?' was repeated, but he went on: 'You've got to leave her alone, when she's at it; you must leave her alone . . . she's bigger than me.' The same question was repeated but he continued as before: 'No, that's the girl who's bigger than me, got to leave her alone . . . you've got to leave her alone when she's at it . . .' 'Is that why she doesn't come to see you?' he was asked, but he merely replied, 'You've got to leave her alone; she has to put everything down.'

Patients with organic mental states demonstrate an extensive distractability. This distractability takes the form of an assimilatory process whereby extraneous percepts are incorporated into the patient's speech, apparently outside awareness. Frequently the content of the patient's utterances is determined by stimuli provided by the interview situation. The following data are taken from a case of senile dementia. The perseverative trend was pronounced in speech. In this instance the author was making notes while the patient was speaking. The patient spoke as follows: 'Kind of cold today. Better with a drop of whisky . . . better when we go back . . . now, do you want to write that in France or in the British Transport thing . . . the British information . . . that's what they call the paper . . . the British paper . . . they'll know how to head it just when you put it in these words . . . that's fine . . . I can't tell you much more . . . I wouldn't put that down, Jimmy, until you see how they carry you through . . . Saturday, they deliver it to you . . .' When asked what was delivered he replied, 'The paper . . . that's all I can mind, Jimmy . . . I cannot tell you anything . . . I don't get the paper . . . you are best not to take too much in case they carry you off . . . I'll not say anything about you . . . I want to mention your name so that you can be papered along with your pals . . .'

In this case the content of the patient's speech resulted from an assimilation of immediate perceptual experience. This applied not only to the author writing on paper but also to the 'British Transport thing' which was derived from an advertisement-type calendar on the wall of the interviewing-room. Recognition of this assimilatory tendency in organic mental states sometimes helps towards an understanding of speech content that appears at first sight to be without any specific determinants; for example, Mr X began talking about the fact that all the patients had to hang their coats on hooks as soon as he saw the author hanging up his coat on entering the consulting-room.

The tendency for speech content to be influenced by random percepts can also be seen when patients are having difficulty in naming objects. In one case, another one of cerebral degeneration, the patient was asked to name a watch. His reply, influenced by the author's pipe and matches lying on the table, was: 'It's a thing I never used in my life . . . plenty watches and knocks I didn't need them . . . all my life . . . never once . . . all the people in my life . . . never needed to use them . . .' This phrase, 'I used it [or them],' is almost always used by individuals when referring to tobacco and sometimes to liquor. When the author began to smoke the patient spontaneously said, '. . . used to use it all my life . . . tobacco, pipe, matches, cigarettes . . . never used them, stopped altogether.'

When this man was later shown a box of matches, he said, 'It's a sparcar . . . it's a cubic . . . a pipe . . .' The word 'sparcar' was a carry-over from his attempt to name a blue Bic pen, his response being

'. . . watch, knocks . . . blue, sparcar, inkcar.' The perseverative trend led to his calling an ashtray 'a gas pipe . . . for keeping off stuff . . . pipes and cigarettes.' Similarly, keys were called 'pipe cloths or time clocks'. It would seem as if the process of word-finding in these patients does not proceed uninfluenced by immediate environmental stimuli and by the perseverative trend. The examples quoted illustrate the manner in which external impressions are assimilated and thereafter inappropriately employed in speech.

Disorders of perception in organic mental states are for the most part confined to the results of the disorganization of the way in which the body and self are perceived. These phenomena were referred to under the appropriate section of the examination scheme. Disturbances of visual perception are less frequent, apart from those cases where misidentifications and hallucinations appear. They have already been referred to in the section 'Object Relations'.

A constant finding in cases of organic mental states is the loss of the capacity to recall immediate impressions. All patients suffering from diffuse cerebral degenerations present a Korsakow-like picture with confabulations and a loss of time-sense. This is usually accompanied by varying degrees of memory-loss for past events. Patients can be roughly divided into two groups, regardless of the exact nature of the cerebral degeneration. In one category the amnesic defects constitute the main clinical manifestations, namely, loss of memory for immediate and past events, so that the patient is forgetful of a dead spouse, of his family, of specific periods of his life experiences, etc. There are serious defects of topographic memory, of words, and of body-parts. An inability to retain impressions accompanies these negative symptoms. In the second category the above-mentioned amnesic signs also appear, but they are accompanied by a series of positive symptoms – namely, misidentifications, perseveration in speech and action, confabulations, and the reappearance of early memories in the form of hallucinatory and delusional experiences. Several instances of this have all been described in some of the clinical illustrations detailed above. Here the patient denies reality and substitutes a false reality consisting of episodes of his past life. Such cases raise a number of interesting questions (Lewis, 1961). Do these patients forget everything about those who were dear to them because such recollections bring too much pain? Or can the amnesia be regarded as entirely due to organic damage? Are the patient's denial of illness and refusal to acknowledge the reality of his environment (the ward and its inmates), and the substitution of a belief that he is still at home or at work, also means of avoiding emotional distress? Are these phenomena to be interpreted as defences in the same way as is usually done with the symptoms of a neurotic or psychotic patient?

Psychoanalytical writers of an earlier generation (see Fenichel, 1945) categorized such phenomena under the heading of pathoneuroses or disease neuroses (Ferenczi, 1916) – in this instance, cerebral pathoneuroses. In their view, cerebral disease led in certain individuals to the active operation of repression, denial, and projection. These mechanisms were initiated automatically apart from conscious intent, and their aim was the annulment of the anxiety and mental pain engendered by the physical effects of the brain damage. The clinical phenomena – the amnesias, confabulations, delusions, and denial of physical defects – were the result of the operation of these mental mechanisms and could not be attributed to damage to specific cerebral areas.

Only certain types of amnesia can be explained on the above-mentioned basis. There are the amnesias for objects and names without affective significance, which seem to be related more to deficiencies in the capacity to attend and intend. It is a commonplace observation that patients suffering from organic mental states have difficulty in reproducing on demand words they have just heard. For example, a patient was unable to recall the author's occupation when asked. The word 'doctor' was inaccessible but not lost because the selfsame patient was accustomed to addressing the author as 'Doctor' whenever he appeared in the ward. On one occasion another patient was told the author's occupation. A few minutes later she could not recall what it was. Afterwards she said in response to a question, 'I didn't hear what you said, Doctor . . .' This example is not unlike the classical observation made by Hughlings Jackson on an aphasic patient who, although unable to utter the word 'no' on demand, could say 'I can't say no.'

Lewis (1961) quotes experimental work supporting the inference made from clinical observation of the type described that registration of impressions occurs at least partially in patients with amnesias due to cerebral disease. It would appear that the defective ability for recall is closely linked to the disturbance of attending and intending. When the patient cannot intend (in this instance recall at will) he also shows disturbances of the attention mechanism in the form of perseveration and distractability.

4. MOTILITY

In organic mental states disorders of voluntary movement can be most easily observed when the patient is asked to carry out simple instructions. Such patients usually tend to sit quietly without making spontaneous movements based on conscious intentions. Where extensive cerebral degeneration has occurred, the investigation of the capacity for voluntary movement may be interfered with by the patient's difficulty in comprehending speech due to an amnesia for words. However, in most cases this complication is limited and patients can cooperate if they are given several opportunities to try to follow the instructions given. Another difficulty in the administration of these tests is provided by the appearance of perseveration, since patients continue with the first movement asked for when presented with the second request.

When patients suffering from organic mental states are asked to perform a simple act, they may react in a number of different ways. First, the patient may not respond at all. Second, he may remain immobile but respond with an echo reaction. This was the case with a senile patient who said, 'Punch on your chin' when asked, 'Point to your chin.' When the examiner demonstrated the action on himself the patient carried it out correctly. However, when he was asked immediately afterwards to lift his left hand he immediately pointed to his chin, revealing a perseverative trend of the 'switching' variety (Freeman and Gathercole, 1966). Third, the patient may carry out the movement, for example tapping on the table or squeezing the examiner's hand, a specific number of times, and then continue it indefinitely or, in the case of the last-mentioned instruction, the grip may pass into a state of tonic contraction. Fourth, the patient makes no response to the instruction, but inquiry reveals that, although he made no movement, he fully understood what was expected of him.

Patients' abilities to make skilled and coordinated manual movements can be examined by employing the simple tests devised by Luria (1966) (see Appendix B). Although the patient appears to understand what is expected of him as a result of several demonstrations, he usually does not succeed. He will be unable to perform the ring-fist test or the first-edge-palm test. One part of the movement may be executed correctly but there is an absence of a smooth transition to the next.

Instead, the test is abandoned or there is perseveration of the first component of the movement.

Similar disorders of voluntary movement to those described have been found by Luria (1966) to occur in bilateral frontal lobe lesions. He has observed that the termination of the movement requested is as difficult as its initiation. Motor perseverative signs, both repetitive and switching, also occur. Luria (1965) has noted that these phenomena can also occur in unilateral frontal lesions. This was so in one case in the series described here. Mr P, who suffered from a glioblastoma of the left fronto-parietal region, presented all the manifestations described

FIGURE 1

for bilateral cases and for diffuse degenerative states. During interviews, Mr P would grasp the edge of the desk with his right hand. The tonic contraction of the flexor muscles rendered him unable to release his grip at will (Levin, 1955).

There are patients suffering from organic cerebral states who show signs of motor perseveration ('switching variety') only when asked to write or draw. Mr X, whose case was referred to earlier, presented the following sequence of phenomena. He was asked to draw a clock; which he did. He was then asked to draw a man (see *Figures 1a* and *b*). He was asked to draw a clock again and he produced (*Figure 1c*), a man with a clock-face.

On another occasion, after drawing a clock and a man (*Figures 2a* and *b*), he was asked to draw a clock again. He responded by drawing a man (*Figure 2c*). He was asked to draw a clock on three further occasions. He drew a man each time (*Figures 3a, b,* and *c*).

FIGURE 2

FIGURE 3

Then Mr X was asked to draw a house. He drew the following and said, 'That's the mouth; there's the chimneys on the top.'

FIGURE 4 'That's the mouth; there's the chimneys on the top.'

Figures 1c and *4* both reveal the influence of condensation on perceptual motor functions.

The tendency compulsively to repeat one component of a drawing was shown by Mr P. His drawing of a house is depicted below (*Figure 5*).

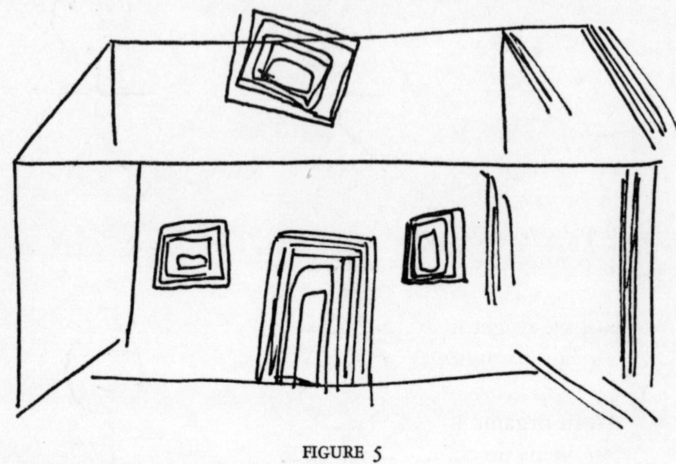

FIGURE 5

These manifestations have been presented because of the similarities to the perserverative phenomena sometimes encountered in the drawings of longstanding cases of schizophrenia (Freeman and Gathercole, 1966).

5. SENSORI-MOTOR ORGANIZATION

The alterations in the motor system – tonus and reflex changes – which may occur in focal and diffuse cerebral disease have been well documentated in the neuropsychiatric litrature and therefore there is no need to repeat them here (Allison, 1962; Mayer-Gross *et al.*, 1954). It is only necessary to recall that catatonic manifestations may appear in focal as well as diffuse cerebral lesions (Schilder, 1928a; Weinstein, 1967). Hypertonia of the limb musculature and catalepsy are not uncommon features. In the case of Mr P, the patient with the tumour of the left fronto-parietal region, there was a rigid catalepsy of the right arm. It is in cases which present catatonic manifestations that negativism is most likely to be encountered.

In the section on perception of the body, an account was given of the various forms of inattention which may occur in organic mental states. A description was also presented of the manner in which sensation may be displaced from one body-part to another or projected into space. Note was also made of the way in which perseveration occurs in the sensory sphere. Face dominance (Bender, 1952) is not uncommon.

6. MANIFESTATIONS OF 'INSTINCTUAL DRIVE' ACTIVITY

(*a*) *Libidinal*

A preoccupation with the mouth, anus, and genitals is by no means uncommon in those cases of organic mental disease where the disintegration of psychological function has been extensive. In one case of general paralysis, the patient, apart from presenting signs of oral dyskinesia, continually put anything within his reach into his mouth. As Mr P's state deteriorated, he constantly fingered his anus. It was quite impossible to get him to desist from this habit, since at this stage of the illness he was quite inaccessible although fully conscious. Genital exhibitionism and masturbation are frequently observed in patients suffering from organic mental states.

The phenomena described above are autoerotic: there is no tendency to involve others in the activities. However, organic brain disease can, in some cases, lead to the appearance of deviant sexual (genital) behaviour. In one patient who suffered from Korsakow's psychosis, homosexual tendencies became manifest and led to his making homosexual advances to other patients. This patient had no previous history of homosexual behaviour.

(*b*) *Aggressive*

Outbursts of rage are frequent in patients suffering from organic mental states. They are most likely to appear if the patient is frustrated in something he wants to do. In this respect his behaviour is somewhat similar to that of the very young child.

7. AFFECTIVITY

Sadness, grief, anxiety, and elation are the most common emotions found in organic mental states. The ease with which affect is generated has often been described. However, the affective response is frequently appropriate, as when the patient may weep when thinking of her dead husband. It is of interest that such a sequence of psychic events may occur in a patient with senile degenerative cerebral changes in whom there is an extensive amnesic defect. These patients (to be discussed further in the next section) are to be compared with those already described who no longer acknowledge such memories and have constructed a delusional reality. That there are patients who, in spite of severe amnesias, still remember their lost object relationships indicates that repression may be the operative factor in those organic mental states in which significant recollections from the past are denied.

8. DEFENCE ORGANIZATION

The instinctual phenomena that make their appearance in organic mental states reflect the extent to which the forces normally exerting control over the direct expression of the drives are disorganized and deficient in their function. A further result of this disorganization is the intrusion of the processes of condensation and displacement (the primary process) into thought and perceptual functions. Condensation leads to misidentifications in the visual sphere, to disturbances of conceptual thought, and to defects of perceptual-motor functions. Concepts are no longer discrete and autonomous; for example, the patient who called the author a 'vegetarian or Victorian' did so as a consequence of condensation affecting the memory traces of words. Condensation affected perceptual-motor functions, leading to Mr X's drawings of the house with the face and the man with the clockface. These data provide support for Freud's (1916) assertion that condensation is not primarily concerned with defence but is a basic property of mental processes.

While it is inappropriate at this point to attempt a designation of the defective functions which permit the intrusion of drives and primitive thought processes, there are several phenomena which should be noted because of their relevance in this context. Earlier, patients with organic mental states were roughly categorized into two groups (see page 109). One group consisted of those patients who had constructed a delusional reality by means of misidentifications and misinterpretations of what was seen and heard and by a denial of reality. The other was characterized by a memory defect only.

The clinical material suggests that two mental mechanisms are at work. In the first group denial is constantly operative. Any percept, the recognition of which would weaken the new reality, is immediately denied or distorted in such a way as to become congruent with it. Simultaneously, memories which may have been distressing are repressed. The patient does not acknowledge that he was ever married, had a family, or that his wife is now dead. The evidence in favour of the view that repression is the cause of the forgetfulness is twofold. First, there is the selective nature of the forgetting: all the experiences from adult life are not forgotten; and, second, all patients with similar organic mental states do not have an amnesia for events which have had emotional significance. In the second category of patients denial plays no part.

The clinical material reveals that organic brain disease may lead to a disintegration of the forces which normally hold the drives and primitive modes of mental activity in check. At the same time, mental mechanisms which serve the purpose of avoiding emotional distress (repression) still retain their effect.

CHAPTER 8

Chronic Schizophrenia and Organic Mental States

At the beginning of the preceding chapter, attention was drawn to a series of clinical phenomena which may be found in both schizophrenic psychoses and organic mental states. Here, an examination will be undertaken of those manifestations in greater detail, as they are to be found in patients suffering from chronic schizophrenia. The data are drawn from fifteen patients whose illness had been active for at least seven years without a remission. In every case the onset occurred in early adult life. In these patients there had been a serious deterioration in all aspects of personality functioning. They were not only cognitively disorganized but also withdrawn from the world and without a systematic delusional reality. They would be best categorized as hebephrenic-catatonic states. In a previous publication (Freeman, Cameron, and McGhie, 1958), detailed descriptions were given of the manner in which thinking, perceiving, and memory were deranged in chronic schizophrenia. A significant omission was the absence of descriptions of the disturbances of voluntary movement and posture which are so common in these conditions. This will be rectified here, and a comparison will be made with the disorders of motility occurring in organic mental states.

The mental functions which are equally disorganized in chronic schizophrenia and in organic mental states are those concerned with attending, concentrating, speech, thinking, memory, and motility. Thus they give rise to distractability, perseveration, echo-phenomena, inattention, and disorders of motility. The mode of presentation will not be based on the examination scheme employed in previous chapters. Instead, the clinical phenomena will be described within the context of the patient's dealings with other patients and doctors in a series of group meetings, as was recounted in an earlier publication (Freeman, Cameron, and McGhie, 1958), and presented under such headings as 'Disorders of Speech', 'Attention', 'Memory', and 'Motility'.

DISORDERS OF SPEECH

The differentiation of speech from thinking disorders is difficult in the schizophrenias. The result has been a tendency to regard speech disturbances as reflecting the underlying disorder of thinking. Here, account is taken of those authors (Kleist, 1960; Fish, 1962) who believe that, in the schizophrenias, a speech disorder exists quite apart from a disorder of thinking. Hence speech disorder is considered as expressing itself primarily in formal defects, whereas thought disorder is revealed by the content of speech.

Chronic patients vary considerably in their speech capacity. There are those who speak freely, but whose speech is so disorganized that grammatical laws are not observed. Then there are those whose speech is halted by blocking almost before it has begun. There are two characteristics of the speech of chronic patients which warrant further description because of their resemblance to the speech disturbances found in organic mental states. They are perseveration and echolalia. A further manifestation worthy of examination is the fact that verbal symbols are not easily or readily available to the chronic schizophrenic patient. In this he again resembles some patients with organic mental states.

Perseveration

Perseveration in the speech of chronic schizophrenic patients assumes two forms. The first is observed while the patient speaks spontaneously; the second when his speech is interrupted by questions or comments from another person. As will be seen, both types reflect the trend towards a compulsive repetition of words or phrases and in a sense are basically similar. As an illustration, during a group meeting Mr O said, 'It's a presumptuous thing to respect someone . . . respect . . . respectable . . . respect . . . he didn't respect money of me but I didn't have it to give to him.' The word 'respect' was repeated continuously during the remainder of his utterance.

The manner in which this word 'respect' made its appearance is worthy of note. Two days earlier, another patient, Mr Z, equally disorganized cognitively, had been talking somewhat incoherently about his Army career in Italy. Mr O continually stood up and walked about the room, picking up pieces of wool or fluff from the floor, while Mr Z was speaking. The author commented, 'Mr O likes to keep everything neat and tidy.' Mr Z muttered, 'He's a billet orderly.' At first it was difficult to make out what Mr O was saying but then the word 'respect' became clear and the following phrase could be distinguished: 'Respect is a foreign word . . . respect . . . a funny word . . . it's had a long run for its money . . . respect from a tanned man.' 'Respect' appeared again on following days, its appearance being reinforced by Mr Z passing wind per anum. In that meeting Mr O alternated his usage of the word between 'respect' and 'respectable'. Two days later, he said, apparently in response to Mr Z making peculiar gestures, 'Chinese respect gestures (jesters) . . . the Chinese guy; he was doing the gestures . . . stinking . . . stinking respect . . . told to respect stinking people . . . respect is a lower word . . . you could write that.' The word 'respect' disappeared from this patient's utterances as the days passed, not to reappear.

In this last example, the perseverative trend was activated by a remark made by another patient. At first sight it seems as if the choice of word was made at random and that affective considerations played no part. However, there are good grounds for believing that in both organic and schizophrenic states it is not just always a completely mechanical affair. The patient suffering from the organic mental state described in Chapter 7, who perseverated about his daughters, was clearly concerned about them. When Mr O was stimulated compulsively to repeat the word 'money' after another patient had said 'Money corrupts', he eventually referred to homosexuality and said, 'He asked me to go into a room and molest him . . . he asked me if I took his money in the room.'

In organic mental states and chronic schizophrenia, once the patient has started on his repetitive speech it is impossible to get him to change the topic in spite of constant stimulation (Bychowski, 1935). Here the switching form of perseveration is evident. This phenomenon accounts for the inappropriate responses so frequently obtained to questions in cases of schizophrenia. For example, Mr O said: 'Someone took him into a room . . . molestation is worse than assault . . . he asked me to go into a room and molest him . . . the man asked if I took the money in the room.' As he had previously referred to a cartoon strip (Rip Kirby), the author asked the patient if he read the papers and where he got them. The patient continued, 'He could speak to an illustration form, he asked if I would molest him in that room . . . molestation is a pretty criminal caper . . . he asked if I was betting on a prostitute . . . the man in the illustration did . . . he would do me in.' Interestingly enough, a discussion about gambling on horse races (betting) had been taking place immediately beforehand.

The material that has been presented indicates that in organic and functional states affective factors are operative in leading to the choice of word or phrase that is repeated, but they do not account for the repetition itself. This appears to be associated with the special state of consciousness existing in both categories of patient. Only such a state can account for the manner in which extraneous percepts are inappropriately assimilated into speech (for example, betting). This problem will be taken up below.

Echolalia

Echolalia is to be found quite frequently in patients suffering from chronic schizophrenia. The patients are usually inattentive and unresponsive. Echolalia bears a striking resemblance to perseveration in so far as there is a common element of repetition. This repetition is automatic and seems to occur outside conscious intent. The stimulus word or words are repeated over and over again without any regard for the context within which they appear. It is not only statements or questions made directly to the patient that are echoed, but anything said directly within his hearing. A patient will repeat parts of a sentence he has overheard: for example, the author remarked to a colleague at the beginning of a group session, 'The roads are dangerous after the snow yesterday.' The patient echoed and repeated 'snow yesterday'.

From a descriptive standpoint, there is little to distinguish the echolalia that occurs in the chronic schizophrenic patient from that occurring in the patient suffering from an organic mental state. When the mental status of patients of each category is scrutinized they are found to have in common a severe disturbance of cognition and volition. Interest in their surroundings is almost nonexistent, and they are unresponsive. Speech, thinking, and recent memory are deranged. The fact that on some occasions the schizophrenic patient appears to have a 'normal' memory or to speak rationally does not contradict the fact that when he presents with echolalic responses his cognitive organization is quite different from that required for environmental adaptation. The clinical evidence suggests that an explanation of echo reactions, just as with perseverative signs, cannot be undertaken without reference to the condition of consciousness obtaining in the patient.

Inappropriate Use of Words

It has frequently been observed that schizophrenic patients manifest considerable difficulty in expressing themselves in the appropriate words. Sometimes the words are employed, but used in the wrong sense. For example, a patient employs the word 'son' to mean either or both 'sun' and 'son', or 'feat' to mean 'feet' or 'feat'. Again, many of these patients have lost the ability to employ pronouns correctly, thus making it difficult to know whether the patient is referring to himself or to the person he is talking to. At times this suggests not only that the patient has lost the sense of identity (the 'I') but also that there is a deficiency in the capacity to discriminate the self from others, as in the case of the patient who said, 'You deliberately rip up the frocks for me to tear.' The difficulty in finding personal pronouns is also to be observed in patients with organic mental states, and was referred to in the previous chapter.

While inferences may be made regarding motivations underlying the difficulty in word expression in chronic schizophrenia, the fact that patients present this specific loss of function cannot be denied. In earlier publications (Cameron, Freeman, and McGhie, 1956; Freeman, Cameron, and McGhie, 1958), several examples were presented of this phenomenon. For example, when chronic patients were being offered cigarettes at a group meeting, one patient, who was withdrawn and uninterested, made an apparently irrelevant remark about bishops: 'There are a lot of bishops about.' At this point the observer (J.L.C.) realized that the cigarettes he was offering were a brand called 'Churchman'. This patient could not employ the words which would have conveyed his feelings about the offer of cigarettes. Even confrontation with this explanation of his utterance led only to his agreeing with what the therapist said. He made no reference to cigarettes.

Observers have constantly been impressed by the fact that the schizophrenic patient who has the greatest difficulty in finding words and using them correctly can on some occasions speak in such a way as to indicate that his speech and thinking are essentially intact. This has convinced many authors that there cannot be a true 'dementia' in the schizophrenias comparable with that obtaining in the organic mental states. Perhaps some light can be thrown on this problem by examining the conditions under which apparently normal speech and thinking arise. The following clinical illustrations are instructive in this respect. The patient who talked about tearing frocks (quoted above), who knew the author well, was having an interview in a room from which it was possible to see the ward clock. At one point in the meeting the patient was asked if she could see the clock. She did not reply. She was then asked if she could tell the time. She made a wholly inappropriate response: 'I'm a nurse, not a doctor.' About five minutes later she said, 'It's 12 o'clock, time for dinner', and got up and left.

The correct employment of words is generally associated with the presence of some need on the patient's part. As a rule, the 'normal' speech ends if the need is satisfied. However, even when the wish is met, the normal speech is not sustained. Attention has already been drawn to the fact that 'normal' speech may arise when the patient is angry. For example, a patient (Miss JB) whose speech was utterly incomprehensible (Freeman, Cameron, and McGhie, 1958) became furious with one of the observers. She had her hands over her eyes; then suddenly removed them, saying angrily, 'It's better to be mad, the mad don't see.' Whether 'normal' speech is activated by a need or by anger, the content is always simple and the speech rarely sustained. It has a certain spontaneous, automatic quality, suggesting that it is not the outcome of reflection and consideration.

As well as finding it difficult to express certain words, chronic schizophrenic patients are often equally handicapped in using proper names. For example, the patient just referred to (Miss JB) was asked to come into a consulting-room. She refused, and sat in a chair outside in the corridor exactly opposite the room of a colleague. His name was on the door (C. E. Gathercole). While the author was sitting with the patient, Mr Gathercole passed by. The patient immediately said, 'You should be a pole or a Jack Tar; we can't all gather from that.' When the author asked her if she knew the name of the man who had passed she replied, 'No, I don't listen like that . . . I listen to the king.'

This patient, as with others described, has lost the ability to employ certain concepts, which may be simple, as in the instances quoted, or complex. In their place, other words are employed that bear a relationship to the inaccessible verbal symbols.

The speech defects described here support the theory originally proposed by Freud (1915) that, in schizophrenia, words are no longer primarily used as a means of communicating information about things and people. These objects have lost their cathexis (interest), and the concepts (verbal symbols) representing them can be employed at any time or place without any reality referent. The interest in specific words or names will depend upon the patient's preoccupations and needs. There will be occasions when words are inaccessible because the patient has no interest in them. At other times they will be used inappropriately as the expression of some attitude or feeling. In organic mental states the thinking disorder affects the process of conceptualization. Things and people retain their cathexis and there is a constant effort to express ideas which signify objects. This is often accomplished by the employment of phrases which act as a substitute for the lost concept. Critchley's (1964) statement that in the schizophrenias there is 'no true inaccessibility of vocabulary but rather it is its utilization which is deranged' is strikingly similar to the theory proposed by Freud.

DISORDERS OF ATTENTION AND CONCENTRATION

A number of phenomena to be observed in chronic schizophrenic states indicate that attention is no longer selective or that it is not assisting in the function of adaptation. Perseveration, which has already been described, is one; inattention and distractability are the others. Inattention has a twofold aspect. Not only is the patient unresponsive to a stimulus directed to him, but at times he apparently pays little attention to his own thoughts as they occur in speech. This is reflected in a divorce between speech and action when the patient expresses certain ideas which he obviously ignores, as his behaviour indicates. For example, a patient whose behaviour was characterized by negativism was given a cigarette. He sat motionless for quite a few minutes without making any attempt to get a light, and continued to do so even when another patient struck a match and offered it to his neighbour. The patient in question was then asked by the author, 'Do you want a light, Mr B?' 'No', he replied, but immediately got up and lit his cigarette from the proferred match. This form of behaviour was repeated in other contexts.

Inattention can occur at the level of sensation, with simple percepts, and with verbal communications. Inattention is not necessarily due to faulty perception. Following a latent period, the response to a stimulus appears but often in a different setting. It is this which leads to apparently incomprehensible statements or replies to questions. Inattention may have close associations with a disorder in reflective or self-awareness, as the last clinical example suggests. In some chronic patients, a series of phenomena can be observed not unlike the non-perception that occurs in some forms of organic mental state. While speech and thinking defects may make identification of the schizophrenic patient's communications difficult, it is usually possible to note a restriction of attention which expresses itself in a denial of all or part of the body. Such patients insist that their bodily movements and functions are foreign to them and must therefore belong to the body of some other person. Usually these patients misidentify to such an extent that they do not acknowledge the nurses and doctors as nurses and doctors or the hospital as a hospital. As in the case of patients demonstrating the syndrome of anosognosia (Weinstein and Kahn, 1950), this form of inattention is part of a wider symptom complex in which are also to be found amnesias, confabulations, perseverative signs, and echo phenomena.

Although Bleuler (1911) described the occurrence of distractability in the schizophrenias, this phenomenon has received little attention until recent years. There appear to be two distinct forms of distractability in chronic schizophrenia. In one, the distractability has a passive quality, in so far as the patient appears to assimilate percepts into his stream of talk without the intervention of awareness. There is no apparent recognition of the inappropriateness of their inclusion. In the second form, the patient appears alert. Here the distractability can be regarded as 'active', in so far as the patient is trying to record all new stimuli to help him confirm or refute his delusional experiences.

It is the passive form of distractability which resembles the distractability found in certain organic mental states and described in the previous chapter. In both categories the content of the speech may be determined entirely by some extraneous percept. During a group meeting a discussion was taking place about gambling. Someone said, 'Mr —— is a professional punter.' After a few seconds Mr O said, 'He could do that because he was a professional naval officer. He was chucked out of the navy on the grounds of having respect.' This patient continued on the theme of professions and professional activities ('professional experiences') for quite some time. Another illustration of this apparently indiscriminate assimilation of overheard speech is demonstrated in the phrase quoted in the section on 'Disorders of Speech'. 'He asked me if I was betting on a prostitute.'

The content of speech may equally well be determined by something the patient has observed or noted. This will be inappropriately incorporated into his speech. Phenomena of the type described provide support for the idea that there is a serious derangement of self- and reflective awareness with respect to what is experienced in the environment. Responses are made to external stimuli automatically, without the intervention of deliberation or intent. In this respect there is little difference between the chronic schizophrenic patient and the patient suffering from an organic mental state. Both respond automatically to external impressions without reflection on what has been registered mentally. The difference between the two states lies in the fact that the organic patient is usually friendly and responsive unless the cerebral degeneration is extreme, whereas the schizophrenic patient is withdrawn and uninterested in human contact. Nevertheless, both clinical conditions show an equal disorganization and/or disintegration of those mental processes which underlie the capacity to selectively attend and reflect on what has been experienced.

DISORDERS OF THINKING

The disorders that may affect conceptual thought in chronic schizophrenia have been well documented in the literature and further data have also been presented in earlier chapters. It only remains to add a few comments that may be of value in comparing the manifestations of disorders of thinking in chronic schizophrenia and in organic mental states.

In the chronic schizophrenic patient the most striking abnormality is that which leads to a breakdown of grammatical construction, thus making speech and writing difficult to understand. The syntactical fault is due to numerous causes, among which may be listed the inappropriate use of words and the appearance of neologisms and paraphasias. The multiple meanings carried by these verbal formations influence the ensuing thoughts in directions that cannot be accommodated by the rules of grammar and logic. The patient who says, 'I didn't have a church wedding, I was history . . .' introduces the inappropriate second phrase because of his preoccupation with delusional ideas surrounding his belief that he is Prince Charles Edward Stuart. Thus the delusional ideas find a special form of representation in speech as a consequence of the thinking defect.

This thinking defect consists in the re-emergence of condensing or syncretic trends, fusing concepts that in normal circumstances are discrete and autonomous. When a woman of 32 shouted out, 'They are dirty, Persian oil and Glasgow Royal! Oil is mental!' she had little regard for conventional meaning. Oil was a condensation product. Contained within this word were recollections and feelings about her unhappy marriage, her stay in Persia with her husband who works for an oil company, and his eventual infidelity. Similarly, a neologism or substitute word can have several meanings, as in the case of 'masterpiece' referred to in Chapter 6, or the word 'ortifice' (a condensation of artifice and orifice). These meanings can only be discovered through knowledge of the patient's past life, present experiences, and circumstances.

Communication can be further disrupted by the patient's tendency to fragment words, to use the part for the whole, or to alter one or more letters in a word. For example, a patient was talking about the law and said, 'He was a galse witness . . . they pounce on evidence . . . the pouncil and do them in.' Patients who corrupt words in this way are quite able to state them correctly on other occasions, although possibly using them inapprorpriately. As was shown in the previous chapter, grammatical construction can be deranged in organic mental states either by an inability to recall words or by paraphasias. While chronic schizophrenic patients also have a difficulty in recalling words, other words are sometimes employed as substitutes.

Chronic schizophrenic patients and patients suffering from organic mental states exhibit different types of thinking. The former have a defect in conceptualization that is apparent in the data presented by the patient. In the latter, the most obvious disturbances are the egocentrism and concrete thinking. It is also possible to discern a concurrent disorder of concept formation (see p. 105) not unlike that encountered in the schizophrenias. In chronic schizophrenia verbal symbols are not irrevocably lost or destroyed. They may reappear intact after having been altered or condensed with other words. However, even when the verbal symbol has regained its correct form it may be used inappropriately. The difficulty that stands in the way of deciding whether or not a thinking disorder occurs in organic mental states similar to that of the schizophrenias results from there being no simple way of discovering whether a paraphasia has a special meaning for the patient.

DISTURBANCES OF MOTILITY

In chronic schizophrenic states, disorders of motility can be described under two headings: first, disturbances of voluntary movements and, second, disturbances of posture. It is the first category of disturbances that will mainly be described here, since it is these manifestations which bear the greatest resemblance to the disorders of motility which may occur in organic mental states. The data to be presented are drawn from patients observed in clinical interviews and from patients who were asked to perform the simple tests described in Appendix B.

A striking feature of the chronic schizophrenic patient is the blocking of voluntary movement. The patient becomes fixed at some stage of a voluntary movement, and it is not brought to completion. This behaviour suggests that a dissociation has taken place between intentions on the one hand and motility on the other. The patient wishes to carry out an act, but nothing happens. This phenomenon is best seen in the case of the patient who enjoys smoking. He is given a cigarette but does not make any attempt to light it. Eventually he is offered matches. He may strike the match, with some difficulty, but instead of lighting the cigarette he continues to hold the match in his hand until it burns his fingers. A similar kind of disconnection between intention and movement is apparent when the patient is asked to carry out a simple task. He may not react at all or he may make an echolalic response, for example, responding to 'Put out your tongue, please' with 'Put out your tongue, please.' Finally, movement may appear after a latent period, but the act is not completed.

A further series of phenomena occurring in the sphere of motility are the repetitive actions that arise when the patient is asked to perform a task. The patient may be asked to nod his head, and will do so innumerable times. When requested to squeeze the examiner's hand three times, the patient squeezes it indefinitely or there is a tonic grasp. Such patients have great difficulty in carrying out Luria's tests (the fist-ring test, etc.) and they frequently manifest perseveration of the faulty switching variety. They cannot pass on to the second movement.

Repetitive manifestations and difficulty in switching to new movements can be observed in the course of the patient's spontaneous activities in the ward or occupational therapy department. One patient, a woman of 28, was able to carry out simple movements, but if she was expected to carry out a complex task she frequently failed. She had little persistence. In occupational therapy she would find it difficult to abandon a pattern of movement and initiate another when, for example, making a basket. This motor perseveration was limited to complicated activities. This patient did not show any repetitive movement. For the most part she sat hunched up in a chair with knees and arms flexed. Spontaneous voluntary movement was most in evidence when she was under the influence of a need or of anger.

This patient could not perform Luria's tests (see Appendix B, items 13, 14, and 15) but she had no difficulty in opening a box of matches,

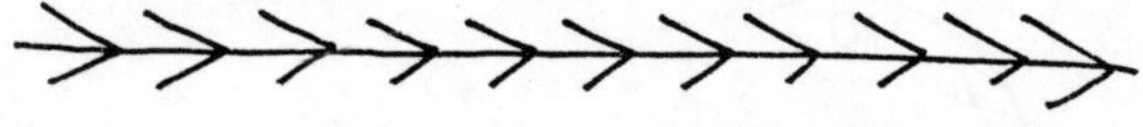

FIGURE 6 'Draw an arrow.'

FIGURE 7 'Draw a man.'

taking out a match, lighting it, and then lighting her cigarette. This state of affairs is not uncommon. Many patients who are incapable of completing simple tests of voluntary movement can nevertheless manage the intricate movements required for eating with knife and fork, lighting a cigarette, or even writing, if, for example, the writing is concerned with an interest such as filling in a betting slip. The selfsame patient, if asked to make a drawing or to copy a design, will show a repetitive tendency (see *Figures 6* and 7) and sometimes perseveration of the switching variety. In *Figure 8* the patient has been asked to draw a bicycle after having just completed the drawing of a clock-face. *Figure 8* can be compared with *Figure 1c* on p. 112, and *Figure 4* on p. 113.

As in the case of speech, 'normal motility' may appear whenever the patient is interested in an object or is motivated by a need or by anger. Observations indicate that the disturbances of motility are more likely to be found when the patient is inattentive, distractable (passive variety), presents echo reactions, and is generally unresponsive. This

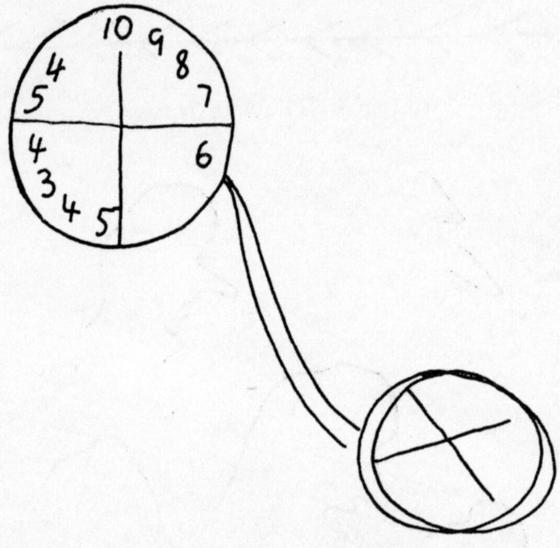

FIGURE 8 'Draw a bicycle.'

suggests, as with speech, that the patient is in a state of consciousness characterized by minimal reflective awareness regarding environmental stimulation. His reactions are disorganized and without aim. It should be noted, however, that, even when the patient appears to regain 'normal motility', it is rarely sustained. When a patient writes, filling in his betting slip, the task is not properly completed. When asked several minutes later about his bet he cannot even recall the name of the horse he has backed.

The phenomena just described are very similar to the motility disorders found in organic mental states, which were described in the previous chapter. As with the chronic schizophrenic patient, the patient suffering from an organic mental state may be able to undertake the complex activities described above, without being able easily to perform the simple tests of voluntary movement. However, even this 'normal motility' will disappear with the progressive cerebral degeneration. Only in very few schizophrenic patients – and even here the diagnosis may be doubtful – does the patient completely lose the ability to act 'normally' when activated by a need such as hunger.

Finally, reference must be made to the undoubted connection that exists between repetitive rhythmical movements of the limbs, particularly of the arms and hands, and masturbation. While this association is not usually established, it was clearly seen in one patient who, for several weeks, was observed to tap his feet for quite long periods or swing his legs from the knee. Sometimes he would repeatedly stroke his hair with his right hand. This repetitive movement would continue indefinitely until his attention was drawn to his behaviour; but even then it would resume after a short latent period. One day he began by swinging his legs rapidly up and down. This was followed by rubbing his head. By this time the autoerotic element in his behaviour had become obvious. Soon he began to rub his genital region. This ceased and he returned to rubbing his head. Within a short time he experienced orgasm.

NEGATIVISM

Negativism is encountered frequently in chronic schizophrenic patients. Current therapeutic practice has tended to reduce the incidence of the active forms of negativism (Bleuler, 1911) so that the most frequent manifestations are of a passive nature. The patient either cannot or will not respond to an instruction or accede to a request. Negativism also affects the patient's response to passive movements of his arms. Attempts to lift his arm, as when testing for catalepsy, are resisted and a pronounced hypertonia of the flexor muscles will be found.

Negativism generally occurs along with clinical phenomena that have already received some attention in this and earlier chapters. Inattention, distractability, and perseverative trends are to be observed, along with ambitendency and a hypertonia of the upper-limb musculature. Ambitendency, which appears to reflect the conflict in the patient's mind regarding certain actions, appears as often in early cases of schizophrenia as in those of long standing.

Although negativism has rarely been described as an important manifestation of organic mental states (senile and pre-senile dementias, brain damage, etc.), patients frequently show an unwillingness, and sometimes a refusal, to cooperate, either during physical examination or in the course of their daily management. The failure to describe this behaviour as negativistic may be due to the belief that it is secondary to a general decline in intellectual functions, particularly inability to understand what is said (receptive aphasia), to the confusion springing from amnesias, and to loss of control of affect.

This position is difficult to maintain when the negativism extends to the patient who resists any attempt to interfere with his current preoccupation, even if this is only walking up and down the ward or sitting in a chair. Strenuous opposition is shown by the patient if the nurse attempts to lead him to the table for a meal or if, for example, his jacket has to be changed because it is damaged. Here there is no question of verbal interchange, yet something within the patient causes him to resist. Like the schizophrenic patient, he will oppose efforts to lift or flex his arms, and an increase of muscle tone will become apparent.

Again, as in the schizophrenias, these patients are found to be inattentive and to manifest pronounced perseverative trends. An explanation of the negativism in organic mental states may be that the perseverative activity, even if limited to the most simple sensory motor functions, cannot be interrupted. When attempts are made to interrupt him the patient responds with negativistic behaviour.

Robertson and her co-workers (1958) have described this perseverative trend which occurs in Pick's Disease under the general heading of rigidity. 'Obstinacy' is the term they use to indicate the presence of perseveration. They state:

> 'Closely related [i.e. to rigidity] and yet dissimilar, was a quality usually described as "obstinacy". Once these patients started an action they could not be deflected from their individual mode of terminating it. Case 1 continued to scatter crumbs for the birds in the garden although she knew that she was expected to use a recently erected bird tray. Case 3 acquired a habit of placing plates of soup in the oven to heat and could not be dissuaded from this although it was pointed out that the resultant pellicle rendered the soup unpalatable. The complex pattern of some of these perseverating actions concealed their essential compulsive nature. Observers therefore, assumed that the patients' exasperating persistence indicated wilful malice.'

It is difficult not to designate some of this 'obstinacy' as negativism. It certainly would be so described if it occurred in a patient diagnosed as schizophrenic.

In the English literature Schilder (1928a) is the only author to make a comparison between the negativism of the schizophrenic individual and that of the patient suffering from cerebral disease. He introduces his comparison by asking if there are organic phenomena which are comparable with the phenomenon of negativism. As answer he offers a number of observations drawn from a case of cerebral arteriosclerosis. He thought that the patient's muscular negativism was comparable to the negativistic tendencies of the catatonic patient. In his discussion of the problem he indicates that, in spite of similarity, catatonic states are never completely identical with the catatonia of cerebral lesions.

Patients suffering from chronic schizophrenia and organic mental states and who present negativistic manifestations have one further common characteristic. In both states a change has taken place in the condition of their cognitive organization away from that necessary for environmental adaptation. Sufficient clinical evidence has been presented to indicate that the capacity to reflect on experiences is diminished or lost and that the ability to form conscious intentions directed to the exterior is weak or absent. It is this state which facilitates the emergence of echo phenomena, perseverative signs, abnormal motility, and inattention. In both clinical categories, organic and schizophrenic, this is the mental status operative concurrently with the negativism.

Differences between the two conditions exist in so far as the mental life of the chronic schizophrenic patient may occasionally alter in the direction of normality with the disappearance of the negativism. This normality, as has already been mentioned, need not be thought of as identical with that of the mentally healthy, since it is automatic and ephemeral in expression. In the organic state the negativism, once firmly established, is never replaced by a comparable improvement in mental function. Once again, the clinical evidence suggests that there are indeed close resemblances between the phenomena of chronic schizophrenia and organic mental states, but the underlying mechanisms cannot be regarded as entirely identical. The discussion of this problem will be taken up later in this chapter.

DISORDERS OF MEMORY

There is general agreement regarding the disorganization of memory in chronic schizophrenic states. This disorganization particularly affects recall. Sometimes the patient appears to have no capacity for short-term recall and yet at other times this function is quite intact. Similar inconsistencies of performance affect long-term and immediate memory. It has frequently been observed that, even when recall is unimpaired, the temporal sequence of the events is distorted and they are often inappropriate to the situation in which they are reported.

In some cases of chronic schizophrenia, memories of life experience prior to the illness are no longer available to consciousness. Observers have remarked on the fact that the amnesia is selective. The patient will deny the fact of his marriage or insist that his parents are not his real parents. The gaps in the life-history as told by the patient are filled in by newly created material which is generally included with the remainder of the delusional reality. In the type of patient described here, there is usually little attempt to confabulate or fill in the memory gaps. For example, a patient said, 'I am forgetting who I am.' Associated with this is an apparent forgetfulness for the symptoms of the acute phase of the illness.

In some cases, memories of the past are reactivated in the form of hallucinations. In one case the patient visually hallucinated pictures of her children. She accused other patients and the doctors of causing this. She did not want it, because it made her too upset. Again, memories may appear in behaviour activated by auditory hallucinations. The same patient accused her persecutors of forcing her to lie on a couch: she complained, 'They make me lie down on a couch and put a pillow under my hips.' Later it was discovered that this was the way in which she had intercourse with her husband. In a case to be described in Chapter 10, a young woman patient hallucinated the sensation of a penis pressed against her body. This was a memory of love-making with her boyfriend.

Memory disturbances in chronic schizophrenia raise two important questions. The first is what role does repression play in these states and the second is to what extent does self-awareness operate in the recall of memories. It is generally assumed that repression is seriously damaged in the schizophrenias. This view is based on the appearance of childhood fantasies and their associated drive attitudes. It is difficult at first sight to reconcile this theory with the observations described above. Patients appear to have little difficulty in dismissing from consciousness thoughts and recollections that would be distressing. They react strongly when efforts are made to get them to remember. When memories appear in the form of hallucinations the patient accuses someone of bringing this about.

The patient who believes that his limb movements or his speech are controlled by an outside force has repressed conflicts regarding the expression of sexual or aggressive wishes. A patient who, for example, complains that he cannot smoke because a force interferes with his using his right arm and hand has repressed his conflict about smoking and/or masturbation. Repression has removed the ideational content from consciousness. In other cases, the ideas and affects are not dismissed from consciousness but they lose their self-reference, as in the instance of the patient who believes that a machine is causing him to have erections and sexual thoughts against his will. Here repression is unable to block the excitation from awareness.

Recent events are easily forgotten but there is no evidence of a permanent impairment of memory. The clinical evidence favours the view that repression operates as easily and efficiently in the chronic schizophrenic as in the healthy individual. The fact that whatever is forgotten, for example a doctor's name or an appointment, is not permanently inaccessible indicates not that the repression is permanent, but merely that a withdrawal of interest (cathexis) from the outside world has momentarily taken place. This view fits easily with the observation that when a patient is recounting a memory that is inappropriate to the situation he is doing so automatically and without the intervention of conscious reflection. Only such an explanation would account for the appearance of the memory at that particular time. The patient is in no way concerned whether it is relevant or not.

Although much of the memory disorder in the chronic schizophrenia can be explained as the result of a withdrawal of interest and a disturbance of reflective awareness, there are other phenomena – the apparent permanent loss of identity, the amnesia for life experiences – which can only be regarded as due to a permanent repression. They must be distinguished from the withdrawal of interest and attention that occurs momentarily and leads to a transient forgetfulness. Such a permanent amnesia is comparable to childhood amnesias that result from a counterforce preventing the emergence of memories. The presence of both permanent and transient amnesias suggests that repression may operate efficiently in the chronic schizophrenias.

DISCUSSION

The purpose of this chapter has been to examine the similarities and differences that exist between the clinical phenomena characteristic of chronic schizophrenia and those of organic mental states. There appears to be a phenomenological identity in a number of different areas of mental function: the problem is whether or not the mechanisms underlying these apparently similar phenomena are the same.

In the second chapter of this book an account was presented of Hughlings Jackson's theory of psychosis; and attention was drawn to the concept of dissolution to explain the loss of healthy adult mental functions. Dissolution had the indirect result of leading to the appearance of less developed forms of mental processes. The characteristic of these processes was dependent on the speed at which dissolution occurred and the depth to which it reached. The phenomena that have been described, whether occurring in schizophrenic or organic mental states, can be organized within the framework of Jackson's theory. These phenomena can be regarded as either the direct result of dissolution or the consequence of it. Thus positive and negative indices of dissolution can be postulated and their expression designated as in the accompanying table. The positive indices are the equivalent of Jackson's positive symptoms, the negative indices equivalent to the negative symptoms. In the following discussion, it is more appropriate to begin with a consideration of the negative indices.

POSITIVE INDICES	NEGATIVE INDICES
1. *Condensation products* (*a*) speech and thinking (*b*) perceptual-motor (*c*) memory	1. *Altered state of consciousness* (*a*) loss of reflective awareness (*b*) loss of mobility of attention (*c*) inattention (*d*) loss of conceptual powers (*e*) loss of short-term memory recall
2. *Repetitive phenomena* (*a*) perseverative signs (i) speech (ii) motility (iii) sensory (b) Echo-phenomena	2. *Disorganization of voluntary movement*
3. *Distractability*	3. *Disorganization of connection between volition (intentions) as indicated in speech and motility*
4. *Negativism*	

In this chapter, attention has repeatedly been drawn to the consideration that the manifestations in both chronic schizophrenic patients and those suffering from organic mental states can only be attributed to the presence of a state of consciousness entirely different from that necessary for environmental adaptation. This state of consciousness is not identified by so gross a criterion as 'disorientation for time, place, or person'. Disorientation itself implies more than the presence of extensive amnesias. It suggests the addition of such positive signs as misidentifications and confabulations. The state of consciousness inferred here is one betrayed by the presence of a derangement of purposive and selective attention, a deterioration in conceptual powers, defects in short-term memory, and, perhaps of greatest importance, loss of the ability to reflect upon what has just been experienced. In both groups, voluntary movement is disorganized to varying degrees and the connection between speech in its receptive aspects and voluntary movement is gravely disturbed.

Alongside these defects in normal mental functions, further forms of unusual mental activity are to be found. The manner in which speech, thinking, perception, and memory find expression could be attributed to the operation of a process of condensation. Distractability is also a common occurrence. Repetitive phenomena of all kinds arise in speech, writing, drawing, and movement. These manifestations have a compulsive, automatic quality and are not easily brought to a halt.

Negativism must also be considered as a positive index of dissolution because it appears in the place of cooperative interpersonal relations. Its appearance is entirely inappropriate. It can be regarded as arising from two sources, both the result of dissolution. The first comprises the outcome of repetitive behaviours and the disconnection between speech and motility. The second is an instinctual and therefore a potentially object-linked source. It can be thought of as a harking-back (regression) to the sexual organization obtaining in the young child at the oral-anal phase of libidinal development. In support of this is the observation that can be made on very advanced cases of cerebral degeneration where a temporal association exists between 'muscular' negativism and a preoccupation with the oral and anal zones.

While many authors have willingly acknowledged that similarities may exist between the chronic schizophrenias and organic mental states, they have usually underlined one major difference. They have pointed out that there are always occasions when the chronic schizophrenic patient's mental disorganization is resolved and for varying periods of time he speaks and acts normally. They believe that this never happens in the organic state, which pursues a deteriorating course. While this last fact is undoubtedly true, two significant observations have been overlooked. The first, to which attention has already been drawn, is that in the chronic schizophrenias the periods of 'normalcy' are exceedingly brief and their appearance is confined to situations in which needs or anger are manifest. Second, little attention has been paid to the 'improvement' in mental function which may occur in patients whose organic state is well advanced.

A case in point is that of Mr X, described in the previous chapter. This patient, whose speech was impaired through perseveration and a receptive aphasia, and who was amnesic in different spheres including topographic memory, was lost while on a bus trip. A party of patients had been taken to a small town about thirty miles from the hospital. When it was time to return, the patient could not be found. The police were notified, and the bus returned to the hospital. Late that night Mr X arrived at his home, to the amazement of his wife. The patient, who under examination could neither remember his address nor recall fresh information after a few seconds, had managed to obtain a lift back to Dundee. He had then walked to the appropriate bus-stop and taken the correct bus to near his home. He had walked the remainder of the way.

In many cases of organic mental state, information and a means of communication are potentially available but inaccessible on demand. In one case, following the removal of the left frontal and temporal lobes, the patient was unable to recall her address when requested but she could comply when asked to write down her name and address. Luria (1966) has described similar phenomena in patients with bilateral tumours of the frontal lobes. These patients were unable to respond to questions or requests directed to them. Often they reacted with simple echolalias. However, they could spontaneously respond to stimuli and even join in a conversation with nurse or fellow-patient. In all these instances the patient had lost the ability voluntarily to initiate speech or action.

When speech and action at a meaningful level arise in patients with organic cerebral states it is most often in the wake of needs or strong emotion. This is in no way different from the conditions attendant upon 'normal' mental activity in chronic schizophrenic patients. There appears to be in both categories an impairment of the processes underlying the voluntary initiation of behaviour. The ability to reflect on what is experienced is deranged, as is the capacity to initiate intentions in response to requests by another person.

While the chronic schizophrenias and organic mental states are similar in having lost the ability voluntarily to initiate behaviour, they differ with respect to the material integrity of the cognitive processes. In the former, speech, thinking, perception, and memory are disorganized; in the latter, there is a progressive deterioration of these functions. The fact that speech and action which have some possible adaptive value may reappear in organic mental states suggests that the similar process which occurs in chronic schizophrenia is not merely due to the reintegration of a previously disorganized apparatus subserving some aspect of cognition (Schilder, 1928b). An explanation along Jacksonian lines accounts for all the phenomena in a more satisfactory way. The apparent return to normalcy in chronic schizophrenia is only apparent. It is an automatic expression of patterns of behaviour which have originated early in the individual's experience and this is why they are closely tied to the needs and to the affects. A permanent disorder is present in chronic schizophrenic patients, but it lies in the area of conscious reflection and voluntary control over stored information and motility.

The refutation of the 'apparatus theory' is important because this theory carries the implication that there is a potent core of health in the chronic schizophrenic patient which is hidden behind the façade of a cognitive defect. It suggests that the patient might at any time return to complete normality. While psychotherapeutic experiences demonstrate that there is in every chronic case some residue of 'healthy life' (Bleuler, 1963), the manner and nature of its expression make it unfitted for ultimately beneficial psychotherapeutic work. Instances of this healthy life in established cases of schizophrenia have been described in Chapter 5. It differs in nature from the 'automatic normalcy' stimulated by need or affect. It is weak and fragile and cannot sustain the slightest stress.

Although emphasis has been laid, in this chapter, on the similarities that exist between organic mental states and chronic schizophrenia, it is necessary to remember the significant differences. These are most apparent in the less severe forms of cerebral disease, and such conditions are less likely to fall within the province of the psychiatrist. When the pathological process is limited in extent the patient retains his interest in the environment, even although he has the greatest difficulty in communicating with it, as is the case with those suffering from aphasic disorders. Patients with organic mental states wish to make meaningful contact with others, and they sometimes can do so even although handicapped by cognitive deficits and motility disturbances. Even some of the patients described in Chapter 7 were able to achieve this. The chronic schizophrenic patient is quite different, as the clinical examples have illustrated. He has no interest in his surroundings and is indifferent to those about him except under the conditions that have already been specified.

The difference between the two states is also reflected in speech and thinking. The concept is basic for thinking that has the aim of communication, and thus language is an integral aspect of interpersonal (object) relations. Concepts appear to the subject as objects (Schilder, 1923). In this regard, the approach to concepts is different from the approach to needs and affects. The patient with an organic mental state may suffer from aphasia and there may be a disorder of thinking characterized by defective powers of conceptualization (Bay, 1963). Nevertheless, this disturbance does not stop the patient from attempting some form of communication through mime and gesture. The patient suffering from chronic schizophrenia has lost interest in 'things', just as he has lost interest in others. In psychoanalytic terms, he has withdrawn cathexes from real objects and their mental representations (concepts). Concept formation is thus deficient because of a lack of interest (cathexis) and not because of damage to the neural substrate. Some words are cathected, others not, depending on the particular 'complex' with which the patient is preoccupied (Freud, 1915). The employment of these words does not imply the aim of communication but is rather the expression of self-love and egotism (narcissism). Disturbance of object-cathexis implies a disorder of both object relations and language.

CHAPTER 9

Depressive Phenomena and Psychosis

Depressive symptomatology may appear alone or in combination with other manifestations of mental illness. Thus it may appear in association with phobias, obsessions, delusions, or hallucinations. When the illness is confined to depressive manifestations alone, it has always proved difficult to decide on the exact nature of the underlying condition. According to some authorities, a depressive illness may fall into one of two categories: neurotic or endogenous depression. Criteria that differentiate these two states have been described on many occasions (Pollitt, 1965). For others this classification is unsatisfactory because it leaves unexplained the presence of precipitating factors in cases that present all the symptoms of an endogenous depression (Henderson and Gillespie, 1961). It also fails to explain why neurotic depressive states sometimes present phenomena, for example, signs of physiological depression, that belong to the endogenous conditions.

There are authors who suggest that recurrent depressive illnesses are the expression of manic-depressive psychosis. When the depressive state is categorized thus it is immaterial whether it is activated by exogenous factors. A series of states will be found, according to this view, ranging from mild to severe. In some, the precipitating factors will be pronounced; in others, inconspicuous or absent. When the psychomotor depression is intense, delusional experiences may arise in keeping with the sense of guilt. The nosological entity manic-depression therefore accommodates a variety of depressive illnesses. In some, the severity of the illness does not preclude insight into the fact of being ill. In others, judgement is impaired, and irrational ideas founded on guilt influence perception and action.

UNCOMPLICATED DEPRESSIVE STATES

1

There is general agreement that a depressive illness cannot be diagnosed purely on a change in mood. The fact that a patient complains of 'depression' does not mean that he is in fact suffering from a depressive illness. A loss of interest in previously enjoyed activities, a general depression of bodily function with varying degrees of loss of appetite and sexual desire, a feeling of helplessness and hopelessness for the future, and sleep disturbance are essential components of a depressive state. In some cases, self-reproaches are an outstanding feature. When present they vary in intensity, and the patient's judgement of their appropriateness may be intact or deficient.

It is unusual for patients who suffer from depressive illnesses to express anger or criticism of others. They are inclined to excuse the shortcomings of those about them and to blame themselves instead. It is, however, not uncommon to find patients who complain of being 'depressed' expressing annoyance and irritability with spouse or children. It is doubtful whether these are cases of depression, for, more often than not, inquiry reveals that they present few of the manifestations typical of a depressive illness. More often, these are patients whose personality functioning is deviated with respect to interpersonal relations, and they have little capacity to accept responsibility for their actions. In contrast to the depressive patient, these patients freely use projection mechanisms and blame others rather than themselves. Conscience is not well developed – again a striking difference from the patient who suffers from a depressive illness.

Depressive illnesses, whether characterized by guilt and self-reproaches or not, are mental states that show a remarkable persistence (Lewis, 1964). This persistence is naturally more pronounced in the more severe conditions. Here, environmental change rarely influences the symptomatology, and when it does it suggests the possibility of an impending improvement. The fact that the symptoms may remain constant over a long period of time, irrespective of treatment with thymoleptic drugs and electroshock therapy, suggests that so-called 'short-cycle' depressive states should be closely scrutinized to ascertain whether they are in fact forms of depressive illness.

The psychoanalytical contribution to the understanding of depressive illnesses began with Freud (1917) and Abraham (1924). They demonstrated that the illness was related to loss. The patient's personality was such as to make it difficult for him to find a substitute. The lost object is internalized, but as a consequence of the ambivalent attitude to the lost object there occurs within the patient a conflict between feelings of love and hate. The hatred that might have been directed against the object because of the abandonment is directed against the patient himself, identified as he is with the lost object. This results in self-hatred leading to self-criticism. Conscience becomes harsh as a result of the hate which has been passed over to the superego. There is a simultaneous desire to preserve and destroy the internalized object.

The loss may not involve a person. The patient may no longer feel satisfied in his relationships. He may suffer a blow to his self-esteem. All this is experienced as equivalent to a real loss. The loss may have been of some years' duration, but the patient's defence against recognizing the loss may have been adequate. Hence, a minor factor resurrecting the old fears may superficially appear as precipitating cause, but the psychic or actual loss bringing about the illness is a direct emotional echo of earlier traumata.

A woman of 40 presented symptoms of depression and insomnia, and signs of psychomotor retardation. Her illness had been precipitated by a disturbed and ambivalent relationship with her father-in-law which had led to his being put into an old people's institution. Unconsciously she identified him with her own father who had died three years previously, but she had displaced all her hate on to her father-in-law, leaving her father a 'good' figure. Shortly after her father's death she had a miscarriage. At the time, she had thought, 'You will pay for this some day,' because she felt she had induced the abortion by excessive exertion. Her husband had not wanted another child and neither had she. She began her illness with cardiac symptoms, including chest pains and breathlessness, very similar to those which had troubled her father during his last illness. At the same time, she complained of uncomfortable abdominal sensations vaguely reminiscent of the movements of a foetus. She had internalized both her dead father and the dead foetus, and both were the subjects of ambivalence. She unconsciously feared they would destroy her as she had wished to destroy them. At the same time she wanted to preserve them. This conflict was externalized in her feelings about her husband and sons. She feared her illness would damage them to such an extent that they would fall ill. Consciously she was unable to admit any hostility towards them.

Freud (1917) made a comparison between mourning and melancholia.

In the former, the essence of the psychical task is to detach the libido from the lost object 'and in the meantime the existence of the lost object is psychically prolonged' (Freud, 1917, p. 245). Each memory of the lost object is re-experienced with full emotional content. This process, in conjunction with the demands of reality, allows of the gradual dissolution of the bonds tying the individual to his object. In depressive states, the situation is complicated by the patient's ambivalence. Here, the process that occurs in mourning is arrested and instead 'countless separate struggles are carried on over the object, in which hate and love contend with each other' (1917, p. 256).

Fears of damaging and destroying those who are near and dear to the patient are frequent in severe depressions. The essential feature of the relationship is the ability of the object to 'absorb' the hostility and aggression of the individual. Hence, with its loss, to maintain psychic homeostasis, the organism must incorporate the object. In such cases, the fears concerning the internalized object are merely projected on to real figures in the patient's environment. Freud suggests that the depressive process may end as a result of the continual disparagement of the object. Hatred, to the point of murder, allows the depressive patient to free his libido from its bondage.

Following the work of Abraham and Freud, Klein (1935) proposed that the appearance of a depressive illness in adult life is due to the reactivation of an infantile depressive state. This consists of feelings which are at their height just before, during, and after the time of weaning. She distinguished two forms of anxiety: persecutory anxiety, which is predominant during the first months of life, and depressive anxiety, which reaches a climax about the middle of the first year. It is the latter which gives rise to the depressive position. Persecutory anxiety relates mainly to dangers felt to threaten the self; depressive anxiety relates to dangers felt to threaten the loved object, particularly through the subject's aggression and greed. Weaning accentuates these depressive anxieties. Klein (1935) considers that the depressed patient has never successfully overcome the infantile depressive position. He has never been able to secure a good relationship with an object, always fearing that his demands will be so great as to bring about the loss or destruction of the desired object.

In more recent years it has appeared to some psychoanalytical observers that the classical theory and its extensions (Klein, 1935) do not provide an adequate explanation for all the forms of depressive illness. This is particularly applicable to those states in which guilt feelings and self-reproach are absent. In an attempt to explain the wide range of depressive phenomena, Bibring (1953) proposed that depression is an affective reaction which reflects an ego-state characterized by a sense of helplessness and inhibition of functions. This awareness of helplessness possibly lies at the root of all depressive illnesses. It is activated by an inability to maintain or reach certain aspirations which, in the course of development, have been established as ideals. A decrease in self-esteem due to tension between ego and ego ideal may be stimulated by various factors with an ensuing feeling of helplessness.

This view of depression does not clash with the classical theory, in which emphasis is given to aggressive conflicts. Clinical experience underwrites the fact that conflicts over aggression are extremely common in depressive states. The aggression is always turned inwards and this can only be regarded as a means of avoiding the guilt that would be provoked by the expression of the aggression in thought or deed. In Bibring's opinion, this self-directed aggression results from the sense of helplessness which precludes its being turned towards the external world.

II

In the following pages an account will be given of phenomena which occur in uncomplicated depressive states as observed during analytic group therapy (Cameron and Freeman, 1955, 1956). Similar observations can be made during the psychoanalytical treatment of depressive states. The present description is of value because it reveals the manner in which patients relate to one another as well as indicating their predominant conflicts and defences.

The group was composed of eight in-patients. The average age of these patients at the onset of the illness was approximately 54, with variations between 39 and 62. The average age was 57 at the time of treatment. The average duration of illness was three years. Each patient had previously been treated with electroshock therapy, without permanent benefit. Of the eight patients, four were married, one was single, and three were widows. In six instances, the patients became ill after an important emotional stress such as death of the husband, serious illness of near relatives, etc. Only two fell ill without any apparent determining event. All the patients were depressed in mood, were without interest, self-reproachful, anorexic, and sleepless. Three patients were extremely agitated. The illness had been continuous in six patients and episodic in two.

The outstanding characteristic of the group as a whole was their intolerance of aggression and their specific response to real or fantasied loss. In dealing with the former, two main defence mechanisms were used: 'turning against the self' and projection; whereas with the latter, denial was the most usual reaction. Wherever the possibility of loss arose, unconscious conflicts over aggression could be discerned. The absence of one of the therapists or of a group member produced signs of deepening depression within the group. On such occasions patients appeared to be seeking for memories to show that they had been responsible for the absence of the missing person. Associations always led to thoughts of death and memories of the loss of spouses, parents, siblings, etc. Dreams were reported in which the death occurred of a person still living. For example, one patient was tormented by a recurrent dream of great clarity in which she received a telegram informing her of her father's death. In her waking hours she spoke of him with the highest esteem and affection. After her father's recent death she dreamt that the husbands of her three best friends had died. Both this patient and one other, who sustained actual loss by death while under treatment, reacted with denial. The symptomatology of the former changed to a hypomania. In one instance of psychical loss resulting from the indifference of her sons, a patient became acutely depersonalized.

The aggressive conflict provoked by loss invariably resulted in bitter self-recrimination. As the patients learnt to tolerate their inner hatred it was observed that the amount of self-criticism diminished and the capacity to be critical increased. Associated with this was a revival of repressed memories where aggressive wishes had been directed against spouses, parents, or siblings, who had subsequently died. For example, one patient had the greatest difficulty in being angry with another group member. When she was eventually able to show these feelings she recalled a painful rivalry situation with a sister whose death was the precipitating factor in her depressive illness. One patient stated that the reason for remaining in hospital was her fear of venting her anger on her aged parents. This event, if followed by their death, would have been a repetition of the situation following her husband's death.

Hatred was not only a threat to others but also to themselves. The patients constantly attempted to maintain 'good' relationships, but this was imperilled by the projective defence mechanism. Others became hostile and critical. The patients unconsciously tried to placate these 'hostile' people by adopting passive attitudes. This was one cause of the dependency which was so apparent. The dependence was for ever creating anxiety. The patients consciously recognized their emotional vulnerability. In the early days of the group the patients apprehensively awaited the termination of the treatment: 'The doctors may at any time be promoted and sent to other hospitals.' The approach of the holidays intensified these fears. Just before the break, these topics were a constant theme. Another anxiety was that they might be dismissed by the therapists for being too demanding. They wondered how anyone could put up with their constant complaints and demands.

The patients' needs from others were enormous and consequently the pressure to remain on good terms was enhanced so that these demands would be met. Previous experiences of rejection when attempting to satisfy such needs were an ever-present warning against showing what the other person (for example, the therapist) might regard as unacceptable. They dreaded rejection and frequently after an outburst in the group expressed fears that they would not be allowed to return.

A report will be given of one patient's history, not only because it presents the specific problems of an individual but also because this woman was followed up for a number of years after the termination of treatment. Her subsequent life-experiences and her reaction to them tended to support the formulations that were made about the factors giving rise to, and sustaining, the illness. The patient was a woman of 57 at the time of treatment. She had already been in hospital for four years. Not only did she show pronounced depressive manifestations but she was acutely agitated.

The following history was obtained from the patient's sister. There were five children in the family, of whom the patient was the eldest. The patient had always been a jolly, friendly type of person who had been very fond of her parents. She had, however, been rather nervous. As a child she had been unable to travel very far on account of diarrhoea. She left school at the age of 14 and worked in an office for nearly two years, leaving because of indigestion. Employment was found for her nearer to her home. Five years later she left work and came home to act as housekeeper to her parents. She became more nervous and irritable and her diarrhoea grew intractable. About this time she became engaged; but when her fiancé went abroad she broke off the engagement, stating she was not well enough to follow him.

She remained at home from this time, being usually cheerful and methodical though troubled frequently by diarrhoea. At the age of 30 a laparotomy was carried out and she had a portion of bowel resected. Since then she had been increasingly nervous and prone to gastro-intestinal disturbances when subject to stress. When aged 42 she married a widower, a man much older than herself. She had to share a home with her brother-in-law and adult step-son, neither of whom she liked. The marriage was not as happy as it might have been as a result of this. Later, the patient's sister told one of the medical staff that the patient had had a serious quarrel with her husband not long before his death. During this quarrel she had threatened to leave him and he had been most distressed. Her husband had died early in the year of the patient's admission to hospital when she was 53 years of age. Following the death she had been increasingly agitated and depressed. Her appetite had been poor and she was losing weight. She was sleepless and much troubled by diarrhoea.

She had two electroshock treatments and left hospital, returning a fortnight later and receiving a course of six shock treatments before being discharged. She was readmitted several times to various hospitals for further shock treatment. Gradually she developed marked obsessive-compulsive tendencies. Her memory was poor and her handbag and cases were bulging with notebooks containing her 'memory'. She could not even decide whether to get up or remain in bed.

During group treatment, the following information was obtained. Her home life from an early age had been an unhappy one. Her mother had always been a distant, cold, demanding, authoritative person. Pleasure of all kinds was forbidden. Even reading was discouraged and she had instead to carry out some trivial household task. Her relationship with her father was not good but he always seemed unimportant to her. Starved of the essential affective relationship, the siblings turned to each other and she was closer to her sister than to her parents. Always, however, she felt excluded and thought that her mother regarded her as less worthy of affection than the others. As she grew older, her difficulty in travelling increased her sense of being different and finally forced her to find work close to her home. Socially, she was never at ease with other people and some alimentary disturbance frequently interfered with any special occasion. Her relations with men were almost nonexistent and she always felt ill at ease in their company.

Her married life, as her sister reported, was punctuated by quarrels and disagreements. The failure to be on good terms with her step-son caused her much unhappiness. His attitude to her was to ignore her as far as possible. She did not feel any easier for being the previous wife's best friend. With her husband she found she was never quite sure of her role, for she felt that by marrying a man older than herself she had missed his youthful ardour. The painful thought always lurked in the back of her mind that he had acquired a housekeeper rather than a wife.

After his death, she brought her parents and sister into her home. While she had been married they had closed ranks completely and she was no longer a member of the family circle. When she came out of hospital, she had felt that she was not wanted. Any attempts on the patient's part to clean up for her mother, previously so meticulous, were interpreted by the mother as a slight on her own housekeeping. The fact that her parents were now old and frail prevented the patient from expressing her indignation. An attempt to go home while under treatment failed. It appeared later that the patient, now freer in expressing her feelings, had quarrelled with her mother, and her sister had come to the mother's rescue.

Once again, the outstanding feature in this case, and the one which led to the onset of the illness, was an intolerance of hatred. The patient's silence, which was so characteristic of her, was a defence against hurting her mother or anyone in her immediate environment. Following a period of absence from the group, she stated that she had stayed away because her presence was harmful to the other group members. She had a constant fear that her 'badness' and her 'difference' from other people would be discovered and she would be rejected by the person to whom she spoke or by the group in which she found herself.

Oral problems were present also. The patient sought constant reassurance, and if this was not supplied by a doctor she would try to force him to take some action by presenting a physical complaint. During her stay in hospital she had been treated in many different ways. Once given a drug, she refused to do without it. She frequently raised the subject of her diet on the ward rounds and any alteration in it caused a profound reaction on her part. Her silence and withdrawal represented not only a defence against anger, and a turning of it inwards, but also a profound regression to a more passive state. Further, by her silence she succeeded in controlling people in the aggressive way in which she really wished to manipulate her family.

Her ambivalence towards her mother was highlighted when, following a therapy session in which she had attacked her mother, she dreamt that she received a black-edged letter notifying her of her mother's death. Her problems with her siblings caused her great pain. Her relationship with one patient in the group who hectored her and tried to push her into recovery was clearly a repetition of her relationship with her sister, who frequently behaved in the same way. Her amnesia represented a protection against the distressing memories concerning her dead husband. The price which she paid for this protection was the painful obsessive-compulsive doubts and attempts to remember day-to-day trivialities.

This patient gradually improved during three years of group psychotherapy. Unfortunately the improvement was insufficient to permit her to go home and live with her sister and parents. She did go home for weekends from time to time. About a year after treatment terminated, her parents died within a short time of one another. Within a few months the patient was making regular visits home and soon felt able to be discharged. This patient was seen on only a few occasions after leaving hospital. She was followed up during the next five years. She remained well, having only minimal symptoms which did not require medical attention. This response to her parents' death offered some support to the psychodynamic formulation of her illness given above.

DEPRESSIVE STATES COMPLICATED BY OTHER PHENOMENA

In the past, it was not uncommon to encounter mental illnesses in which symptoms of depression of the kind described above were accompanied by delusions, the content of which may best be described as melancholic. The patient believed that he had caused damage to those near and dear to him. His guilt was so intense that he felt that he deserved punishment, and that this awaited him. He misinterpreted what went on around him in these terms. In such states it was not difficult to envisage that the delusional reality stemmed from the depressed mood and the sense of guilt.

Today it is unusual to find such striking cases of melancholia. Patients are met who are afraid that in some way unknown to them they may have done something which will harm others. However, close questioning indicates that the patient does not believe consciously that he is responsible for what he imagines may be happening. For example, a woman patient seen on two successive days spoke as follows. On the first day she said, 'I feel I am causing all the trouble that is going on . . . people seem to be difficult and awkward. They look sort of queer . . . I feel people are looking at me. I feel as if people are saying I am God but I am not God, I am just myself . . . I was praying there wouldn't be a war.' On the second day, she said: 'I can't be to blame for all this – no one can be – whatever is happening, nothing much happened in here [in hospital] . . . I feel all right . . . maybe they are to blame or God's to blame . . . it may not be to do with any of us.'

Behind the patient's concern is a fear that one or more persons unknown to him have brought this situation about. He feels himself to be a victim, a passive agent rather than an active instigator. Sometimes this persecutory element achieves considerable prominence and the patient's reactions to auditory hallucinations with an accusatory content is one of anger as well as anxiety. He does not believe that these criticisms are justified. In this respect he differs from the melancholic patient who felt the blame to be appropriate.

Sometimes the depressed patient presents another kind of misinterpretation of his environment. This takes the form of the belief that for some unknown reason he is being subjected to a form of investigation or trial. In these cases, environmental events are distorted to fit into the patient's delusional idea. Here it is as if conscience is externalized, the patient feeling he is constantly under surveillance and that if his behaviour is adequate he will pass through the ordeal successfully. It is unusual for these patients to feel actively persecuted or to be hallucinated.

A further category of complicated depressed states is composed of that small group of young patients, usually between the ages of 18 and 25, who present delusions and hallucinations. In some respects they are reminiscent of the melancholic patients of earlier generations in that they reproach themselves bitterly for fantasied injuries which they think they have caused. Apart from misinterpretation of environmental events, they show visual misidentifications, and in their speech there is a blocking and omission of thought impossible to distinguish from that which occurs in established cases of schizophrenia. These young patients cannot find a connection between their behaviour and the dreadful things which they imagine are happening to their friends and families. Often there is the conviction that it is a conspiracy directed against them personally.

Illustrative of this form of psychosis was the case of a single woman of 23 – a schoolteacher who was admitted to hospital on account of a severe depression of mood, anorexia, and sleeplessness. This patient was retarded in both thought and action. She reproached herself for having killed her mother, for having attacked other patients in the ward (untrue), for being promiscuous, and for having caused the Crucifixion. She saw herself as being the cause of accidents and disasters which she read about in the paper or saw on television. She had to be made to keep clean and attend to her appearance. Sometimes she was capable of entering into a conversation; at other times she was quite unresponsive.

This patient frequently misidentified those about her. She believed an older patient in the ward to be her aunt who had come back from the dead. She thought that everything that went on around about her was concerned with her and was caused by her presence. She believed she was in a convent, possibly the convent in which she had passed some of her school-days. She thought the ward sister was one of the nuns. She was convinced the author was her father. At another time she believed she was in prison. The reason for this was her belief that she had murdered her mother. At another time, she believed her body was being used for experiments directed from the television. This patient made a good response to electroshock treatment and there was a disappearance of the depressive symptoms and the psychotic manifestations. At a later date she revealed that the symptomatology had occurred following a sexual experience with a male friend.

Finally, reference must be made to those cases of recurrent severe depression where hallucinatory and delusional manifestations dominate one or more episodes of illness. Two cases will be described, both of which were followed up for two years after the phase of psychosis. The first patient, a married man with two children, was 46 years of age when he fell ill with a depression. He complained of depression of mood, he found himself weeping without cause, and he was for ever criticizing himself. He had suicidal intentions. His concentration and memory were such as to make work difficult. He was admitted to hospital and treated with electroshock therapy. The improvement was not sustained but he gradually recovered with the aid of thymoleptic drugs.

About six months later, he relapsed and had to be readmitted to hospital. He was again very depressed in mood, lacking in interest, and sleepless. He was very self-critical. This time he responded well to electroshock treatment. His improvement lasted only about three months and he had to be readmitted to hospital for a third time. It was noted that the depression did not seem so pronounced as previously and that he appeared rather suspicious. He admitted that he felt something peculiar was happening. At home, he had the idea someone was tampering with his mail. He thought his birth-certificate had been stolen. His wife reported that he was keeping to himself and not mixing with others as heretofore. During his period in hospital, it was observed that he found a significance in trivial events. He wondered if the masons were active at his work, turning people against him. These ideas were dissipated with the aid of phenothiazine drugs.

He remained in hospital for eight months. After discharge, he was at home only a few weeks before he had to be readmitted. He now revealed that he was sure he was being followed and watched. He believed his wife was trying to poison him. He said the newspapers and wireless were constantly making references to his affairs. He could not think properly; unknown forces put thoughts into his head and took them out again against his will. He heard voices calling him a cheat and liar. This made him very angry. A well-known author had extracted his (the patient's) whole life-history by means of radiography, and written a book about him. Life was torture, and he was actively suicidal. During this period there was no sign of depression of mood or self-reproach. He remained in hospital for eleven months.

Treatment with phenothiazines led to the gradual disappearance of these psychotic manifestations. They were replaced by a feeling of fatigue, depression of mood varying from mild to severe, and frequent bouts of weeping. On account of mental and physical fatigue he was unable to work. This patient was seen weekly for a period of over two years from the time of his last discharge from hospital. His mental state never varied from that just described and on only one occasion did he seem to become suspicious. He never recognized that his experiences during his last stay in hospital were irrational. It is likely that the phenothiazines kept the delusional ideas at bay, but it is significant that for nearly a year in hospital his symptoms did not respond to these medications. It is possible that the delusional ideas receded spontaneously, to be replaced by the chronic depression that existed over the two years of out-patient attendance. During the meetings the patient was always pleasant in manner and responsive. He spent most of the time talking about his symptoms and his anxiety about them. Relations with his wife and daughter remained good. During the sessions it emerged that the most likely precipitant of the illness was his mother's death, which occurred three months before he attended the psychiatric out-patient department for the first time.

The second case is that of a single woman of 42. She was a

schoolteacher who began to find it difficult to concentrate at work. Her appetite was poor, she lost weight, and she was depressed in mood. She had an unpleasant sense of inferiority and found it difficult to hide this from her pupils and her colleagues. She was referred to the psychiatric department of a general hospital and was advised to undertake a course of electroshock treatment as an out-patient. She made a good response to this therapy and remained well for almost a year.

Almost a year after her first attendance she had a relapse with almost identical symptoms. In addition she complained of hearing voices which were criticizing her. She had developed the idea that the voices were coming from the wireless. Admission to hospital was arranged, and she remained there for three months. It was noted that she was not particularly depressed but more concerned with the voices, which she now regarded as a form of persecution. The voices gave her instructions. They told her to do certain things, some of which were trivial, others which frightened her. She thought the voices were sometimes answering her own thoughts. The voices appeared to come from the vicinity of each ear, sometimes from the walls of the room in which she sat. She gradually became to believe that there was a conspiracy to keep her in the hospital. She became very suspicious of the medical staff and was not cooperative. She misinterpreted any request as a means of increasing control over her. Treatment with phenothiazines had little effect. She discharged herself from hospital against advice.

She remained out of hospital for three months. According to the sister with whom she lived, the hallucinations varied in intensity and the patient became increasingly upset. She had to return to hospital and this time she remained for six months. A gradual improvement took place, with the hallucinations and persecutory delusions gradually disappearing. The patient was seen regularly at the out-patient department for the next twenty-two months. During this time there were two occasions when the psychotic manifestations made their appearance. From time to time she showed signs of a depressive illness but these did not reach such an intensity as to require hospitalization. It was impossible in this case to find out the immediate stimulus for the onset of the illness.

COMPLICATED AND UNCOMPLICATED DEPRESSIVE STATES

The comparison between complicated and uncomplicated depressive states that will now be undertaken can best be accomplished by classifying similar and dissimilar phenomena with the aid of the examination scheme.

I. OBJECT RELATIONS

(*i*) *Nature of the Relationship with Real Objects*

In the uncomplicated depressive states, the patients were able to create a therapeutic alliance when offered the opportunity of treatment. They were capable of making relationships with other patients. It is apparent from the material described that transferences developed which could be employed for therapeutic purposes. The treatment of the patients differed little from that of patients suffering from neuroses. Difficulties arose when patients expressed their resistances through an intensification of the depression with accompanying suicidal wishes. Further problems were presented by patients who could not pass beyond a monotonous repetition of symptoms. Such obstacles were often sufficient to obstruct therapeutic progress entirely.

The patients with complicated depressive states were incapable of bringing about the conditions necessary for psychotherapeutic intervention. They were withdrawn and sometimes quite inaccessible. Where persecutory delusions were present, the therapist and other medical and nursing staff were rapidly assimilated into the complex of irrational ideas. Misidentifications of doctors, nurses, and other patients with figures drawn from the patient's current and past life and vice versa also made communication difficult. Even when the delusional reality receded, it was almost impossible to make the kind of contact with the patient that would allow him to discuss the problems that clearly had a connection with the symptoms. Contact was possible only when the patient had a complete remission of symptoms or when depressive manifestations remained alone.

(*ii*) *Nature of the Relationship with Delusional Objects*

The complicated depressive states presented all kinds of relationships to delusional objects. In this respect these patients were very little different from those who are sometimes diagnosed as suffering from paranoid schizophrenia or paranoid psychosis. Passivity feelings, thought insertion, delusional perceptions, and hallucinations could all be observed. All such phenomena were completely absent in patients with uncomplicated depressive states.

2. PERCEPTION OF THE SELF, SELF-REGARD, AND PERSONAL IDENTITY

There is no serious derangement of these mental processes in uncomplicated depressive states, apart from varying degrees of loss of self-regard and anxieties about bodily health. These anxieties can be pronounced and take the form of a chronic hypochondria. In the complicated states a variety of disturbances may affect perception of the self as well as self-regard. As in the cases described, patients may feel they have lost the autonomy of the self – bodily and mental functions seeming to be under the control of outside influences. Changes in the body-image may arise, as in the case of a patient who felt her body getting bigger and bigger. This was seen as being caused by some outside force.

3. STATUS OF THE COGNITIVE FUNCTIONS

In uncomplicated depressive states the form of speech and thinking is intact. The flow of speech may be affected, and in severe cases there is a retardation. This contrasts with the complicated cases where omissions and derailments in speech may occur. This was to be seen in the case of the depressed young schoolteacher described above. Here there was an omission of connecting words and phrases which made her speech difficult to understand. Her utterances were usually punctuated by long pauses. On one occasion she asked, 'Am I in hospital . . . is that my mother who comes up . . .?' After a pause she continued, 'The nurse brought these budgerigars in here.' [There were two budgerigars in the patient's room at the time of the interview.] 'She did this to let me know I talk rubbish.' She was silent for some seconds and then added, 'It's painful to have a baby.' There seemed no connection whatever between her remarks about the budgerigars and about childbirth. She was asked if she could explain the connection. With some difficulty she said, 'The birds are coloured blue and green like Rangers and Celtic football teams . . . there's that woman next door with a baby.' In fact there was a patient, suffering from a puerperal depression, in the next room who had her baby with her.

This last remark about there being a patient with a baby next door provided the connecting link between the budgerigars and birth. It appeared that the day before the budgerigars had been in the other patient's room. This was the bridge between the two apparently disconnected utterances. For several days previously the patient had been affected by having the woman with the baby next door. One day she said, 'I was holding a baby between my legs just now,' and at other times she asked some question or other about childbirth.

Magical thinking is commonplace in these complicated depressive states and provides the basis for the delusional ideas, whatever their nature. Disorders of concept formation are uncommon. Reference has already been made to the visual misidentifications that may appear in these complicated cases.

4. MOTILITY

Sometimes complicated cases show a disorder of motility. These patients may adopt certain postures. In these cases it is usually easy to discover that the behaviour is undertaken for fear of damaging or harming others.

5. SENSORI-MOTOR ORGANIZATION. Not relevant.

6. MANIFESTATIONS OF 'INSTINCTUAL DRIVE' ACTIVITY. Not relevant.

7. AFFECTIVITY. Not relevant.

8. DEFENCE ORGANIZATION

The psychoanalytical treatment of severe uncomplicated depressive states has shown that the mechanisms of introjection and projection play a central role in dealing with the drive and object-relationship conflicts. Some clinical material that supports this formulation has been described earlier in this chapter. Accentuation of self-reproaches, depression of mood, and despair can be seen to occur under conditions when aggressive tendencies are activated. This is brought about by introjection. This mechanism can be observed in the transference situation during the psychoanalytical treatment of depressed patients.

In complicated depressive states there is a profound withdrawal from objects. Introjective mechanisms continue to operate as in the uncomplicated cases, but there also a disorganization and regression both of ego-functions and of the drives. Repression as it affects repudiated childhood fantasies appears to be in abeyance, and these fantasies find conscious expression. As in schizophrenia and paranoid psychosis, the loss of the real world is substituted partly or wholly by a delusional reality. Projective mechanisms can be seen to be at work both in the exteriorization of unacceptable wishes and in the superego.

THE CONCEPT OF DEPRESSIVE PSYCHOSIS

The grouping of severe uncomplicated depressive illnesses into the class of psychoses has never found universal acceptance among clinical psychiatrists (Roth, 1963) – hence the terms 'endogenous depression', 'physiological depression', etc. The term 'psychosis' carries with it the idea of alienation. The patient is estranged from life and from himself. Psychosis implies a break with reality and an impairment of judgement of such severity as to support belief in irrational ideas which lead to maladaptive behaviour. This conception of psychosis is taken directly from Freud (1924). In psychotic illness there is a derangement of all those mental functions which ensure adaptation to the environment. Not only is the patient alienated from the external world, but the mental representations of that reality are disorganized also.

In severe depressive states characterized by self-reproaches, judgement is deficient. The patient is not alienated from others or from himself. Frequently he recognizes that his self-criticism is inappropriate. The depth of his depressive mood or the other symptoms cannot be regarded as evidence of psychosis, unless it is accompanied by features that bring the condition into the category of 'complicated' depressive states.

The position adopted here is that uncomplicated depressive illnesses are not psychoses in the sense outlined above. Freud (1924) made this distinction in differentiating melancholia from the category of psychoses. In his view, based on his structural theory, the melancholias belong to the group of narcissistic neuroses, in which the conflict lies between ego and superego. In psychosis, the area of disturbance is between ego and the outer world. Depressive states are closer to the psychoneuroses, and it is a fact of clinical experience that depressive symptoms are frequently combined with anxiety, phobias, and obsessive-compulsive phenomena. Depressive states in pure culture have a characteristic natural history. However many attacks there may be, the symptoms rarely change in form or content. Patients have been met whose depressive attacks have occurred at regular intervals for forty years without any change in the symptomatology. Reference to hospital records has confirmed this finding.

From a purely descriptive standpoint, it is difficult to find a way of classifying complicated depressive states if they are not to be allocated to such categories as manic-depressive psychosis. This diagnosis can sometimes find justification in the fact that the condition remits spontaneously or with antidepressive drug treatments, and that relapses occur periodically. However, neither outcome is invariable, and clinical data have already been presented that show that a patient may have only one attack of complicated depression amid a series of uncomplicated depressive illnesses. It is also too easy to find a so-called premorbid cyclothymic personality in these 'atypical' patients and to use this to justify the diagnosis of manic-depressive psychosis. The evidence presented in support of such personality traits is often weak in the extreme, being based on the patient's or relative's reports in response to leading questions. Finally, a family history of depressive illness cannot be invoked in support of a diagnosis of manic-depressive psychosis, since this kind of family may equally give rise to a schizophrenic psychosis. Reference will be made later to the concept of the cycloid psychoses (Leonhard, 1961) which attempts to differentiate 'complicated' depressive states from manic depression.

Scandinavian psychiatrists have recognized that patients in whom depressive manifestations play a leading role cannot all be placed within the category of manic depression. Faergeman (1963), in his study of psychogenic psychoses, employs Schneider's classification, which includes the category of emotional syndromes. Under this heading are included depressive syndromes (reactive depressions or melancholiform reactions; psychogenic depressions; psychically precipitated melancholias; depressive syndromes including pre-schizophrenic episodes) and states of elation. Faergeman points out that in certain of these depressive illnesses follow-up demonstrated the eventual appearance of a schizophrenic illness. This and other studies suggest that the pathological process operative in complicated depressive states is not a unitary one. Mayer-Gross and his co-authors (1954), for example, state that manic-depression and schizophrenia can occur in one and the same individual. In this they are following the views of authors quoted by Faergeman (1963).

The psychoanalytical theory of psychosis finds no difficulty in accommodating the phenomena presented by complicated depressive states. It emphasizes the differences in the psychological structure underlying the depressive manifestations, on the one hand, and the accompanying or alternating psychotic phenomena, on the other. It also attributes the clinical manifestations to varying degrees of regression affecting the ego and the drives. In the same way the evolution-dissolution theory is not embarrassed by the great differences in the clinical phenomena. The extent of the dissolution must vary from patient to patient, and it is the nature of the individual that will govern it. In uncomplicated depressive states the dissolution is limited, being confined to those systems regulating self-esteem (ego-ideal systems in psychoanalytical theory). The derangement of these systems leads to their childhood precursors making a reappearance resulting in an emotional vulnerability inappropriate for adult life.

According to the view taken here, straightforward depressive states – whether considered to be reactive or endogenous – are not psychoses in the strict sense of the term. Clinical experience repeatedly confirms that these illnesses run a characteristic course, and that constitutional and hereditary influences play a part in the aetiology. The fact that some of these depressions alternate with manic and hypomanic states justifies the use of the concept of manic-depression. Criticism is only made of the additional word 'psychosis'. Where a delusional reality makes its appearance, there is every reason to believe that a new process of illness has supervened which is only indirectly related to the depressive manifestations.

CHAPTER 10

The Concept and Diagnosis of Schizophrenia

The diagnosis of schizophrenia is entirely dependent upon the conception of the illness held by the examining psychiatrist. For this reason it is logical to discuss both these problems in the one chapter. The concept of schizophrenia may be very wide, very narrow, or something in between. There are some authorities (Langfeldt, 1960) who wish to restrict the diagnosis, and thus their conception is similar to the state Kraepelin designated dementia praecox. There are others who similarly wish to restrict the use of this nosological category, but they feel that it should not only be confined to patients whose illness runs a deteriorating course. As a consequence, various descriptive criteria are postulated (Schneider, 1959) which when met indicate the presence of schizophrenia. Nearly all attempts to define what schizophrenia is are based on the presence or absence of clearly designated clinical phenomena. In spite of all these efforts, controversy regarding diagnosis continues around those patients who present abnormalities of mood and psychomotor excitement. There is little agreement about the relationship of delusional and hallucinatory states to the schizophrenias.

In the English-speaking countries the tendency has been to gloss over the difficulties which the clinical phenomena all too frequently present and to cling to the diagnosis of manic-depressive psychosis or paranoid schizophrenia. The inconsistencies that exist between one aspect of the clinical picture and another are ignored under the compulsion to establish a diagnosis. French and Scandinavian psychiatrists (Ey, 1959; Pichot, 1967; Faergeman, 1963) have left the problem rather more open and have refused to commit the clinical phenomena to two or three major diagnostic groupings. Thus they recognize delusional and hallucinatory states existing independently of schizophrenia. The German authors (Kleist, 1960; Leonhard, 1961) have also tried to do justice to the complexity of the clinical manifestations by introducing new categories of schizophrenic and non-schizophrenic psychosis. Unfortunately these attempts have only resulted in the description of symptom complexes which rarely appear in pure culture.

THE CONCEPT OF SCHIZOPHRENIA

I

The clinical phenomena described in earlier chapters provide the basis for a concept of schizophrenia. This material was presented in accordance with an examination scheme that has the aim of embracing all the varieties of clinical data that may arise in psychotic illness. This approach was thought to be essential because a theory of schizophrenia must take into account all the changes that have affected psychomotor functions in the individual case.

In patients whose mental state was described in Chapters 5, 6, and 8, who were diagnosed as schizophrenic on the basis of symptoms and outcome, emphasis was laid on three groups of clinical phenomena – namely, the manner of expression of disorders of object relations, of cognition, and of motility. This division of the phenomena into groups is basically artificial, since they are all so closely interrelated. However, it will be adhered to in this instance for clarity in presentation.

In each case the patient had lost his capacity to relate to others in a manner that would provide emotional satisfactions and offer a reasonable means of adaptation to his surroundings. The extent of this loss varied from patient to patient, and even where it was most severe an ability to behave spontaneously and respond occurred when needs were uppermost. Alongside this loss there appeared in varying degrees a preoccupation with delusional and hallucinatory experiences. When this was present the patient always gave the impression that it was of greater significance and importance to him than the reality of his environment. In the long-stay wards of all mental hospitals there are patients who have constructed elaborate delusional systems by which they regulate their lives. The question which has never been satisfactorily answered is whether such patients are basically similar to those to whom reference has just been made. In a practical sense they are identical because of their inability to exist in the community. Apart from this, however, significant differences exist, particularly in the spheres of speech, thinking, memory, and motility.

When the cognitive status and the motility of the schizophrenic patients were investigated significant changes were found throughout. It was observed that many of the abnormal forms of cognition and motility could be attributed to the activity of a process of condensation and to a trend towards compulsive automatic repetition. Whenever such processes were operative in speech, thinking, or memory, the patient was found to be utterly detached from the world of objects – using this term in the psychoanalytical sense. He was inattentive, unresponsive, and negativisitic. He would be found to be distractable in the passive sense and to manifest echo reactions. Cataleptic signs and hypertonia of the limbs were present in addition to the repetitive trend in motility. Some patients remained in this state for long periods, while others presented such a condition intermittently.

In the chapter on organic mental states, clinical data were presented showing that many of the abnormal forms of psychomotility which appeared could also be attributed to the operation of mental processes characterized by a trend towards condensations and automatic repetition, the latter possibly reflecting the inherent inertia of mental processes. It was phenomena influenced by this kind of mentation that most resembled the cognitive and motility disorders of the schizophrenias. These manifestations were most commonly observed when the patient had largely lost his capacity to relate to others. At such times negativistic behaviour was not uncommon.

It was proposed that a special state of consciousness obtained in both categories where there was little capacity to reflect on the self and on immediate experience. If 'normal' or 'improved' mental activity suddenly appeared, only to vanish again, it was due to the operation of automatic, involuntary, learnt speech or action stimulated by need or strong emotion. When the operation of mental processes characterized by condensing and repetitive trends can be inferred, it is indicative that the organizational level of both cognitive and volitional functions is specific for the patient in this particular phase of the illness. This organizational level is quite different from that required for purposive attention. It is also distinct from that obtaining in day-dreaming and hypnagogic state. It most clearly resembles the cognitive organization of the dream in so far as condensations provide one of the principal components of the dream-work. The theories advanced by both Freud and Hughlings Jackson provide equally satisfactory explanations for the appearance of the clinical phenomena. They indicate why the volitional and cognitive processes assume their characteristic form. The psychoanalytical contribution goes further by revealing how the content of these phenomena is determined.

The phenomena to which attention has been directed, and the mechanisms underlying them, are not limited to long-standing cases of schizophrenia. They may also be found in patients who have just fallen ill. In the case of the patient described in Chapter 4, repetitive phenomena, echo reactions, and passive distractability accompanied an extensive withdrawal and detachment. During one such withdrawn period the patient wrote down the following:

$\pounds 55555 - 17 - 0$

$55\ 5\ 557.170$ miles

$$7 \times \frac{55{\cdot}557170}{22}$$

$7 \times 2525\ 325\frac{10}{11}$

$17\ 6\ 77261\frac{4}{11}$ miles diameters of earth

$$\frac{55557170}{3} = \text{VOLHUME OF earth}$$

$$55557170 \times 5357\frac{170 \times 5}{3}\ 55557170$$

$55551707 \times 55555710 \times 5555577557 = \text{Christ}$

$$\frac{55557170}{0} = \text{A}$$

$$\frac{55555770}{\text{A}}$$

$555755170 \times 55557170 \times 55557170 = \text{Christ}$

$$\frac{5555551717}{3} = \text{Exhume}$$

The number 5 referred to the number of his ward. He bitterly resented being detained there. The 'A' underneath one of the series of figures was the first letter of the surname of an occupational therapist to whom he was much attached. He believed that he was Christ, and 'EXHUME' and 'VOLHUME' and 3 are connected with the resurrection. While the content of this production can be understood as a response to his environmental and delusional experiences, the nature of the representation must be attributed to the activation of mental processes with a repetitive-compulsive quality. Condensations affected his visual perception and his thinking.

This patient was of particular interest because of the elation which appeared coincidental with his recovery. Its presence highlighted and provided a contrast with the fact that so many of his delusional ideas had a melancholic content. Some months after his discharge from hospital he fell ill again. This time not only did he present similar features to those described in Chapter 4, but intermittently he was elated in mood and over-active. This over-activity occurred in both thinking and action. He presented flights of ideas, clang associations, and punning. This hypomanic activity alternated with phases characterized by withdrawal, inattention, perseveration, persecutory delusions, and hallucinations.

II

It is clinical experiences of this kind which raise the question of how psychomotor depression and excitement are to be integrated into a theory of schizophrenia. What relationship does the depressed or over-active psychomotility bear to the remainder of the disordered mental processes? Can it be regarded as the primary disturbance which through its own momentum leads to a cognitive disorganization, to delusions and hallucinations? This view is not hard to sustain when speech and thinking are either accelerated or retarded with a consequent fragmentation of words and phrases. In the same way it is not difficult to assume that wish-fulfilling or self-damaging fantasies may achieve a reality for the patient under the influence of intense elation or depression.

Psychomotor excitement and depression rarely occur except in relation to environmental objects. In this respect the states in which these phenomena occur differ qualitatively from schizophrenic reactions. Psychoanalytical observers have shown repeatedly that the depressed patient is concerned for the safety of the object, he is concerned for its welfare. The schizophrenic patient is either indifferent to the fate of the object or fears persecution. It is impossible to provide an adequate explanation for depressive or manic states unless the factor of conscience is considered. The psychoanalytical concept of the superego takes into account not only the activity of the conscience of the healthy adult but also the unconscious component. It is this unconscious component which can be held responsible for the self-accusations, misinterpretations, and delusions which the patient believes to be justifiable, and can be regarded as consistent with the depressive mood. In hyperactive states, conscience appears to be in abeyance, and wishes and actions find a free expression. Outbursts of violence, rage, criticism, and sexual activities on all levels of libidinal development are not restrained.

When patients with manic-depression (uncomplicated depressive states) are closely observed, it is apparent that there is an absence of that radical alteration in the state of consciousness which has already been described in the chronic schizophrenic and certain organic mental states. There is no sign of that specific loss of volition, that derangement of the ability to reflect on experience, passive distractability, echo reactions, or perseverative signs. Thus when the symptomatology is confined to the psychomotor depression or excitement and its immediate effects on cognition, it stands in contrast to the phenomena described in earlier chapters. Problems arise alike for theory and practice when patients are encountered who present either an alternation between psychomotor over-activity and schizophrenic symptomatology, as in the case described in Chapter 4, or different combinations of symptoms.

The following case history is relevant. A young woman of 18 fell ill in 1963. The illness had an acute onset some months after her mother's death. She stopped eating, and was mute and negativistic. Treatment with electroshock therapy led to symptomatic improvement. During the remainder of the hospital stay she did not show any delusional or hallucinatory phenomena. The condition was diagnosed as a depressive illness. About a year later she had to be readmitted to hospital. She had gradually become uninterested in and withdrawn from life. Immediately prior to admission she became acutely anxious, saying she was afraid of her father. At one moment she feared he might assault her sexually, at another that he was a homosexual. She wondered if she was homosexual. Gradually she improved and appeared to have gained insight into her irrational ideas about her father.

Four months after the second discharge from hospital she relapsed once again. She had not settled well at home. Between periods of depression of mood and apathy she was elated and excited. It was the physical and mental over-activity which led the father to consult the general practitioner.

When admitted to hospital she was observed to be distractable; anything and everything took up her attention. Her speech was characterized by flight of ideas. She would roar with laughter. After some days this passed and she became withdrawn and uninterested in herself. She neglected her appearance. After a month the over-activity returned and continued for several months. Gradually she improved and was discharged. Unfortunately she only remained symptom-free for two to three months, and in April 1966 had to be readmitted. At this time she complained that at work and in the street people were saying that she was a homosexual. They were telling one another that she masturbated. During the rest of her stay in hospital she was alternately over-active or withdrawn. She was discharged at the end of 1966.

An opportunity to obtain more information about her mental state was provided when she relapsed five months later and had to be readmitted to hospital. Initially she was giggly and talkative. She said to the author, 'I'm still hearing voices . . . I've the feeling I've done something wrong . . . I thought I was odd when my periods were irregular . . . maybe it's masturbation.' At the next meeting she was dejected in mood – she wished she was dead. She was worried about cancer (her mother had died of a tumour) – 'My parents were too old when I was born' (the patient was an only child). During the course of these comments she hallucinated – she heard someone saying 'dirty old man.' She laughed and went on to ask if it was right for a man and woman who were unmarried to live in the same house. She was sure she was an embarrassment to her father.

At the third meeting she was still very talkative. She revealed her fear that she might have sexual feelings for her father. She said that she sometimes felt a penis pressing against her abdomen. In the following weeks she provided unequivocal evidence of the presence of auditory hallucinations. She asked the author, 'Do you hear voices?' when there was no noise audible. She said she heard someone talking about masturbation and she burst out laughing. At another time she said someone said she was a virgin. Again on occasions she heard the word 'jealousy'. Very often it was impossible to be sure if she was hallucinated or merely misinterpreting noises or faint speech overheard outside the consulting-room.

During this time she was noisy and unrestrained. She occasionally exhibited her genitalia or struck out at another patient. She sexualized the relationship with the author. She believed he was hypnotizing her and arousing her sexually – 'You don't love me, you hate me, you're frustrating me.' During the day she complained to the nurses that her mind was interfered with by the wireless and television. She had no control over her thoughts or feelings and they were being directed in certain ways. The women in the ward were saying she was a homosexual – they were teasing her because she was unmarried. She objected to all these experiences to which she was subjected and considered them a persecution.

Frequently her statements regarding hallucinations or ideas of influence or passivity were made calmly without the presence of pressure of speech or excitement. She complained that she heard a boy's voice saying, 'She's virginal.' She believed she was in electrical contact with her father and by this she meant sexual contact. As during previous admissions to hospital, the over-activity gradually abated. This was not related to the treatment by phenothiazine drugs, which had been administered from the time of her admission. In spite of the change in mood and behaviour, she continued to express ideas of the type described. The only difference was that she was rather reluctant to participate in meetings. At no time, however, was she ever completely unresponsive or inattentive. She never displayed any signs of negativism or a motility upset.

This patient exhibited manifestations which are generally regarded as signs of a schizophrenic illness. The belief that action, thought, and feeling was controlled, the interference with the processes of thought, and the gradual falling-off of spontaneity and initiative are indicative.

Another category of case which tests the conceptual and diagnostic powers of the psychiatrist is the patient who presents a mixture of over-activity and depression alongside phenomena that may appear in a case of schizophrenia. A case in point is that of a woman of 38 who was admitted to hospital in a state of excitement and restlessness. She could hardly be confined to bed. She kept up a rapid and continuous flow of speech which was difficult to follow. From among the welter of associations the following was perceived: 'I am fit enough to eat all the food I get – I am not afraid to die – my husband is getting near middle age – he needs exercise. I am writing too fast for my husband . . .' At this point the speed of associations made it impossible to record the next statements. She was extremely unhappy and wept copiously. As in the sample of her speech quoted above she occasionally interpolated into her stream of talk extraneous percepts (the author writing, in this instance). She did not appear to be concerned that this rendered her remarks illogical.

During the meeting with the author she showed that there were moments when she could not really differentiate herself from him – as in the remark 'I am writing too fast . . .' or again, 'I cannot hear very well', when he asked her to repeat an almost inaudible utterance. Most striking was her complaint of a flushed face (in fact her complexion was deathly pale) when the author arrived flushed and breathless from hurrying to keep the appointment. Comparison of both faces simultaneously in a mirror did not influence her conviction as to the appearance of her face. Similarly she had the greatest difficulty in discriminating between her husband and herself, frequently referring to characteristics of her husband as if they were her own and attributing some of her own traits to her husband. There were periods when she misidentified the older patients in the ward with her mother. All these phenomena occurred against a background of an accurate orientation for time and place. Although this patient was constantly depressed in mood she was not truly self-critical. She was worried about the effect of her illness on her children but she did not blame herself in any way. She was never hallucinated or deluded. Only after treatment with phenothiazine drugs did the over-activity decline in intensity, to leave the depressive mood more conspicuous.

This patient presented a number of features which are described as occurring in schizophrenic states. She gave the impression that she was in an altered state of consciousness with reduced self-awareness. This may be inferred from the passive distractability and the condensations leading in the visual sphere to misidentifications and in interpersonal relations to some deficiency in self-object discrimination. In this respect she was quite different from the previous patient described. In that case there was no sign of passive distractability, nor did phenomena appear in thinking or perception that could be attributed to condensation.

Patients who present symptoms of a depressive nature against a background of psychomotor over-activity are generally categorized as mixed manic-depressive states. However, this nosological entity does not easily encompass patients who reveal their preoccupation with a psychotic reality characterized by misinterpretations, misidentifications, hallucinations, and delusions. Frequently these delusional experiences have a persecutory content. It is well known that these illnesses usually remit spontaneously or with the aid of physical treatments. Kasanin (1933) introduced the concept of the schizo-affective state to make allowance for those cases which show a mixture of schizophrenic and manic-depressive features. The idea of a mixed or atypical state has never been well received. According to Mayer-Gross *et al.* (1954) it is unsatisfactory to allocate clinical conditions to a nosological group only on the basis of their not fitting into other groups and when they are without aetiological, psychopathological, or prognostic affinities. They suggest that atypical states should be included in either schizophrenia or manic-depressive psychosis.

This solution is not satisfactory because it tends to obscure the problems presented by the atypical cases. Their frequency has led to the proposal that these states should be separated from both schizophrenia and manic-depression. The Scandinavians, for example, introduced the concept of a reactive psychosis to ensure the differentiation of these and other states from schizophrenia. A further attempt to refine the concept of schizophrenia by dealing specifically with these atypical states has been made by Leonhard (1961). He considers that they often belong to a group of psychoses which are neither schizophrenia nor manic-depression. In Leonhard's opinion these cycloid psychoses always remit without a defect state. These conditions bear great similarity to the schizophrenias but can be distinguished from each other on clinical grounds alone. Three different categories of cycloid psychosis have been described – a motility psychosis, a confusion psychosis, and an anxiety-elation psychosis. A characteristic feature is that they are bipolar illnesses – two contrasting states can occur in the one illness.

In the motility psychosis, hyperkinesia and akinesia occur, but there is no mixture as in catatonia. This is a differentiating criterion. In the confusion psychosis, there is incoherent thinking. During the excited phase there is pressure of talk and misidentifications, while in the inhibited phase there is retardation or stupor; affectivity is not affected. It is the inhibition of thought which leads to misinterpretation of the environment. However, other significant schizophrenic signs are absent. The mood swings of the anxiety-elation psychosis help to make the diagnosis, in spite of ideas of reference and delusions, usually with a grandiose or melancholic content. Unfortunately for this formulation, overlapping occurs between the different forms of cycloid psychosis, and thus atypical states have to be postulated. Leonhard admits that there are times when it is difficult to make a distinction between schizophrenia and cycloid psychosis. This implies that the diagnosis is eventually made on the outcome rather than on the clinical picture during the illness.

III

The next problem to be discussed in any attempt to form a concept of schizophrenia is the place of clinical states characterized predominantly by delusions and hallucinations. These conditions, which rarely appear before the end of the third decade, are usually free from disorders of cognition and there is no serious disturbance of affect. Psychiatrists are still divided in their opinions about the relationship between these paranoid syndromes and schizophrenia (Faergeman, 1963). For some (Mayer-Gross *et al.*), paranoid psychoses are to be included within the group of schizophrenias, while for others (Batchelor, 1964) these are separate conditions with their own aetiology, phenomenology, course, and outcome. The controversy is no nearer being settled than it was fifty years ago, and this situation is likely to continue as long as some psychiatrists feel obliged to place syndromes within disease entities. In this context it is only relevant to consider how the clinical manifestations that constitute the paranoid syndromes relate to the phenomena that occur in schizophrenia and how they can be understood with the aid of the dissolution and regression hypotheses of Jackson and Freud.

An account of a typical case may be helpful. When the patient, a single woman of 40, was first seen it would have been impossible to know that she suffered from a mental illness. Only gradually did she reveal the nature and the extent of her irrational ideas. She believed that she was being tortured by genital sensations. She believed that these sensations were not hers, but those of unknown men. She said that male genitals were literally inside her, and that men were continually masturbating. At other times she believed that a woman was stimulating the man's penis. She further maintained that she could tell the kind of man it was from the sensations. Sometimes he was coloured, at other times thin, and sometimes fat. These beliefs could be correlated with the physician who was in charge of her case; in fact a coloured doctor, a thin doctor, and a fat doctor had looked after her on different occasions. At a later time she announced while in a state of 'union' with one physician that the man whose genital was inside her was 'extremely brainy'. She said, 'I am a composite person.'

Apart from the genital experiences, the patient believed that she was the recipient of all the suffering in the world. If a woman was ill with chest pain she had chest pain; if another was in labour she experienced her labour pains. This patient's grandiosity revealed itself in numerous ways. When angry with a doctor she told him that those who went against her always ended in serious trouble, and she cited instances. She insisted that she was no ordinary patient, and her identification with Christ was clear in her assertion that she was born to bring peace to the world and as a result had to bear the sufferings of humanity.

In this case there was a profound alteration in the way in which the self was experienced. The boundaries of the self were disordered, thus leading to a form of merging with others. Apart from this phenomenon there were no other indications of the effect of condensation. When the patient was seen the illness had been in a stationary state for a long period. She had first consulted psychiatrists about nine or ten years earlier, but her mental upset had been present before. A period of mental disturbance had led to her first period of hospitalization, of which no details were available. Is it possible that there were other positive signs present at that time reflecting the presence of condensations and other primitive mental activity?

In another case of similar type an opportunity was afforded of observing the kinds of phenomenon that appear at the onset of an illness characterized by delusions. The patient was a single woman of 45 who was completely dominated by persecutory ideas. These ideas had been present for several years. At the time of admission to hospital, she was difficult to make contact with and quite self-absorbed. Only after a few days did she indicate something of her experiences. She misidentified nurses and patients. She thought the hospital was a place where humans were changed into animal form and this was to be her fate. She believed the world was about to end. Sometimes she thought the sun was about to crush the world, and when she had this thought she felt breathless as if her body was being crushed also. During this experience she had the conviction that she was the centre of some mysterious happening. As the weeks went by she developed the idea that the author was hypnotizing her and controlling her mind. This was merely an aspect of her conviction that unknown forces were interfering with her mental and bodily functions.

Once over the acute phase, this patient did not show any indications which might have suggested a disturbance in the capacity to reflect on experience nor did she have difficulty in communicating what was experienced. In this respect she was similar to the first case described. Both the patients were reasonably attentive and free of upsets in the sphere of motility. These patients are typical of cases variously diagnosed as paranoid schizophrenia or paranoid psychosis. The onset is gradual, so the exact manner in which the illness began is often difficult to ascertain. By the time the patient comes into contact with the psychiatrist the delusional ideas are firmly established and dominate his mind to the exclusion of all else.

Such clinical evidence as is available indicates that, possibly at the beginning of illnesses later to be categorized paranoid schizophrenia or paranoid psychosis, there is a brief period when the patient passes through a phase in which there is a profound alteration in the state of consciousness. This may in some cases lead to distractability, inattention negativism, perseverative signs, thinking disorder, and misidentifications. This phase may be extremely brief and so later the patient has no recollection of it. Whether such a phase occurs may depend upon the rapidity of onset of the illness.

IV

As a prelude to the presentation of a concept of schizophrenia, it will be useful to return once again to a description of some of the outstanding clinical features that were found in established cases of schizophrenia and in certain organic mental states. The presence of such phenomena as inattention, lack of interest, passive distractability, echo phenomena, perseverative signs, and negativism was taken to indicate the presence of a special state of consciousness in which reflection on immediate experience was deficient. Additionally the speech, thinking, memory, and perception of these patients was found to be influenced by a process of condensation.

The clinical data thus appeared to be governed with respect to their form by two influences which can only be regarded as representing the manner in which mental processes operate when more advanced mental functions are in abeyance. The first is the trend to condensation, the second an automatic repetitive tendency. Both find their expression in the mental life of the healthy and in those suffering from neuroses. There, however, their expression is curtailed and not allowed free play as occurs in chronic schizophrenia and organic mental states.

Automatic repetition reflects the basic inertia of mental processes. Together with the tendency to condensation it reflects the qualities of what is mental. Such considerations are based on Freud's view (1940) that the true essence of what is mental is not to be discovered in conscious processes. Consciousness is only one quality of the mental governed by its own special laws. Taken from this standpoint, psychological development consists of those means whereby the innate, autonomous trend towards repetition and condensation are progressively limited in order that they may not interfere with the aim of environmental adaptation.

Condensation alters cognition as much in organic mental states as in the schizophrenias. Conceptual thinking and perceiving assume the characteristic forms already described. In organic mental states, condensation is not evoked for the task of constructing a new reality although the results of condensation in perception (misidentifications, synaesthesiae) may be employed at times to assist in such a purpose. The phenomena presented by organic mental states support Freud's (1916) belief that the tendency to condensation is a primary mental quality and that only secondarily does this become involved in defence and the elaboration of a psychotic reality. In the schizophrenias an additional factor operates. It is this which differentiates the schizophrenic patient from the patient with an organic mental state – namely the withdrawal of object-directed cathexes.

In Chapter 2 an account was given of Jackson's theory of mental illness. He proposed that the form of the positive symptoms would depend on the speed and extent of the dissolution, the type of individual in whom dissolution took place, and the influence of local bodily states. The various manifestations which appear in all psychotic states can be explained with the aid of this hypothesis. The situation in chronic schizophrenia and organic mental states results from a deep and extensive dissolution affecting all aspects of mental functioning. This leads to positive symptoms – the result of the emergence of condensing and repetitive trends. Power (1957), following Jackson's views closely, has designated fusion (condensation) and repetition as the predominant influences at work when dissolution or evolutionary reversal results from a disturbance of the 'highest cerebral centres' as occurs in organic mental states, post-convulsive states, and the psychoses.

In both the chronic schizophrenias and the organic mental states the dissolution is not resolved. Under certain conditions, however, there is an automatic expression of speech and motility which gives the impression of normality. Over and above this there always remains a fragment of healthy mental activity which only makes its appearance under special circumstances. This is to be seen in the chronic schizophrenias as a result of the action of drugs or during psychotherapy. This improvement is, however, rarely permanent or sufficiently powerful to offset the results of dissolution.

In recent cases of psychotic illness the dissolution can be equally extensive, leading to phenomena indistinguishable from those of chronic schizophrenia. This will be accentuated if the onset is acute, indicating a rapid dissolution of healthy mental functions. Clinical experience demonstrates that this 'deep' dissolution need not be permanent and the patient may either recover the lost functions or suffer an impairment of varying degrees of severity. Associated with the dissolution are all the positive manifestations which have received so much attention in this book. The diagnosis of the clinical state is generally based on the positive symptoms, and it is this which has given rise to so much confusion.

Jackson's theory demonstrates that once dissolution of any extent occurs then hallucinations, delusions, and alterations in the form taken by cognitive processes must occur – this resulting from the intrusion of modes of functioning belonging to early phases of development. An example of this is the effect of dissolution on the speech regulation of voluntary movement. Luria (1966) has described experiments that show that in a child under the age of three speech does not play the decisive role in regulating voluntary movement. It follows from Jackson's theory that many of the positive signs of functional psychosis are essentially non-specific. This view is supported by the fact that many organic diseases, both intra- and extra-cerebral, may produce positive signs indistinguishable from those of the functional psychoses. Epilepsy, syphilis, brain damage, and other organic mental states may be quoted here, apart from intoxication with drugs. The investigations conducted by Slater *et al.* (1963) into the schizophrenia-like psychoses of epilepsy are a case in point. The schizophrenias and the epileptic psychoses cannot be differentiated on the basis of positive symptoms. Both states may disclose delusions, hallucinations, and an altered state of consciousness. They can be distinguished, however, by the presence of the negative signs typical of the schizophrenias – namely the loss or the distortion of the world of objects. The only exception to this is when the altered state of consciousness in the epileptic patient reaches the point when meaningful contact with others is abandoned.

Freud (1911) recognized the importance of the part which dissolution played in leading to the signs and symptoms of psychosis. He called the dissolution 'an internal catastrophe'. Like Jackson he appreciated that delusions and hallucinations were not the direct expression of the disease. Freud regarded the results of dissolution – the delusions and hallucinations – as attempts to regain the world of reality. In contrast to Jackson he envisaged these phenomena as having purpose and aim. Freud discerned that 'this attempt at recovery' (Freud, 1911) was not the disease itself. He thought that the core of the disease lay in the disruption of ties with the environment.

Bleuler's theory of schizophrenia (1911) also followed along the lines laid down by Jackson. He did not attribute equal significance to all the clinical phenomena presented by a patient suffering from schizophrenia. He regarded the delusions, hallucinations, motility disorders, and negativism as reactions to a basic defect which was the essence of the illness. This defect was to be found in the loosening of the associations, ambivalence, and autism. These were the primary symptoms. The remainder, the delusions, hallucinations, etc., constituted the secondary symptoms. Later writers have not maintained this basic theoretical distinction. This has had the result of secondary (positive) symptoms being afforded an importance similar to and sometimes greater than that accorded to the primary (negative) symptoms. The positive symptoms have thus come to be looked upon as the essential features of schizophrenia upon which the diagnosis should be based. This state of affairs has materially contributed to the confusion now surrounding the diagnosis of schizophrenia.

It was Freud who filled the gaps in Jackson's theory. He stressed the importance of Jackson's third factor – the type of individual in whom dissolution takes place. It is unnecessary here to provide an account of the psychoanalytical theories of psychosis based on the study of innumerable cases of schizophrenia and allied states (see Freeman *et al.*, 1965), beyond referring to the fact that psychoses are initiated by conflicts that are in themselves no different from those which lead to attacks of neurotic illness.

As was indicated in Chapter 2, Freud based his theory of psychosis on that evolved for the neuroses. The sequence of anxiety and/or guilt arising from conflict, regression to fixation points, and eventual symptom formation occurred. Inherent in this theory is the concept of defence. Psychotic symptoms are regarded as essentially defensive, with the aim of neutralizing anxiety and/or guilt regarding wishes and attitudes towards objects in the real world. Melanie Klein and her followers have elaborated this theory in their work with psychotic patients.

The defence theory of psychosis may not be altogether correct. Is a theory suitable for the explanation of neuroses applicable to the psychoses? Federn (1943) was perhaps the first psychoanalytical writer to cast doubt on a psychopathology of psychosis modelled too closely on the psychoneuroses. As is well known, Federn (1948) disagreed with Freud's hypothesis (1911) that the first phase in, for example, schizophrenia is the detachment and withdrawal of libido from objects, and that the positive symptoms are the result of a second phase – an attempt at restitution. According to Federn (1948), a disturbance of the ego cathexis leads to a loss of the ego boundary. Ideas are no longer distinguished from perceptions. The alteration in the ego leads to a state where ideation, affect, and bodily sensation appear to arise from the environment. The resulting falsification of perceptual experience is followed by mistaken judgement and conclusions.

Federn (1948) demonstrated on innumerable occasions that the first delusions that substitute for actual events and the first falsifications that replace a correct apprehension of reality can be attributed to occurrences of the previous day in the patient's life. These events occur long before there is an actual break with reality. Nor did Federn (1943) agree that the symptoms of schizophrenia were the outcome of defence, as in the psychoneuroses. He believed that the first signs of the illness occur independently of a defence against the drives, against the environment, or against the demands of the superego. He said (1948): '. . . the psychosis itself is no defence but a defeat. It is a defeat of an ego which has ceased to be able to defend itself against the impact on the instinctual demands, the requirements of external reality and the conflicts which derive from them.'

Federn's theory has several important implications over and above its being consistent with the dissolution-evolution hypothesis. First, it suggests that the defect in schizophrenia is to be found in a personality organization that is vulnerable both in its relations to objects and in its cognitive organization. Second, it raises the possibility that the psychotic symptoms (the positive signs) are only indirectly linked with the unconscious conflicts that initiated the dissolution. Third, it challenges the view that the aim of the symptoms is the provision of a defence against the conscious recognition of the conflict.

In the initial stages of a psychotic illness it is not difficult to note that the patient employs certain manœuvres to keep thoughts that cause anxiety and guilt from consciousness. At this stage there is a defensive activity no different from that of the psychoneurotic patient. However, once the delusions and hallucinations appear, little effort is made to conceal the nature of the conflicts and fantasies associated with the onset of the illness. In this respect the psychotic manifestations differ entirely from psychoneurotic symptoms, where the main purpose of defence is concealment of the repressed from consciousness. The preservation of the psychotic reality – the delusions and hallucinations – ensures a continued repudiation of these openly expressed libidinal and aggressive fantasies. The preservation is dependent upon a provision of new ideational material which will reinforce and strengthen the structure of the psychotic reality. Freud (1924) has pointed out that this new material is derived from memory traces and from fantasies which the patient created in earlier times. It is also obtained from current experiences in the home or the hospital ward. Such material is utilized regardless of the nature of the delusion, that is, whether its content is grandiose, persecutory, or depressive.

Evidence has already been presented that shows that repression may continue to act efficiently in established cases of schizophrenia. This should not be regarded as surprising, because the dissolution does not effect the entirety of the patient's mental life, as Freud (1914) was quick to demonstrate. The loss of functions due to dissolution have their counterpart in the positive symptoms – catatonic manifestations and/or a delusional reality. Repression and denial are recruited to preserve the *status quo*.

The psychotic reality sometimes provides a means of adaptation. The delusions and hallucinations can be regarded as a means of shoring up the ego, and threats to their status provoke anxiety. This is due to the dread of a further dissolution, to a return to the 'internal catastrophe'.

The hypothesis which has been developed does not imply the need for a radical revision of Freud's theory of psychosis. It emphasizes the necessity of laying stress on factors other than those of conflict as the principal agent determining the form of the clinical phenomena as distinct from the content. Such a modification still leaves open the possibility, as far as causation is concerned, that infantile experiences may be such as to lead to fixations and thus to one kind of predisposition to the illness. Dissolution exposes these fixations and they may contribute to the nature of some, but not all, of the positive symptoms. These fixations must be assumed to have arisen in the context of interpersonal (object) relations, and they would therefore contribute to the subsequent distortion of the capacity to make adequate and satisfying relationships.

A case can be made for the view that the schizophrenias are cerebral pathopsychoses – that they are cerebral disease psychoses. Careful review of the clinical phenomena has shown that defence mechanisms are initially effective in their function – that in fact the ego is partially intact. The schizophrenic patient avoids what is distressing and anxiety-provoking by denial, projection, and repression, as does the healthy individual. Condensations, the tendency to compulsive repetition, and the expression of instinctual drives, lead to the characteristic clinical phenomena. In explanation of this intrusion of a primitive (unconscious) form of mentation, recourse must be had to some constitutional-hereditary weakness in the neural substrata which ordinarily hold the primary process in check.

The view presented here follows the theory (Bellak, 1958) that schizophrenic symptomatology may make itself manifest in any mental illness whether initiated by mental conflict, physical disease, or drug intoxication. The mode of expression is initially through an altered state of consciousness (an 'amentia symptom complex'). The clinical state is regarded as resulting from the most far-reaching dissolution of mental function with the resultant intrusion of the primary process. Delusions, hallucinations, and the form of thinking and perceiving which makes the psychotic reality viable are non-specific phenomena.

The essential feature distinguishing the schizophrenic patient from all those other states – functional or organic – that present schizophrenia like phenomena is the deterioration of ties with the object world. It is not purely the result of the intrusion of the primary process because this occurs in all the conditions leading to the positive symptoms. In schizophrenia the cathexes (interest and drive) investing people and things are deranged and this applies equally to their representations in the mind. This deterioration of object-directed cathexes occurs simultaneously with cognitive disturbances, again the result of decathexis, with resultant misinterpretations and falsifications of experience, as Federn (1948) described. The deterioration of object cathexes is the principal negative symptom in which lies the core of the illness. This can be regarded as the essence of the schizophrenic process (Freud, 1911).

In certain individuals the schizophrenic process is not resolved, for reasons which are unknown. These patients form the group of established case of schizophrenia. At the same time, even in such cases, there remains a remnant of healthy mental life even although its expression has many of the qualities of infancy and childhood (Cameron, in Freeman, Cameron, and McGhie, 1965). The clinical examples presented in Chapter 5 demonstrated this fact. This being so there is always the possibility, even in the established case, of a development and strengthening of this non-psychotic part. Such knowledge must influence views on the treatment, course, and prognosis of the illness. At the same time, the psychosis itself does not necessarily die out even although the patient no longer shows striking positive symptoms. Psychotherapeutic work with apparently 'burnt-out' schizophrenic patients has shown that even the original symptomatology may reappear with the intense affects that characterize the recent case. The theories of Jackson and Freud make allowance for the variety of clinical phenomena which occur in psychotic states and the changes, both favourable and adverse, which may arise in the course of the illness.

THE DIAGNOSIS OF SCHIZOPHRENIA

There are two aspects to the diagnosis of schizophrenic psychoses. One of these is straightforward, the other is fraught with problems and complexities. The first is the differentiation of schizophrenic from organic brain disease, drug reactions, and metabolic disease. This facet of the diagnostic problem is simplified for the psychiatrist by the presence, in these conditions, of observable phenomena that are largely independent of the patient's subjective experience and his own. The diagnosis can be arrived at on the basis of relatively objective phenomena – physical signs and laboratory tests. The differentiation of the schizophrenias from other functional psychoses is hindered, as has already been indicated, by the absence of such objective information.

There is general agreement that reliable diagnosis in schizophrenia is difficult to achieve because of the lack of a refined clinical method which can take into account the major variables which influence the patient's symptoms and behaviour at the time of examination. This difficulty has provided a major obstacle to research in schizophrenia when attempts have been made to correlate symptoms with physiological and biochemical findings. It also introduces an element of unreliability into the assessment of drug effects in this condition.

Currently two distinct trends can be discerned in the approach to the problem of reliable diagnosis. One derives from the psychoanalytical approach to psychosis, the other from academic and clinical psychology. According to the former view, a comprehensive and realistic account of the symptomatology, at any stage of the illness, can only be obtained by a careful study of the patient in the course of his relationship with the psychiatrist, nurse, occupational therapist, and others over an extended period of time. Studies such as those described in Chapters 5 and 6 demonstrate the great variability that characterizes the signs and symptoms of a psychotic illness. In conjunction with other clinical studies, they suggest that both intra- and inter-patient variability must be regarded as a primary characteristic of psychosis.

Recognition of the problems referred to above, and an awareness of the unreliability of clinical concepts and diagnostic categories in the hands of different observers, have led some psychiatrists and psychologists to try to obtain a degree of control over the phenomena even at the risk of losing sight of important clinical information. They have attempted to bring order to the field by imposing a form of structure to which both phenomena and observer must conform. They have introduced ordered interview techniques and rating scales which can be examined for inter-observer reliability and whose results can subsequently be submitted to statistical treatment. These methods have provided valuable data about major clinical manifestations.

The research task lies in the future, but at present it is valuable to have an instrument which will assist the clinician in directing his attention to all possible areas of abnormal mental functioning. The examination scheme has a place here. This scheme was not devised as an alternative to the generally accepted methods of mental examination or as a base for a destructive attack on current diagnostic procedures. Clinical states must be allocated to nosological entities, but this does not mean that phenomena inconsistent with the particular category should not be given their proper importance and significance. As the examination procedure is in no way associated with or derived from schemes of diagnostic classification, its concern is primarily with the raw material of observation. Once all the phenomena are gathered, then the discussion about diagnostic categorization can best be undertaken.

With knowledge in its present state, it is impossible to assert with confidence that a mental illness having features considered here to reflect the activity of a schizophrenic process, or phenomena considered by others to indicate the presence of a schizophrenic illness, will remit, follow a relapsing course, or progressively deteriorate. Even follow-up studies have not proved helpful, and patients categorized as 'process' schizophrenia have remitted, while so-called reactive cases have deteriorated (Astrup and Noreik, 1966).

The problem is further aggravated by the disagreements between psychiatrists about the criteria necessary for the diagnosis of schizophrenia. Attention has already been drawn to the fact that too much emphasis is laid on positive symptoms when the problem of diagnosis arises. Positive symptoms are not specific for schizophrenia – whether they are delusions, hallucinations, motility disorders, or perseverative signs. They represent the reaction to different pathological processes – some of which can be easily identified. Epilepsy and brain damage due to degenerative and vascular changes are representative of the 'organic' variety. Most often, however, there is no such physical change in the brain and recourse must be had to the 'functional' concept. Delusions and hallucinations do not indicate the presence of a schizophrenic psychosis, but their presence in a patient suffering from a disorder of speech, thinking, perception, and voluntary movement will raise the possibility of such a diagnosis.

The terms 'schizophreniform psychosis', 'reactive psychosis', 'psychogenic psychosis', 'nuclear schizophrenia', 'cycloid psychosis', 'schizo-affective state', 'pseudo-neurotic schizophrenia' reflect the attempt to give recognition to the variety of abnormal processes – the actual pathological events – which give rise to the non-specific positive symptoms. With knowledge in its present state, the diagnosis can rarely be absolute unless it is based on the final outcome of the illness. This often means a revision of the original diagnosis, as the follow-up studies show. There will always be doubt, particularly in those cases where the predominant manifestations are of a delusional nature.

Steps towards improving the standard of diagnosis can be made by spending as much time as possible with the patient and obtaining information from all those who have had contact with him. The data obtained in this way, and categorized in accordance with the examination scheme, do not make the task of diagnosis easier. The procedure has, however, the merit of revealing the extent of the heterogeneity that exists in abnormal mental states.

CHAPTER 11

Treatment of the Psychoses

At the present time there is no specific treatment for psychotic illnesses. The phenothiazine and thymoleptic drugs can only be regarded as symptomatic treatments, although this in no way undervalues their beneficial effects. Lack of exact knowledge about aetiology and pathogenesis means that their mode of action is unknown. No one can predict with confidence whether a patient will make a good response or not. In this respect these treatments are used empirically in the same way as electroshock therapy. This situation is in part brought about by the heterogeneity of the clinical phenomena that occur within nosological entities. No two schizophrenic or depressed patients are identical in behaviour, symptomatology, personality, or in the processes underlying the clinical manifestations.

Follow-up studies in the case of schizophrenic states indicate that drug treatment does not necessarily lead to the kinds of change that would allow the patients to be regarded as cured. At best, many are sufficiently improved to enable them to live outside hospital. They have lost the striking and more extreme forms of symptoms, but their capacity to relate to others remains deficient, as does their drive to work. As yet there is no completely reliable information about the psychosocial state of these patients who have been discharged from hospital. Several publications indicate that all is not well in this respect (Mandelbrote and Folkard, 1961; Gillis and Keet, 1965; Wing *et al.*, 1964) it would appear from these follow-up studies that the adjustment of many patients suffering from schizophrenia and living in the community is poor or marginal. They suffer from symptoms that are very similar to those found in patients who are confined to hospital. Crises of various kinds arise from time to time causing difficulties in the family, with neighbours, and with the police.

The administration of drugs can only be regarded as one aspect of the treatment of the psychoses. In the absence of specific measures, the management of the patient's illness assumes a major importance in much the same way as it does in those cases of physical illness which are little understood and for which there is no curative therapy.

Psychotherapy

It is in the sphere of patient management that the knowledge which has been gained from the psychotherapeutic treatment of individual cases can be employed. Psychotherapy is in no stronger position than drug treatment or electroshock therapy when it comes to making claims about therapeutic efficacy. As with drug treatments, psychotherapy is successful in some cases and not in others. As far as contemporary psychiatric practice is concerned, individual psychotherapy is a major undertaking and only in a very few cases is it a practicable proposition. Committed as psychiatrists are to the treatment of numerous patients suffering from all kinds of serious mental illnesses, there seems little point in a preoccupation with a psychotherapy of psychosis that implies the continuous treatment of patients for many years with no guarantee of a successful outcome.

It is, nevertheless, important to refer to some of the conditions which are necessary for undertaking psychotherapy with psychotic patients and to the phenomena which may be found during this treatment. It is only with the aid of this information that programmes of management can be designed. It is an interesting thought that, in spite of the theorizing about the technique necessary in the psychotherapy or psychoanalysis of the psychoses which has taken place over the last twenty-five years, the majority of therapists indicate that their main effort is directed towards contacting the healthy elements in the patient. This was Federn's (1943) position, from which he advocated that emphasis must be laid upon building up a positive relationship with the patient.

Federn (1943) was the first to demonstrate that as long as the positive relationship exists it is possible to get the patient to examine the falsification of perceptual experience and thinking that provides the raw material for misinterpretations and delusional ideas. In favourable instances the patient becomes aware of the means whereby the distortion has come to pass. Patients often attribute a defect in cognition to a persecutor. They insist that loss of memory is due to the persecutory activity. Sometimes it is possible to show the patient that what he has forgotten is something that he does not wish to remember and by attributing the amnesia to a persecutor he externalizes the problem. As long as the patient is well disposed to the therapist, then work of this type can proceed with a gradual building up of a sounder discriminatory capacity and reality-testing.

Sometimes contact can be established with the non-psychotic, healthy mental function of a withdrawn schizophrenic patient provided certain needs are satisfied. In such cases interest in the doctor and nurse follows the need for food, cigarettes, or the knowledge that their psychic preoccupations will be given full attention. Disappointment leads to a withdrawal from the doctor or nurse and sometimes to an outburst of anger. In patients of this type the tie with the world of reality is fragile and tenuous. While it remains intact it is possible, as Federn showed, to observe changes in the patient's appraisal of the environment in the direction of normalcy. Even if only for a brief period, the patient will, for example, recognize that his misidentifications are a product of his imagining. In this way he indicates that he has not lost the capacity to learn – to alter his perception of reality on the basis of real experience. Loss of the object world is accompanied by a return of the delusional perception.

It is in cases of this type that interpretative psychotherapy meets with little success. The altered state of consciousness which obtains in these patients is such that they are not in contact with the therapist. Their cognitive processes are characterized by a profound inertia and condensations. The former has the effect of putting the patient out of phase with the therapist. For example, the patient will assimilate something of the therapist – an aspect of his appearance or a fragment of what he has said. This material finds a repetitive representation and, as in cases of organic mental state, the perseverative trend cannot be dispelled by verbal interventions. The latter, condensations, lead to the phenomena which have been described in earlier chapters.

This does not mean that patients of this kind are beyond therapeutic influence. Clinical experience has revealed that over a period of many years a gradual strengthening of the healthy elements in the patient may occur. Concomitantly there is a return of the capacity to intend and attend for the purpose of adaptation to others and to the environment. These changes are usually associated with an emotional attachment which gives the patient a sense of safety and security. This may come from the institution itself or from an undeclared attachment to nurse, doctor, relative, domestic cleaner, or some other figure in the patient's immediate circle. The follow-up studies to which reference was made earlier in this chapter indicate that deterioration is not the general rule in these severe conditions and that improvement can take place. Such improvements can in part be attributed to the phenothiazine drugs, in so far as they ameliorate the impact of the psychosis on the residual healthy mental activity, thus giving it a better chance of development.

In cases of paranoid psychosis the psychotherapist is sometimes agreeably surprised to observe that the patient responds enthusiastically to his approach. Positive feelings predominate and the therapeutic contact does not seem so different from that in a case of neurosis. This favourable impression is soon dispelled as the patient inexorably draws his delusional complex into the treatment situation. The psychiatrist soon becomes a persecutor and treatment is broken off. In cases where the psychotic disturbance is also characterized by a cognitive disorganization, the psychiatrist is misidentified and a kind of merging occurs. The patient attributes features of his physical and mental self to the psychiatrist and simultaneously identifies with certain aspects of the latter.

In psychotic states the processes necessary for the dissipation of the abnormal manifestations cannot find an optimal development. This is due to two factors. First, the patient is incapable of relating to another person other than on the basis of the immediate satisfaction of needs, whether physical or psychological. In such instances lack of interest and the altered state of consciousness result in an inability, and in an absence of a wish, to learn about the nature of the psychotic ideas and percepts. Second, even when a psychotherapeutic process has been initiated it is easily disrupted by the delusional reality making its appearance in the patient-therapist situation. The vivid and compelling nature of this content captures the patient's attention and distracts him from the task of examining his misinterpretations of the environment.

This outcome is not inevitable and there are many patients who present with delusional ideas who are capable of proceeding to the development of a therapeutic alliance with the therapist and to beneficial therapeutic work (Salzman, 1960). In these cases there is sufficient object libido, to use a psychoanalytical term, for the patient to develop working transferences. As the literature attests, these transferences, in contrast to those encountered in the neuroses or depressive states, are not well controlled. This leads to various kinds of problem, as is illustrated by the case of the female student described above (p. 166). It will be recalled that she was an only child and that her mother had died of cancer. She lived alone with her father. When the illness began the patient became preoccupied with a series of irrational ideas. She believed her father was a homosexual; she was convinced she was a homosexual. She heard people saying this at work, in the street, and even at home when no one was there. She eventually fled the house in panic, fearing that her father was going to assault her sexually. Later in the hospital she confided that she had experienced sexual feelings for her father.

During the course of the psychotherapy erotic tendencies made themselves manifest in the direction of the author, just as they had done with her father. In the case of a neurotic patient who developed sexual fantasies towards the therapist it would be possible to call on the reasonable, healthy part of the patient and demonstrate that these manifestations were a repetition of the father relationship which now acted as a resistance to the progress of the treatment. In time, this resistance may be dissolved. In the present case the patient was too involved with her ideas, there was no reasonable ego to appeal to, and her controls were defective. Knowledge that it was the loss of the mother which had led to the backward movement (the regression) of mental life and the appearance of childhood instinctual attitudes led to the treatment and the patient's care being continued by the ward sister, who was able to help the patient to regain control. Continuation of the treatment with the author would only have heightened the sexuality and the anxieties to which it gave rise.

This case and many others show that even when transferences develop they are unstable and unreliable. These transferences do not include what are sometimes referred to as psychotic transferences (negativism, persecutory attitudes to the therapist, therapist-patient merging), which are of quite a different nature (Freeman *et al.*, 1965). The transferences which appear may fluctuate between friendliness and idealization, on the one hand, and dislike and hatred, on the other. As there is no evidence as yet that attempting to work through these difficult periods with the patient leads to benefit, it is still appropriate to follow Federn's advice (1943) and pass the patient over to a female colleague or nurse until such time as the disturbed phase has passed.

Psychotherapy, which consists essentially of an interpretative technique, has a place in the treatment of certain psychotic states where the cognitive disorganization is limited and where there is still the capacity for the development of genuine employable transferences. While these are patients who would reach a remission of symptoms with drug treatment alone, the psychotherapy adds to the quality of the remission. It helps the patient to widen his life-experience and avoid pathological solutions to object-relationship conflicts.

Psychopathological Evaluation and Management

Conditions are such in the average mental hospital that the psychotherapy of individual cases must be confined to a very small number of patients. Other methods must therefore be found to employ the insights gained from the study and treatment of single cases. The symptoms and conflicts of each patient must be discovered in as much detail as possible so that the management will be such as to speed recovery rather than hinder it. It is here that the examination scheme described in Chapter 3 can be of use. With its aid an assessment can be made of the different clinical phenomena and of the patient's capacity for relationships. Object-relationship capacity must be examined from the point of view of the level on which it finds expression and the conflicts which accompany it.

At the outset of contact with a recent or long-stay patient suffering from psychosis, the psychiatrist cannot tell to whom the patient will make an attachment. It is only by constant observation and discussion with nurses, occupational therapists, and others that this information will become available. However ill the patient may be, he has not entirely lost the wish to make contact with others. The fact that limited emotional attachments do occur in psychotic illnesses, however chronic, means that some therapeutic influence is possible. The psychiatrist's task is to find out if such a capacity exists and where it is directed.

At the same time the psychiatrist must also have some knowledge of the patient's principal conflicts if management is to have a beneficial effect. For example, it is inevitable that some patients have to be confined for their own safety, and then the psychotic reality often results in a worsening of the patient's state by leading him to believe that he is surrounded by persecutors. Confinement with patients of the same sex may have adverse results for another reason. If a patient is preoccupied with problems of sexual identity and as a consequence of the illness experiences his body as wholly or partly female he may believe that he is attracting or will be attracted sexually to his fellow-patients. Very often the uncooperative, aggressive, or terrified behaviour of patients can be traced to these causes – the intrusion of the psychotic reality or the appearance of homosexual tendencies in consciousness. Analytically orientated psychiatrists, understanding that both kinds of experience may arise in psychosis, are on the alert for their occurrence. When they make their appearance appropriate steps can be taken to relieve the patient's fears by transferring him to a situation where his freedom is not restricted.

The Role of the Nurse and the Occupational Therapist

Management is an extension of the psychotherapeutic process into the ward and into the occupational and recreational therapy departments. This psychotherapeutic process proceeds independently and without interpretative procedures. It is not concerned with making manifest the conflicts that are related to delusional ideas. The essential task is to help restore the cognitive functions and judgement. This can only be effected on the basis of an emotional attachment by the patient to nurse, therapist, or doctor. The successful application of this procedure is entirely dependent upon harmonious cooperation between all those who care for the patient. This approach was pioneered by Maxwell Jones (1952). It requires a conception of the nurse and the therapist as individuals who can assist the patient to a better level of mental health. This influence is to be exerted systematically through knowledge of the patient's psychopathology and not by intuition, which is notoriously unreliable.

This management programme requires that nurses and therapists shall be educated for their therapeutic task. It is not so long ago since the training of the psychiatric nurse was confined to biological, medical, and surgical subjects. Psychology consisted of lectures or instinct and memory. The psychiatric nurse had to employ common sense because her training had not provided her with a means whereby she could actively organize her interchange with patients. This lack of appropriate training was emphasized in a report on psychiatric nursing carried out by Manchester Regional Hospital Board (1955). It stated:

> 'The core of the curriculum should be the study of human relationships as these may exist between individuals and within groups. The main object of such study is to equip the nurse with a skill in dealing with individual patients and in group work and to give her an understanding of the influence groups may have on human behaviour.'

The questions which immediately arise are how is the nurse to develop skills in dealing with individual patients, how is she to understand them, and how is she to acquire knowledge about the way in which the mentally ill relate? This information and the necessary techniques can be acquired through clinical work simultaneously used as an educational experience. This demands the active participation of the psychiatrist, either in a formal teaching programme, or informally in the working situation in the ward.

Doctors and nurses have always known that when people fall ill with either physical or mental disease, changes take place in their personality functioning. They lose certain characteristics and acquire others. They show less initiative and independence. They may be subject to self-preoccupation and to rapid mood changes. There is a change in the quality of their relationships. These changes are even more pronounced when an individual enters hospital as a patient. He becomes dependent on others and manifests a sensitivity which was previously foreign to his temperament. The rational, reality-orientated attitude to the doctor and nurse, the awareness of their limitations, physical, emotional, and intellectual, is submerged in the wish for an omnipotent and omniscient figure who can bring immediate relief for the mental or physical sufferings.

In psychoanalytical terms a regression has affected the patient's mental functioning. In neurosis the patient behaves to those around him in the same way as he did in childhood. A spontaneous transference neurosis has developed. These spontaneous transferences are common-place in hospital and they explain the inappropriate emotional reactions and behaviour which some patients show. These manifestations demonstrate that transference phenomena are not confined to the consulting-room alone but can appear in different situations given the appropriate conditions. The psychotic patient may show similar transferences, but in addition he also presents other phenomena, which have been described in earlier chapters.

One important difference exists between the spontaneous transference neurosis which appears in hospital patients and that which occurs in the course of psychoanalytic therapy. In psychoanalytical treatment the transferences are 'working transferences' developing in a patient whose personality is still sufficiently intact to throw off the effect of the regression once he has left the consulting-room. In the hospital patient, the spontaneous transferences are an expression of a weakened personality. The regression continues as long as the patient is ill. The spontaneous transferences are expressed in inappropriate situations and towards individuals who are often unprepared for them. These spontaneous transferences are neither quiet nor controlled. Sometimes the patient is demanding and aggressive. This can lead to anxiety on the nurse's part. At other times the nurse becomes the 'reincarnation' of all those who have disappointed the patient in the past, and this leads to overt and latent aggressive reactions of all kinds.

Nurses vary in their capacity to bear the reactions of patients who suffer from mental illness. Aggressive behaviour is difficult for some and easy for others. Some nurses can accept the excessive demands which patients make, while others are extremely intolerant of this stress. A similar variation of response is found when patients complain that the treatment has not helped or that they are worse rather than better. In this inconsistency of response – tolerating one manifestation and not another in the same patient – the nurse is similar to the young mother who can help her child easily through some phases of its early development and not others. The reason is the same in both cases – namely that the appearance of specific behaviours in the patient or child stimulates repressed complexes in the nurse or mother with ensuing defensive reactions, which may take the form of withdrawal, depression of mood, anger, or disgust. We must regard these reactions as potentially antitherapeutic.

The nurse is thus liable to develop transferences to the patient. The difference between nurse and patient is that the nurse's transferences are less intense and under some degree of control. In the patient's case the transference reactions have a compulsive quality and they are easily set free. The nurse may unconsciously regard the patient as sister, brother, mother, or father and tend to react to him as if this was so. She may also relate to the psychiatrist, ward sister, or matron as if they were in the parental role. Fortunately she has the traditional administrative structure of the hospital to help her deal with reactions to her colleagues and to the medical staff. Nursing tradition and the hierarchical staff structures are a positive therapeutic influence in so far as they help the nurse or occupational therapist to contain inappropriate reactions which might otherwise impede a patient's progress.

These considerations indicate that little good may come of a nursing education policy which aims at radically altering or sweeping away traditional nursing or staff structures. The sudden disappearance of these structures could lead to widespread anxiety and confusion on the part of nursing staff who would then feel bereft of the support which they provide. The task of psychiatrists is to modify existing nursing practice so that it becomes effective in the treatment of mental illness.

This can only be done by widening education within the existing structure.

The nurse – and the occupational therapist – can learn about the patient and obtain the knowledge that will allow her to participate positively in the treatment. She can come to understand her counter-transferences if she is given the opportunity to study individual patients under supervision. With student nurses a great deal of preparatory work can be done by holding informal education meetings in the ward. This helps the nurse to get to know the psychiatrist, and over a period of time she will lose her anxiety and express her opinions about a patient. These informal meetings can be essentially didactic, in so far as their content may consist of a discussion of a single case. At first, simple descriptions of patients' illnesses, and of the treatment and prognosis, are sufficient. The main purpose of the meetings is to allow a relationship to develop between the student nurses and the psychiatrist – a relationship which will give the nurse confidence to report in detail what she observes and how she feels when in the clinical situation. These meetings can be of service in providing the clinical background for theoretical material which the student nurse receives at the nursing school.

For those nurses who show an active interest in the psychology of the psychotic patient, the next step can be their spending time with patients in the manner described by Cameron, Laing, and McGhie (1955). These workers describe an experiment conducted with a number of chronic schizophrenic patients. Although it did not set out to be an educational experience for nurses, this was perhaps its most valuable result. They selected eleven female patients who were considered so disturbed that they were confined to the ward and only allowed into the courtyard for exercise. Two nurses – neither of whom had more than four to five years' experience – were delegated to look after these patients. The patients and nurses were allocated a large, bright, newly decorated room which was comfortably furnished. Magazines, materials for making rugs and baskets, and sewing and knitting equipment were provided. The patients remained in the room until 5 p.m. and then returned to their ward. The nurses were asked to provide a daily report on the patients' behaviour. Regular discussions were held with the nurses once or twice a week.

For the first weeks the patients were indifferent to their new surroundings, but gradually one or two began to sew or read. In the first months the nurses, in the absence of any definite instructions, devoted themselves to encouraging the patients – they approved and disapproved as they thought appropriate. They tried to teach them better table manners and to discourage 'unladylike' behaviour. They were worried about the patients running away, since the door was not locked.

As the months passed changes became apparent in most of the patients. They paid more attention to their appearance and many were sewing, drawing, or making rugs. Some of them took over small tasks such as making tea or setting the table for lunch. They began to relate to one another in a way that had never occurred before. The nurses were now much less anxious and noticeably more relaxed. They felt the patients were becoming more sensible. Cameron and his colleagues had no doubt at this point that the change lay as much with the nurses, who were now more confident and at ease.

There was a setback when one of the nurses left for her annual holiday and a substitute was put in her place. The patients became easily upset and quarrelsome. Housework and baking, which had become one of the main activities, ceased. No one went out for walks, alone or accompanied. The other permanent nurse became less tolerant. She was sharper with the patients, criticizing and reproaching them, much as she had done at the beginning of the project. When the regular nurse returned, the patients improved once again.

At the meetings held to discuss the behaviour of the patients, every effort was made to encourage the nurses to speak freely and frankly. They soon came to realize that their observation and opinions were valued. This increased their confidence. As far as possible, policy decisions were made at these meetings with the agreement of all present. In the course of the meetings opportunities were always available for showing the nurse how the patient reacted to her in a positive or negative manner. In this situation, the positive ties were very obvious in the pronounced identifications which took place – the patients coming to behave like the nurses. Considerable attention was given to showing the nurses how important they were for the patients and how the patients reacted if they (the nurses) were absent or unavoidably disappointed them.

The nurses did not fail to be impressed by their own experiences, particularly when they were detached from the immediate work situation through discussion. They came to see that the patients' behaviour depended almost entirely upon the state of their relationship. As long as this relationship remained on a reasonable level, the patients maintained their improved state. If the attachment was threatened in any way the improvement disappeared, at least temporarily.

This is one method by which nurses can learn something of the nature of psychotic illness and how the symptoms are closely tied to the state of the patient's interpersonal relations. It is also a method whereby a nurse can come to realize that occasionally her behaviour is motivated by fear of the patient – not necessarily of the patient's aggressiveness, but of some characteristic which has a disturbing quality. In the course of discussions the nurse can come to see that although speech makes it easier to communicate with patients it is misleading to think that words are essential for the development of a therapeutic relationship. In the experiment everything points to the fact that patients responded primarily to the emotional climate of their immediate environment and only secondarily to words.

It is through personal experience that the nurse or occupational therapist will gain the kind of knowledge which is essential if she is to participate positively in a therapeutic programme. It is sometimes thought that the imparting of psychological insights to nurses is too difficult an undertaking – that the nurse cannot understand and apply the complex ideas and concepts which the psychiatrist employs.

This is not a valid argument. When technical terms are used only after a description of the phenomena they represent the nurse rapidly comes to appreciate their meaning and usefulness.

Nurses and occupational therapists are always keenly aware of their patient's emotional turmoil. They are often handicapped by the lack of a frame of reference within which they can order their observations. It is this lack which prevents and discourages them from communicating their observations to their medical colleagues. The kernel of all therapeutic techniques in psychiatry is a positive relationship between patient and nurse or patient and doctor. The nurse must become aware of the obstacles within the patient which impede the development of this relationship and the forces which may destroy it once it has appeared. The nurse is in a position to allow the patient to unburden himself of his fears about the illness and hospitalization. The progressive ventilation of fears strengthens the positive tie. In psychosis this emotional bond is severely tested and sometimes broken, as in the case quoted in Chapter 5. Through personal contact with patients and discussion of case material, the nurse becomes an active therapist – not as a substitute for the psychiatrist but as an independent member of the treatment team.

The Therapeutic Programme

The therapeutic approach to the psychotic patient will be based on a psychopathological evaluation of the case. This must be carried through whether the patient is suffering from an illness of recent onset or of long duration. The evaluation is dependent, as has already been mentioned, on information obtained from all those concerned with the care of the patient. Once this information is available steps can be taken to construct the best possible plan of management.

In the recent case some reliance will inevitably be placed on drug therapy in leading to an amelioration of the symptoms and perhaps to a complete remission. Whether such a favourable outcome ensues or not, knowledge of the patient's conflicts may help to avoid relapse. For example, a young man's illness was precipitated by his father's death. He proceeded to a remission with the aid of drugs. His delusional ideas disappeared and he was discharged. Within a few months he had a relapse and had to be readmitted to hospital. A detailed investigation of the psychopathology revealed that the content of his delusion consisted of the belief that his father was still alive. He was sure he had seen him in the street. He was convinced that his mother was behind a plot to get rid of his father. In his relapse he spoke a great deal about his anger and fear of his employer who clearly stood in the father relationship. This and other evidence suggested that it was he who had entertained death wishes against his father, which he had subsequently projected onto his mother. In the psychosis he brought his father to life again – he saw him in the street. His case history is reminiscent of Hamlet.

It was obviously not enough to repeat the previous therapeutic approach and send him home. However, he had either to live away from his mother, who obviously accentuated his conflict, or he had to be provided with the support the discussion of his problems might bring. After several weeks of such discussions he was discharged home, but this time he was seen regularly as an out-patient by the author who now stood *in loco patris*. This time there was no relapse, and the patient remained well at a two-year follow-up.

Only an examination of the patient's psychopathology will reveal who is the best person to undertake the therapeutic task. In the case described in Chapter 4, his excellent relationship with his sister led to a female doctor being encouraged to undertake regular meetings with the patient. However, it is not necessarily the psychiatrist who will be the main agent in the management programme. The nurse or occupational therapist may turn out to be the one with whom the patient establishes an emotional bond. The further development is dependent on a team approach, with the psychiatrist providing support and help for the nurse or nurses concerned.

The employment of group techniques will depend upon the orientation of the staff psychiatrists and the manner in which patient responsibility is organized. If conditions are favourable, the group approach can be of value for recent cases. The psychotherapeutically minded psychiatrist is in a favourable position to undertake this kind of treatment because of his knowledge that the forms of relating that will develop in the group will be predominantly repetitions of relationships that are currently taking place in the hospital ward or that occurred at home or in childhood. While patients with severe neuroses and depressive states are more suitable for this form of treatment, psychotic patients can also benefit from its use. Here, as with individual treatment, the deviant nature of the capacity to relate leads to serious difficulties. However, even when the positive therapeutic influence is limited, the psychiatrist obtains a very clear picture of the patient's illness and the manner of its development.

Group therapy, like all kinds of therapeutic intervention, requires the closest cooperation with the nursing staff and any doctors who are directly concerned with the patients. Reference has already been made to the manner in which patient's reactions may spill out from the consulting-room into the ward and finding expression with other patients and nursing staff. This is why it is necessary that nurses and doctors must be especially knowledgeable about individual patients and cognizant of the way in which patients transfer attitudes and behaviour to them from husbands, wives, parents, and siblings.

Sufficient has been said about the management of the chronic patient here and in other publications. The part the nurse and occupational therapist have to play is paramount. However, they cannot be expected to continue their therapeutic work at a high level unless they are continually supported by senior members of the medical staff. Their presence indicates that the care of the long-stay patient is as important and as essential as that of the recent case, who will more likely than not proceed to a complete or partial remission. Only a certain degree of improvement can be expected in the case of the long-stay patient, and this is dissipated easily enough to the discouragement of those who care for him. The constant presence of a senior staff member at continuing regular discussions helps to offset this discouragement because the reasons for relapse frequently become apparent. The factor of morale is decisive in the management of the chronic patient. This can only be maintained when leadership is offered by the psychiatrist and through the continuing cooperation of all those involved in patient care.

At the beginning of this chapter attention was drawn to the fact that the treatment of the psychotic patient is entirely empirical if it is confined to drug therapy. This empiricism can be radically reduced if use is made of the knowledge obtained from psychoanalysis. It offers a method of psychotherapy for psychotic patients, but of even greater importance is its capacity to provide guide-lines for the construction of programmes of management in which nurses and occupational therapists can play a decisive part. Not only do such programmes frequently lead to success but their application prevents the activity of anti-therapeutic processes.

Appendix A
EXAMINATION SCHEME

1. OBJECT RELATIONS

(i) Nature of the Relationship with Real Objects

Describe the types of real object relationship that appear in the course of the illness. Is the patient interested in the object only as a source of need satisfaction? Is the object easily given up? Does the object exist in its own right apart from the patient's needs and is there concern for the object? Is there a low frustration if the need is not met? Does the relationship carry with it such features as the wish to protect the object, or jealousy or envy of the object? When interest and concern for the object arise, do they remain or are they liable to disappear? Does the object relationship remain viable following the expression of aggression arising from a disappointment with or separation from the object? A note should also be made of the kinds of object-relationship content that make themselves manifest. Is this oedipal or pre-oedipal in type? If the object exists in its own right, what part is played by heterosexual object cathexes, on the one hand, and homosexual cathexes, on the other? Is there inappropriate concern and anxiety for the object? Does the patient feel persecuted by the object? Does he irrationally over-value the object? Is the patient negativistic and unresponsive?

(ii) Nature of the Relationship with Delusional Objects

Describe the form in which the fantasy objects find representation. Does this occur by means of misidentification, through hallucinatory experiences, through the effect on bodily and mental sensibility or by the construction of imaginary objects? Where possible, details should be provided of the nature of the misidentifications and of the fantasy (delusional) objects. The modality in which the hallucinations occur and their content must also be noted. An account should be given of the patient's attitudes to the delusional objects. Is he friendly to, hostile to, or dependent on these fantasy objects? Again, a description should be presented of the attitudes of the delusional objects to the patient as he sees them: are they advising, friendly, reassuring, critical, or persecutory? Are the fantasy objects related or connected to real objects that exist in the present or existed in the past? Are the fantasy (delusional) objects condensed with real objects in the present?

2. PERCEPTION OF THE SELF, SELF-REGARD, AND PERSONAL IDENTITY

Note whether there is adequate investment of the boundaries of the self and the self-representations. If so, is this constant or is it subject to derangements during the course of the illness? Is there evidence of a loss of stability of the self as reflected in disturbances of self-object discrimination resulting in a projection (externalization) of self-representations and/or a merging with the object leading to transient identification? Are there specific changes in the physical characteristics of the body as experienced subjectively, and loss of autonomy of the self as indicated by such phenomena as flexibilitas cerea and automatic obedience? Is there a disturbance of personal and sexual identity? Are there indications of a disorder of the self as evidenced in increase in intensity of bodily sensations, perceptions, thought, and affect, in hypochondriacal preoccupations, in changes in the body-image, in an over-valuation of the self, and in exaggerated belief in the effect of thought and action? Is there an awareness of disintegration of the self, a weakness or loss of bodily or mental functions?

3. STATUS OF THE COGNITIVE FUNCTIONS

(*a*) Give details of disorders of verbalization as expressed through speech. Is grammatical construction adequate? Is there obstruction or 'derailment' or omission in the flow of associations? Are words changed in form? Do paraphasic phenomena occur? Is there evidence of perseveration or echo phenomena? Are there indications of a fluctuation between normal and abnormal verbalization and vice versa? Does obstruction of speech ever give way to fluent verbalization? What is the content of speech when this occurs? What are the conditions under which blocking becomes manifest? Is there evidence of the patient's failure to comprehend the speech of others?

(*b*) Provide information about those instances where thinking has assumed a magical, omnipotent quality. Describe the operation of the primary process when it influences the thought processes.

(*c*) Is the patient able to sustain attention for purposes of ordered thinking and speech and for appropriate reactions to environmental stimuli? Are there signs of distractability? Does this distractability emanate from the patient's attempt to understand his experiences or is the external stimulus experienced passively outside consciousness, only secondarily making its appearance in speech? Is there a fluctuation between states of inattention and purposive, directed thinking? Is the change to normal attention related to the anticipation of the satisfaction of a need or to delusional or hallucinatory experiences?

(*d*) What is the state of the perceptual functions? Are the modalities adequately differentiated? Is there evidence of synaesthesiae? In the sphere of visual perception, is there any disturbance of size, shape, or distance constancies? Are percepts experienced more intensely than normal – for example, noise or colour? Are percepts experienced concretely? Does the eye or ear have a symbolic significance with the patient? Does the patient perceive a physical change in his body? Can he discriminate one individual from another? Are there condensations of visual percepts and memory traces leading to misidentifications? Is there evidence of hallucinations in one or more of the sensory modalities?

(*e*) Note whether there is an obvious defect of short-term or remote memory? Are memories deranged with respect to their temporal sequence? Is there repression of significant life experiences prior to the onset of the illness? Do memories make their appearance in the hallucinations or delusions?

(*f*) Is there faulty judgement arising from anxiety and/or guilt?

4. MOTILITY

Are there disturbances of voluntary movement? Is the patient able to act and complete an intention or command? Does motor blocking occur during the course of a voluntary act? Is there evidence of ambitendency? Note the presence of motor perseveration, repetitive movements, and echopraxia. Describe any disorders of posture. Note whether there is flexibilitas cerea or postural persistence. Are there periods when voluntary movement occurs normally? What kind of verbal content and affect are associated with the transition from abnormal to normal motility and vice versa? Note the fantasies associated with the disorders of motility. Is voluntary movement disturbed by auditory or visual percepts?

5. SENSORI-MOTOR ORGANIZATION

Evidences of hypotonia, hypertonia, and asymmetrical tonus states should be noted. Similarly diminution or absence, accentuation and asymmetrical reactions of the tendon reflexes should also be recorded. Attention should be paid to the possible presence of tonic reflex responses particularly in those cases presenting with hypertonia of the upper limb musculature.

Are there signs of inattention to tactile and painful stimuli? Where there are indications of displacement (disturbed localization) of sensation from one body-part to another this should also be noted. Attention should be given to the presence or absence of face dominance. In the course of examination of motor and sensory systems perseverative signs frequently occur.

6. MANIFESTATIONS OF 'INSTINCTUAL DRIVE' ACTIVITY

(a) *Libidinal*

Indications of autoerotic behaviour (genital or pre-genital) should be described. Is there evidence of heterosexual or homosexual behaviour? Does the patient manifest exhibitionistic or scoptophilic tendencies?

(b) *Aggressive*

Detail manifestations of overt, outwardly directed aggression. Note possible stimuli for the evocation of aggressive outbursts. Is there an association between the expression of aggression and changes in such signs of disturbed motility as catalepsy, motor blocking, and ambitendency? Are aggressive outbursts followed by these disorders of motility? Is aggression directed to the body or to the mental self in the form of self-reproaches?

7. AFFECTIVITY

Describe all expressions of affect. Are these manifestations appropriate or inappropriate? Detail the accompanying ideational content. If there is an absence of affect, note the form of object relations and the motility disorder, if present.

8. DEFENCE ORGANIZATION

Examine the status of the defence organization. As this organization is always disrupted in psychosis, details must be provided of those phenomena which indicate a far-reaching disruption of repression. A record should be made, first, of libidinal and aggressive drives which have found direct expression in action (see Section 6) and, second, of fantasies springing from all levels of libidinal development. Similarly, details should be provided of adverse changes in the mechanisms of identification and reaction formation. A full account must be given of the part played by those defences which are close to the primary process and in development have their principal operation prior to the complete establishment of the ego. Thus detail the activity of reversal of aim, denial, turning in on the self, projection, displacement, etc. Finally attention should be drawn to those instances where control of the instinctual drives has been handed over to objects. Note whether these are real or delusional objects or a condensation of the two.

Appendix B

TESTS FOR DISORDERS OF MOTILITY

No.	Instruction	*Time to initiate act*	*Time to complete act*	*Indicate presence or absence of perseveration type and degree if present*
1	Close and then open your eyes			
2	Put out your tongue			
3	Shake your head			
4	Point to your right ear			
5	Touch your left elbow with your right hand			
6	Clap your hands three times			
7	Touch the table			
8	Touch my hand			
9	Point to my right ear			
10	Pass me over that pen			
11	Touch my left knee with your right hand			
12	Grip my fingers three times			
13	Ozeretskii's Test (dem.)			
14	Fist-Ring Test (dem. three times and give three trials)			
	(i)			
	(ii)			
	(iii)			
15	Fist-Edge-Palm (dem. three times and give three trials)			
	(i)			
	(ii)			
	(iii)			

References

ABRAHAM, K. (1924). Manic-depressive states and the pre-genital levels of the libido. In *Selected papers on psycho-analysis*. London: Hogarth, 1942. New edn. London: Hogarth, 1950; New York: Basic Books, 1953.

ALLISON, R. S. (1962). *The senile brain*. London: Arnold.

ANGEL, R. W. (1961). Jackson, Freud and Sherrington: 'On the relation of mind and brain'. *Amer. J. Psychiat.* **118**, 193.

ASTRUP, C. and NOREIK, K. (1966). *Functional psychoses: diagnostic and prognostic models*. Springfield, Ill.: Thomas.

BATCHELOR, I. R. C. (1964). The diagnosis of schizophrenia. *Proc. Roy. Soc. Med.* **57**, 417.

BAY, E. (1963). Aphasia and conceptual thinking. In L. Halpern (ed.), *Problems of dynamic neurology*. Jerusalem: Hebrew University of Jerusalem; New York: Grune & Stratton, 1964.

BECK, S. J. (1967). Schizophrenia: interadaptation of person, family and culture. In J. Romano (ed.), *The origins of schizophrenia*. New York: Excerpta Medica Foundation.

BELLAK, L. (1958). *Schizophrenia: a review of the syndrome*. New York: Logos Press.

BENDER, M. B. (1952). *Disorders in perception: with particular reference to the phenomena of extinction and displacement*. Springfield, Ill.: Thomas; Oxford: Blackwell.

BIBRING, E. (1953). The mechanism of depression. In P. Greenacre (ed.), *Affective disorders*. New York: International Universities Press.

BION, W. R. (1957). Differentiation of the psychotic from the non-psychotic personalities. *Int. J. Psycho-Anal.* **38**, 266.

BION, W. R. (1958). On hallucination. *Int. J. Psycho-Anal.* **39**, 341.

BION, W. R. (1959). Attacks on linking. *Int. J. Psycho-Anal.* **40**, 308.

BLEULER, E. (1911). *Dementia praecox or the group of schizophrenias*. New York: International Universities Press, 1950; London: Allen & Unwin, 1951.

BLEULER, M. (1963). Conception of schizophrenia within the last fifty years and today. *Proc. Roy. Soc. Med.* **56**, 945.

BYCHOWSKI, G. (1935). Certain problems of schizophrenia in the light of cerebral disease. *J. nerv. ment. Dis.* **81**, 280.

BYCHOWSKI, G. (1943a). Disturbance of the body image in the clinical picture of psychosis. *J. nerv. ment. Dis.* **97**, 310.

BYCHOWSKI, G. (1943b). Physiology of schizophrenic thinking. *J. nerv. ment. Dis.* **98**, 368.

CAMERON, J. L. and FREEMAN, T. (1955). Observations on the treatment of involutional depression by group psychotherapy. *Brit. J. med. Psychol.* **28**, 224.

CAMERON, J. L. and FREEMAN, T. (1956). Group psychotherapy for affective disorders. *Int. J. Grp. Psychother.* **6**, 235.

CAMERON, J. L., FREEMAN, T. and MCGHIE, A. (1956). Observations on chronic schizophrenia. *Psychiatry* **19**, 271.

CAMERON, J. L., LAING, R. D. and MCGHIE, A. (1955). Patient and nurse. *Lancet* (2), 1384.

COOPER, D. (1967). *Psychiatry and anti-psychiatry*. London: Tavistock Publications.

CRITCHLEY, M. (1964). The neurology of psychotic speech. *Brit. J. Psychiat.* **110**, 353.

DELAY, J. (1957). Jacksonism and the work of Ribot. *Archs. Neurol. Psychiat.* **76**, 505.

EY, H. (1959). Unity and diversity of schizophrenia. *Amer. J. Psychiat.* **115**, 706.

FAERGEMAN, P. M. (1963). *Psychogenic psychoses*. London: Butterworth.

FEDERN, P. (1943). Psycho-analysis of psychoses. In *Ego psychology and the psychoses*. New York: Basic Books, 1953; London: Imago, 1953.

FEDERN, P. (1948). Mental hygiene of the ego in schizophrenia. In *Ego psychology and the psychoses*. New York: Basic Books, 1953; London: Imago, 1953.

FENICHEL, O. (1945). *The psychoanalytic theory of neurosis*. New York: Norton.

FERENCZI, S. (1916). Disease- or patho-neuroses. In *Further contributions to the theory and technique of psycho-analysis*. London: Hogarth, 1950; New York: Basic Books, 1952.

FISH, F. J. (1962). *Schizophrenia*. Bristol: Wright; Baltimore, Md.: Williams & Wilkins.

FREEMAN, T. (1967). The clinical contribution to the study of the origins of schizophrenia. In J. Romano (ed.), *The origins of schizophrenia*. New York: Excerpta Medica Foundation.

FREEMAN, T. (1969). Signs, symptoms and course of schizophrenia. In L. Bellak and L. Loeb (eds.), *The Schizophrenic syndrome*. New York: Grune & Stratton.

FREEMAN, T., CAMERON, J. L. and MCGHIE, A. (1958). *Chronic schizophrenia*. London: Tavistock Publications.

FREEMAN, T., CAMERON, J. L. and MCGHIE, A. (1965). *Studies on psychosis*. London: Tavistock Publications.

FREEMAN, T. and GATHERCOLE, C. E. (1966). Perseveration – the clinical symptoms in chronic schizophrenia and organic dementia. *Brit. J. Psychiat.* **112**, 27.

FREUD, A., NAGERA, H. and FREUD, E. F. (1965). Metapsychological assessment of the adult personality. *Psychoanal. Study Child* **20**, 9.

FREUD, S. (1900). *The interpretation of dreams*. *S.E.* **5**.

FREUD, S. (1911). Psycho-analytic notes on an autobiographical account of a case of paranoia (dementia paranoides). *S.E.* **12**.

FREUD, S. (1914). On narcissism: an introduction. *S.E.* **14**.

FREUD, S. (1915). The unconscious. *S.E.* **14**.

FREUD, S. (1916–17). *Introductory lectures on psycho-analysis. S.E.* **15** & **16**.

FREUD, S. (1917). Mourning and melancholia. *S.E.* **14**.

FREUD, S. (1923). *The ego and the id. S.E.* **19**.

FREUD, S. (1924). Neurosis and psychosis. *S.E.* **19**.

FREUD, S. (1940). *An outline of psycho-analysis. S.E.* **23**.

GILLIS, L. S. and KEET, M. (1965). Factors underlying the retention in the community of chronic hospitalised schizophrenics. *Brit. J. Psychiat.* **111**, 1057–1067.

HENDERSON, D. and GILLESPIE, R. D. (1962). *Textbook of psychiatry for students and practitioners.* 9th edn, revised by D. Henderson and I. R. C. Batchelor. London: Oxford University Press.

HOFFER, W. (1954). Defensive process and defensive organisation. *Int. J. Psycho-Anal.* **35**, 194.

HOSKINS, R. G. (1946). *The biology of schizophrenia.* New York: Norton; London: Chapman & Hall.

JACKSON, J. HUGHLINGS (1894). The factors of insanities. In *Selected writings*, Vol. 2, p. 411. New York: Basic Books, 1958; London: Staples, 1959.

JASPERS, K. (1963). *General psychopathology.* 7th edn. Manchester: Manchester University Press; Chicago: University of Chicago Press.

JONES, M. (1952). *Social psychiatry.* London: Tavistock/Routledge. Under the title *The therapeutic community*, New York: Basic Books, 1954.

KASANIN, J. (1933). The acute schizo-affective psychoses. *Amer. J. Psychiat.* **13**, 97.

KLEIN, M. (1935). A contribution to the psychogenesis of manic-depressive states. *Int. J. Psycho-Anal.* **16**, 145. Reprinted in *Contributions to psycho-analysis 1921–1945.* London: Hogarth, 1948.

KLEIST, K. (1960). Schizophrenic symptoms and cerebral pathology. *J. ment. Sci.* **106**, 246.

LAING, R. D. (1960). *The divided self.* London: Tavistock Publications.

LAING, R. D. (1967). The study of family and social contexts in relation to the origin of schizophrenia. In J. Romano (ed.), *The origins of schizophrenia.* New York: Excerpta Medica Foundation.

LANGFELDT, G. (1960). Diagnosis and prognosis of schizophrenia. *Proc. Roy. Soc. Med.* **53**, 1047.

LEONHARD, K. (1961). Cycloid psychoses – endogenous psychoses which are neither schizophrenic nor manic-depressive. *J. ment. Sci.* **107**, 633.

LEONHARD, K. (1965). Discussion of M. Bleuler's 'Conception of schizophrenia within the last fifty years and today'. *Int. J. Psychiat.* **1**, 516.

LEMKE, R. (1955). Neurological findings in schizophrenia. *Psychiatrie Neurol. med. Psychol.* **72**, 26.

LEVIN, M. (1955). Perseveration at various levels of complexity, with comments on delirium. *Arch. Neur. Psychiat.* **73**, 439.

LEVIN, M. (1960). Motor function in mentation, imagery and hallucination. *Amer. J. Psychiat.* **117**, 142.

LEWIS, A. (1961). Amnesic syndromes. *Proc. Roy. Soc. Med.* **54**, 955.

LEWIS, A. (1964). General review of depressive conditions. In E. Beresford Davies (ed.), *Depression*. (Cambridge University Postgraduate Medical School, Symposium on Depression, 1959.) London: Cambridge University Press.

LIDZ, T. (1967). The family, personality development and schizophrenia. In J. Romano (ed.), *The origins of schizophrenia*. New York: Excerpta Medica Foundation.

LURIA, A. R. (1965). Two kinds of motor perseveration in massive injury of the frontal lobes. *Brain* **88**, 1.

LURIA, A. R. (1966). *Higher cortical functions in man*. New York: Basic Books; London: Tavistock Publications.

MANCHESTER REGIONAL HOSPITAL BOARD (1955). *The work of the mental nurse*. A survey organized jointly with the University of Manchester. Manchester: Manchester University Press.

MANDELBROTE, B. and FOLKARD, S. (1961). Some factors relating to outcome and social adjustment in schizophrenia. *Acta psychiat. Scand.* **37**, 223.

MAYER-GROSS, W., SLATER, E. and ROTH, M. (1954). *Clinical psychiatry*. London: Cassell; Baltimore, Md.: Williams & Wilkins, 1955.

PICHOT, P. (1967). Recent developments in French psychiatry. *Brit. J. Psychiat.* **113**, 11.

POLLITT, J. (1965). *Depression and its treatment*. London: Heinemann; Springfield, Ill.: Thomas.

POWER, T. D. (1957). A psychiatrist looks at epilepsy. *J. nerv. ment. Dis.* **125**, 279.

POWER, T. D. (1965). Some aspects of brain-mind relationship. *Brit. J. Psychiat.* **111**, 1215–23.

ROBERTSON, E., LE ROUX, A. and BROWN, J. A. (1958). The clinical differentiation of Pick's disease. *Brit. J. Psychiat.* **104**, 1000.

ROSENFELD, H. (1952). Transference phenomena and transference analysis in an acute catatonic schizophrenic patient. *Int. J. Psycho-Anal.* **33**, 451.

ROTH, M. (1963). Neurosis, psychosis and the concept of disease in psychiatry. *Acta psychiat. Scand.* **39**, 128.

SALZMAN, L. (1960). Paranoid states – theory and therapy. *Archs. gen. Psychiat.* **2**, 679.

SCHILDER, P. (1923). *Medical psychology*. New York: International Universities Press, 1953; London: Bailey & Swinfen, 1954.

SCHILDER, P. (1926). *Introduction to a psychoanalytic psychiatry*. New York: International Universities Press, 1951; London: Bailey & Swinfen, 1951.

SCHILDER, P. (1928a). Akinetic states, stupor and negativism. In *Brain and personality*. New York: International Universities Press, 1951; London: Bailey & Swinfen, 1951.

SCHILDER, P. (1928b). Psychic and organic apparatus. In *Brain and personality*. New York: International Universities Press, 1951; London: Bailey & Swinfen, 1951.

SCHILDER, P. (1950). *The image and appearance of the human body*. New York: International Universities Press.

SCHNEIDER, K. (1959). *Clinical psychopathology*. 5th edn. New York: Grune & Stratton.

SCOTT, R. D. and ASHWORTH, P. A. (1965). The 'axis value' and the transfer of psychosis. *Brit. J. med. Psychol.* **38**, 97.

SCOTT, R. D. and ASHWORTH, P. A. (1967). 'Closure' at the first schizophrenic breakdown. *Brit. J. med. Psychol.* **40**, 109.

SHATTOCK, D. (1950). Somatic manifestations of schizophrenia. *J. ment. Sci.* **96**, 32.

SLATER, E. and BEARD, A. W. (1963). The schizophrenia-like psychoses of epilepsy. *Brit. J. Psychiat.* **109**, 95.

STENGEL, E. (1963). Hughlings Jackson's influence in psychiatry. *Brit. J. Psychiat.* **109**, 348.

STENGEL, E. (1964). Psychopathology of dementia. *Proc. Roy. Soc. Med.* **57**, 911.

STROMGREN, E. (1965). Schizophreniform psychoses. *Acta psychiat. Scand.* **41**, 483.

WEINSTEIN, E. A. (1967). Symbolic aspects of ego function. In J. H. Masserman (ed.), *The ego*. New York: Grune & Stratton; London: Heinemann Medical.

WEINSTEIN, E. A. and KAHN, R. L. (1950). The syndrome of anosognosia. *Arch. Neurol. Psychiat.* **64**, 772.

WING, J. K., MONK, E., BROWN, G. W. and CARSTAIRS, G. M. (1964). Morbidity in the community of schizophrenic patients discharged from London mental hospitals in 1959. *Brit. J. Psychiat.* **110**, 10.

WOLFF, H. G. (1963). Dementia. In R. L. Cecil and R. F. Loeb (eds), *Cecil-Loeb textbook of medicine*. 11th edn. Philadelphia: Saunders.

WYNNE, L. C. and SINGER, M. T. (1963a). Thought disorder and family relations of schizophrenics. *Archs. gen. Psychiat.* **9**, 191.

WYNNE, L. C. and SINGER, M. T. (1963b). Thought disorder and family relations. *Archs. gen. Psychiat.* **9**, 199.

ZANGWILL, O. (1964). Psychopathology of dementia. *Proc. Roy. Soc. Med.* **57**, 911.

Index